The Official Book of the

ANTIQUE AUTOMOBILE

Club of America

Robert C. Lichty

A 60-year history of dedication to the automobile

Published by

700 E. State Street • Iola, WI 54990-0001
Telephone: 715/445-2214

Please call or write for our free catalog of automotive publications.
Our toll-free number to place an order or obtain a free catalog is 800-258-0929
or please use our regular business telephone 715-445-2214
for editorial comment and further information.

Library of Congress Catalog Number: 98-84624
ISBN: 0-87341-481-0

Printed in the United States of America

Table of Contents

Acknowledgments

Thanks to all—from those who just made a few great suggestions to those who contributed artifacts and research materials—who contributed to this monumental task. Special thanks to the history committee that worked throughout the project.

Thanks to...

Frank Abramson, Eastlake, Ohio/Philadelphia, Pennsylvania
William Abramson, Eastlake, Ohio
Adam Anderson, Upper Darby, Pennsylvania
Richard "Bud" Armstrong, Grafton, Wisconsin
L. Scott Bailey, England
Ed Baines, Canton, Ohio
Elinore Berkey, Orrville, Ohio
Earl H. Beauchamp, Montrose, Maryland
William Bomgardner, Hershey, Pennsylvania
Art Bragg, Sprucetown, Virginia
David W. Brownell, Bennington, Vermont
Bob & Virginia Burke, Vienna, Virginia
Ken Buttolph, Iola, Wisconsin
George Campbell, Hughesville, Pennsylvania
Vince Chimera, Fort Lauderdale, Florida
Harold Coker, Chattanooga, Tennessee
Joseph "Corky" Coker, Chattanooga, Tennessee
Roland Dunkelberger, Hershey, Pennsylvania
Bob Hall, Carlisle, Pennsylvania
Lunetta Harrington, Sandy Springs, Georgia
Thomas A Herman, San Antonio, Texas
Chris Hennevig, Pottstown, Pennsylvania
Leslie R. Henry, Dearborn, Michigan
Ronald Hvezda, Towawanda, Pennsylvania
William S. Jackson, Hummelston, Pennsylvania
Ron Kowalke, Iola, Wisconsin
Victor Losquadro, Staten Island, New York
Donna Martini, Wilkes-Barre, Pennsylvania
John Myer, Cropwell, Alabama
Kim Miller, AACA Library and Research Center, Hershey, Pennsylvania
William Miller, Linthicum, Maryland
Gary Muehlhauer, Johnson City, New York
Chris Perry, Winton, North Carolina
Willard Prentice, Timonium, Maryland
C.L. "Doc" Pressler, Canton, Ohio
M.G. "Pinky" Randall, Houghton Lake, Michigan
Janet Ricketts, Tarpon Springs, Florida
Willis Selle, Turtle Lake, Wisconsin

Jeanne H. Smith, Hershey, Pennsylvania
William H. Smith, Hershey, Pennsylvania
Frank T. Snyder III, Mountain View, California
Warren Steele, Harrisburg, Pennsylvania
Dr. J. Stanley Stratton, Chambersburg, Pennsylvania
David Strong, Thief River Falls, Minnesota
William Swigart III, Huntingdon, Pennsylvania
Dick Teeter, Mound, Minnesota
Franklin Tucker, Seven Lakes, North Carolina
William Tuthill, Binghamton, New York
Robert Wallace Sr., Upper Darby, Pennsylvania
Chris Werndly, Cedar Grove, New Jersey
Ernie Youens, Mobile, Alabama

Even greater thanks to those, past and present, who acted as a personal inspiration to me not only throughout this project, but over the past 30 years that I have been involved in the AACA as well. They are my true heroes of automotive history preservation.

The original fourteen founders of the Antique Automobile Club of America, and...

David W. Brownell, Bennington, Vermont
Bud Bryan, Los Angeles, California
Henry Austin Clark Jr., Glen Cove, New York
Terry Ehrich, Bennington, Vermont
Chester L. Krause, Iola, Wisconsin
Skip Marketti, Sylmar, California
LeRoi "Tex" Smith, Driggs, Idaho
William H. Smith, Hershey, Pennsylvania
Ruth Franklin-Summerlad, Cleveland, Ohio
Diane Vaughn, Carlisle, Pennsylvania

Thank you to the man who championed the need to document the rich history of the Antique Automobile Club of America to the AACA board. He was also instrumental in helping me make contact with many of the key people mentioned above that made this book possible:

Ronald V. Barnett, Union Grove, Alabama, 1991 AACA National President

The biggest thank you of all goes to the members of my family who have endured my auto collecting passion and the time and dedication this historic effort took away from family life:

Herbert and Isebell Denzer, New Philadelphia, Ohio
Harold C. and Nancy K. Lichty, my parents, North Canton, Ohio
Rosemary G. Rubin, my wife, Canton, Ohio
Christopher C. and Curtiss C. Lichty, my sons, Canton, Ohio
Donna L. Lichty, my sons' mother (deceased), Akron, Ohio

Foreword

by William H. Smith, AACA executive director

This is a very special book about a club, its members, its history and how it has managed to reach its 63rd year.

It started in Philadelphia, Pennsylvania, in the mid-twenties when our founding fathers began to enjoy the old cars. The Philadelphia Auto Show asked them to take part in the auto show and share their cars with show visitors. Taking a car to the show meant one was to participate in the Derby, a timed run of approximately 60 minutes from Coatsville, Pennsylvania, to the Auto Show. Of course, we have to remember that these Derbies took place in the cold month of December, which tells us a little bit about these participants who would later found the Club. The prize for the Derby was sometimes $5.00 and other times it was four quarts of oil. Having talked with some of these participants, I know the real prize was the challenge of completing the Derby in the cold and sharing their old cars with visitors to the Philadelphia Auto Show.

Interest grew and the Derbies led to outings. Those participating came to the realization that it was now time to form a club. The year was 1935 and 14 people gathered in Philadelphia to form the Antique Automobile Club of America. The Duryea in the logo came from a postcard advertising a circus, "The Greatest Show on Earth," where the 1896 Duryea was on display.

The Bulletin, AACA's first newsletter, started in 1937 and was used to get members to the first outings, where members took part in cranking contests, tested their driving skills, and came in period clothing.

In March of 1941, AACA held its first Annual Banquet at The Old Bookbinder's in Philadelphia, Pennsylvania. To this day, the Club holds it Annual Meeting in the Philadelphia area.

World War II came and slowed progress of the Antique Automobile Club of America. In spite of the war, in 1944 the Board met and selected Packard Blue and Brass as the official colors and the Bulletin would now become the Antique Automobile.

Next, the bylaws were amended to allow the formation of Regions & Chapters. As I review this material, I am continually amazed at the foresight of the Club. The Illinois Region was formed in 1946, becoming the first Region in the Club. 1946 was also an important year because it saw the revival of the Glidden Tour™.

The Club was growing and in 1954, there were 4,500 members. The AACA Board of Directors approved the first National Fall Meet to be held that same year in Hershey, Pennsylvania.

In 1959, William E. Bomgardner was hired by AACA as business manager and the National Headquarters office was opened in the Hershey Museum building. The 1960s roared past with growth, international travel, additional National Spring and Fall Meets, and Regions and Chapters now numbering 80.

The AACA made a bold move to a new home in the 1970s, purchasing a former Milton Hershey School home at 501 West Governor Road in Hershey. The new National Headquarters with its 2.7 acres of land was a wonderful move for the Club, and with membership at 25,000, it gave a permanent facility for serving the members.

The next big event was the AACA Library located on the second floor of the AACA Headquarters. In 1977, the Alfred S. Lewerenz Collection was purchased by the Library and it was soon apparent that there was a need for a new building. Regions and Chapters rallied with support and in May 1985, during the 50th year, the groundbreaking was held for the new AACA Library & Research Center building.

1985 marked the Golden Jubilee of AACA, a year-long celebration. We enjoyed a kick-off banquet in Philadelphia, Pennsylvania, at the 49th Annual Meeting. On hand to help celebrate were Frank Abramson, first AACA president, and his wife, Fran; founding member Ted Brooks and his wife, Ruth, and family; and founding member Ted Fiala and his wife, Sue. The Antique Automobile Club of America's week-long Golden Jubilee Tour was held in the Valley Forge in Philadelphia, Pennsylvania, area.

In 1986, I came to AACA National Headquarters to become Executive Director. As I look at the Club and my experiences in it, I see a wonderful Club, a very satisfying hobby, and a means of preserving the history of the automobile and its hundreds of related objects.

The 1990s have arrived and the Club remains healthy having gone through many changes with the years... the passing of old and faithful members, environmental pressures and concerns, and, thankfully, a new generation of members, many of whom embrace the 1960s and 1970s era vehicles, just as I did those old Fords. I'm grateful that we can go from a Model T to a Mustang and have a place for each in this Club, along with everything from a truck to a motorbike.

Reflecting on our achievements, I believe the "25 years or older" qualification for vehicles at National Meets helped the continued growth of AACA. We can all take pride that we have what is believed by many to be the finest judging system for any multi-marque club, with many single marque clubs asking for our assistance to develop their own judging systems. We have more than 400 Regions and Chapters in the Club today.

The AACA Board of Directors consists of 21 members from all walks of life, all dedicated hobbyists. The AACA Library & Research Center, with its 15 Board members, boasts one of the most up-to-date collections on the East Coast.

Looking ahead, the AACA Museum, Inc., a newly formed entity, has purchased 25 acres of land near Hershey to build an exciting vehicle museum for the enjoyment and education of all.

William H. Smith

Introduction

The idea for this book began several years ago during the annual Winter Meeting of the AACA in Philadelphia. It was my observation that the number of the club's notable founders was dwindling and I thought "someone" should do a book on the history of the club soon.

In talking up the idea at the convention, it was unanimous among my many old friends from twenty-five years of being in the organization that, yes, I was correct; there should be a book. But who would write it? Who would publish it?

As with any good idea or suggestion, the burden to find these answers always comes back to the person who first thinks of or suggests it. Bill Smith, Ron Barnett and Pinky Randall especially encouraged me to find an author and publisher. The authorship stuck, with Ron offering to head up a committee to supervise the project at the AACA's end. We put together a prospectus for the book and showed it to several publishers who were all interested.

My former employer from Wisconsin, Krause Publications, stepped forward with the first and best offer to AACA and myself to produce the book. That product is what you are holding in your hands.

What was to take a year actually took two. I wish I had four. Some contributors dallied in getting materials to me, and as a result I am sure I caused Krause Publications some anxious moments. With such a large story to tell, I was constantly finding new twists and turns in the overall theme. There are still many subjects that I wish we could have expanded upon. Of course, there were items that should be included in this history that never found their way to us.

The story of the AACA is a rich and illustrious one. It is but one of many dedicated organizations devoted to the enjoyment and preservation of the antique automobile and its history. From the region and chapter presidents, board and national officers, to the folks who have diligently brought us such fine publications as *Antique Automobile*, we truly have a club in which to be proud.

As you read this book and enjoy the many wonderful photos we have collected in this mission, I hope you sense the same things that I did. One of longing for the simpler times that fostered this wonderful organization and the era in which amazing cars could be and were collected, preserved and restored. The idea of finding a Duesenberg on a used car lot, or a Mercer in a city garage were concepts that I was too young to have even considered as possible. Yet, we have many members still with us who did just that. You will see photos of club events with Stutz, chain-drive Mercedes, Bugattis and the like, touring or just resting at a roadside inn while club members meet. It was an era when a Cord would have been as likely to be in the parking lot as a Mustang is today. What a time it was for car hobbyists, one I wish I could have been part of first hand.

I hope this book is an inspiration for you to participate in AACA to its fullest. One that will encourage you to drive and display your antique cars, so that younger members can experience vehicles that they may never see in action any other way.

As Ted Fiala said in one of his many addresses of the AACA membership at the annual Philadelphia meeting, "Here's to the AACA, may it never run out of gas!"

Bob Lichty

Prospectus

The Antique Automobile Club Of America

Interest in early automobiles became evident in the Philadelphia area before 1932. In that year the officials who conducted the Philadelphia Automobile Show decided to inaugurate, as an added attraction, a derby in which cars twenty-five years, or older, could participate. Prizes were offered for longest distance traveled, appearance, age, and road-worthiness of car. Although many aspects of the feature left room for improvement, the affair was such a success that it was continued with modifications each year until 1940, when the automobile show was discontinues. Some of the participants in the early derbies soon realized that a group or organization of old car owners would serve to promote the aims of old car operators, so in November 1935 the Antique Automobile Club of America was formed with fourteen charter members. The activities decided to hold other events of interest. It was in this year that the Club Bulletin first appeared.

From this start the Club has now grown until it boasts a membership of 150 enthusiasts scattered over the United States and England. The original Club Constitution was redrafted, and meetings were held every month at the home of some member. It was found that the enthusiasm and interest aroused in the collection and exhibition of the early cars grew very rapidly. At the present time the Antique Automobile Club holds its own annual outing in which 25 to 30 cars participate, and it has inaugurated an annual banquet which proved to be a tremendous success in 1940. In addition, there have been many activities of a minor nature including participation in local parades and pageants, as well as short tours to nearby points of interest.

Since the founding of our club, two very active clubs have been formed in other sections of the country. This has served to promote a feeling of mutual interest between the more widely members, due in part to the fact that a great many enthusiasts belong to all three of the clubs.

The original thought in limiting membership to owners of vintage cars has been discarded, because it soon appeared that there were many collectors in allied fields who were tremendously interested. Their collections include emblems, nameplates, lamps, horns, books, catalogs, literature, advertisements, and pictures. In addition we have found many who are simply fascinated in seeing and talking about the cars and former experiences, although they are in no way collectors.

While one of the chief purposes of our organization is to promote good fellowship among those who have this common interest, there is, nevertheless, a more fundamental reason for the hobby.

We who are living in the period 1900-1950 are witnessing one of the most extraordinary changes that has yet come over the human race in such a short period of time. This change can be traced directly to the introduction of the self-propelled vehicle, which, of course, in turn led to the practical application of the aeroplane. It is entirely fitting that the history and the models of this momentous period should be preserved for generations to come, and not only preserved passively in a museum, but actively in order to show how they operated. It is necessary to collect and record, from those who can still remember, the trials and tribulations which accompanied the early days of motoring. Some of our older members recall vividly their first-hand experiences during those times. Younger ones have had it handed down to them by word of mouth. Others of us can remember how, as youngsters, we were permitted to squeeze the bulb horn, or perhaps to hand tools for frequent repairs.

All in all, we sincerely feel that ours is a worthwhile hobby which will, in years to come, prove of tremendous historical interest, and we extend a cordial invitation to anyone, regardless of age or sex, whose interest has been aroused, to join us in this fascinating pastime.

The Roots
of
Auto
Collecting
and
Restoration

It is hard to imagine a 1905 automobile as only being thirty years old when the AACA was created in 1935. Make a mental picture of any 1905 automobile and think about it; in 1935, this ancient vehicle would be the equivalent to a 1968 car. While cars of the late sixties are beginning to look old, especially due to their enormous size, one could argue that cars have changed a lot less in the past thirty years than in those first thirty years of motoring.

Yet, even by the 1930s, many stalwart hobbyists recognized the historic value and interest in ancient automobiles. Many of these cars simply remained in use and required upkeep. Some hobbyists found the amazing old vehicles fun to drive, and in some cases, highly exhilarating. The thrill of a rapid Sunday afternoon cruise in your Mercer raceabout could hardly be compared to a trip in a conservative '30s sedan.

Car museums where almost unheard of until the 1940s, but you can bet that collections of great cars were already beginning to be amassed by those with the foresight to save this small part of mobile history.

Now, ask yourself, should you be stashing away great hordes of sixties, seventies, even eighties cars now? Will the day come when the cars we drive daily have changed so much that you will long to cruise in your AMC Pacer, a Gremlin,

1935 Lincoln LeBaron convertible. (OCW)

14

Pinto, Cosworth Vega, maybe a Corvette or Mustang. Don't scoff; there are already clubs for most of these cars, plus more interesting marques such as DeLorean, Bricklin, Checker, even the once common VW Beetle. As the AACA "25 year" rule comes into effect you will see all of these cars pop up on the show field at Hershey and other national events. After all, as this book is written in 1998, we will see 1973 cars entering the show competition for the first time. Can a '73 Cadillac Fleetwood get your juices flowing the same way a Pierce-Arrow or a Peerless did years ago? Will a Maverick Grabber evoke thoughts of thrilling countryside drives the way a Stutz Bearcat once did.

To the thirty-five year old who road his bicycle to the Dodge dealer to see the new Mopars arrive in the fall of 1973, these cars are just as important to his feeling of nostalgia. His thoughts of paisley polyester bell bottoms and disco music will evoke those same powerful nostalgic memories as a Model A does for a seventy-year-old, or a '57 Chevy does for a sixty-year-old.

It is nice to see younger people entering the hobby as they learn to enjoy and covet the cars from prior to their own nostalgic memories. Even though we are seeing the great collections disperse and fewer and fewer people pursuing the actual act of full restorations, the interest in early cars is on a resurgence. However, we will see a rebirth in restoration as older restorations are re-restored. Possibly, parts will become available as the need demands. And we may again see these great cars regulated to trailers and concours judging fields instead of the highway.

Only time will tell where the hobby of car collecting and restoring is headed. But, let's all hope the automobile will always be an important leisure and business factor for all of us and the generations to come. Our advise, drive your old cars, give rides to anyone who wants one, especially the young. AACA is making a concentrated effort to attract the youth market and so should you if we are going to preserve the memory of the car for future generations.

Minnesota Manual For Motorists

1919
Compiled by Julius A. Schmahl—Sec. of State

1. It is not necessary for the driver of a motor vehicle to blow-up when he has a blow out.
2. A motor vehicle is not an aeroplane; don't try to fly
3. Roads were made to travel on—not to burn up.
4. Women drivers of motor vehicles should be given special consideration and watching.
5. The driver of a motor vehicle on the public highways of this state, meeting or overtaking any horse, or other draft animals driven, or in charge of a woman, child, or aged person, shall not pass such animal and driver at a speed greater than four miles an hour.
6. If every driver of a motor vehicle would carefully consider the rights of others, his own would need no consideration.
7. No driver of a motor vehicle was ever brought into court charged with the offense of driving too carefully.
8. Don't argue with another owner that you have the better car unless you are bigger than he is.
9. If you hunt game from a motor vehicle in Minnesota, the Game Warden will hunt you.
10. The most obnoxious animal in the world is the Road Hog. He is as objectionable as any other hog, and you can't eat him.
11. Toot your own horn loud and long when necessary.
12. Do unto other motorists as you would have them do unto you when you find them stuck on the highway.
13. When the other arm is occupied, be sure to drive slowly.
14. There are two laws governing the "Right of the Road": The Law of Courtesy and The Statute Law. The Statute Law will seldom be violated if the Law of Courtesy is strictly observed.
15. All motor vehicles must be provided with an adequate horn, bell, or other device for signaling.
16. If you must monkey with a vehicle, buy one of your own.

The beginning... the first twenty-five years

Prior to the formal organization of the Antique Automobile Club of America (AACA) in 1935, interest in old vehicles was somewhat rare. Nevertheless, many enthusiasts were fascinated by those cars of our automotive forefathers. It is this author's guess that as early as the 1920s, some men began stuffing away those earliest relics of the automotive birth era. Remember, the entire auto industry was officially only 39 years old. The last Model T Ford had only rolled off the assembly line eight years previous.

The AACA, America's oldest and most respected antique car association, has had a profound influence on the preservation of antique cars among enthusiasts. In this introductory section on the AACA, we will take a brief chronological look at the highlights of the club from its inception in 1935 through its silver anniversary 25 years later. Some of the important developments in the auto industry that led to the club's formation will also be highlighted. Many specific events in its history will be given greater detail throughout the remainder of this book.

In 1985, William E. Bomgardner and Henry E. Krusen interviewed three of AACA's founding fathers: Frank Abramson, Theodore Brooks, and Theodore Fiala. This trio, the only founders still living at that time, had many interesting insights. They not only offered their thoughts on the history of the AACA, but also on the roots of automobile collecting and restoring as a whole.

On the Plaza at the 1938 Philadelphia Auto Show: Earl Eckels' 1912 Stanley, George Hughes' 1909 Hupmobile, and Ralph Weeks' 1909 Maxwell.

This photo of a participating 1904 Ford was taken at the January 1938 Philadelphia Auto Show at Convention Hall.

Ted Fiala told how his stepfather had offered him an old car that he had found while cleaning out a Philadelphia estate carriage barn. At the time, Fiala was not even sure if he wanted such an old vehicle. He told his friend and co-worker at Universal Gun Company, Frank Abramson, about the car. Abramson thought the two could have some fun fixing the old vehicle and driving it around, so they went back to Ted's stepfather and accepted the offer. The car, a 1906 Waltham-Orient, would turn out to be the very vehicle the two would use to found the AACA.

Fiala and Abramson also used the car to advertise Wilson's Cafe at 53rd and Walnut Street in Philadelphia, Pennsylvania. After their regular day jobs, the budding entrepreneurs would drive around in the Orient, an automotive equivalent of a sandwich board sign, promoting Wilson's Cafe. The two would wear gay-'90s suits and handlebar mustaches, driving around until at least midnight. They would

The Orient decked out for advertising "Bundy" typewriters on the streets of Philadelphia in 1935. (OCW photo)

Ted Fiala and Frank Abramson in the Orient at the Philadelphia Auto Show.

This 1907 Waltham Orient was a prize winner in the annual derby held yesterday in connection with the opening of the Philadelphia Automobile Show. Left to right are Fred C. Nicholson, Frank Parker, Frank Abramson and Theodore Fiala, of this city; Guy A. Willey, president of the Philadelphia Automobile Trade Association; and William S. Canning. A total of 22 cars, all 25 years of age or over, were entered in the derby.

then go back to Wilson's, be paid, have some beers, watch the floor show, and then go home. Before long, other companies wanted the two to advertise for them with the ancient vehicle as well. With the money earned utilizing the 1906 Waltham-Orient, the two enterprising young men bought a second car, a 1910 Hupmobile. As of this writing, Abramson still has the same Waltham-Orient. This vehicle is currently (1998) on display at National Headquarters.

Brooks recalled falling in love with a 1914 Buick owned by a neighboring doctor, who had put the car on blocks many years earlier. The doctor gave Brooks the Buick, starting a life-long affair with antique automobiles. He was already driving the car in parades and local events when he heard about the antique auto derbies in Philadelphia. It was at one of these derbies that he met Abramson and Fiala.

Abramson and Fiala started entering the Philadelphia Automobile Derbys in 1933, the third year for such events. The derbies were linked to the new car exhibits in Philadelphia. Commercialism, which would be unheard of in the later days of the organization, was much alive in the 1930s. Cash to individual car owners was a big part of what brought this initial group of old car enthusiasts together in 1935. They were each paid a small amount of money from the auto show promoters to bring their antique vehicles to the event. From those roots came what was to

Frank Abramson and Ted Fiala pose with the 1906 Orient at the 1988 Franklin Mint car show in Wawa, Pennsylvania. (Vince Chimera photo)

21

The ever-present Walter "Sparky" Matter and his Model T at the '48 Devon show. (Chris Hannevig photo)

The 1906 Waltham Orient in front of Frank Abramson's home in Philadelphia in the late 1980s. It is interesting to note that Abramson told us the car was called a 1907 for years, and with research he found it was truly an '06. That is why you will find conflicting dates listing the car in AACA records and even in this book.

become the largest, most respected, old car organization in the world, the Antique Automobile Club of America.

It seems ironic that the new cars that filled the streets and the Philadelphia auto show in 1935 are highly prized collectibles today—although it would not be until 1960 that those new cars would become accepted into AACA judging. In 1960, those contemporary cars would reach 25 years old; that would be the same year as the club's Silver Anniversary. The 25-year rule would come and go several times in the club's history.

Contemplate this simple list of contemporary 1935 cars and imagine what really constituted an antique automobile: 1935 Buick series 90 convertible coupe, 1935 Cadillac V-16 Imperial limousine, 1935 Chrysler Imperial Custom Airflow, 1935 Duesenberg model J convertible coupe, 1935 Ford V8 convertible sedan, 1935 Hudson Deluxe eight convertible coupe, 1935 Hupmobile Aerodynamic sedan, 1935 Lincoln K LeBaron convertible coupe, 1935 Packard Twelve LeBaron All-weather Town Car, 1935 Pierce-Arrow production Silver Arrow coupe, and 1935 Studebaker President Eight Regal roadster. This is a tiny list, but you get the idea. Even the Marmon "16" had only been off the market for two years. Any one of these cars would be a highly coveted hit at an AACA event today.

The AACA officially formed in 1935. Its roots, however, date back to 1931 when the Philadelphia Trade Association prepared for its annual auto show. It was decided that a rally for old cars would be an exciting draw for the show. Early cars would be expected to drive under their own power to the event. Owners of old cars were asked to drive their vehicles in what was labeled the "First Antique Automobile Derby." The event was very successful and repeated for a number of years, each year the number of entrants increasing.

An individual named Fred Nicholson was linked to a number of such derbies, which became reliability runs for cars 25 years old or older. In each derby, the participants had to drive from any point 25 miles from Philadelphia. As they left, the participants had to telegraph derby judges with their starting time. Time checks and traffic tests were the basis for derby prizes. Additionally, there were prizes for showing the cars, manufacturer trophies, and even cash awards.

Some of the most popular starting points were Phoenixville, Trenton, and Wilmington, Delaware. Because it was winter, drivers had to bundle up in the wee hours of 4 a.m. Tire and mechanical problems could throw the most enterprising automobilist off pace before arriving in Rayburn Plaza. The participants would gather in front of Convention Hall and were expected to remain in the plaza, in the cold, to answer questions from the throngs of people heading inside to see the new cars. The old cars were a constant source of curiosity for the crowds.

It was in January, during the 1935 auto show, that the car owners sat in Rayburn Plaza answering questions from spectators, talking amongst themselves about antique cars, and complaining about their treatment by derby officials. The car owners wanted more prize money and recognition for braving the weather and generally adding to the overall success of the commercial event. Ted Fiala and Frank Abramson sat in their 1906 Waltham-Orient, participating in the discussion and paying a great deal of attention.

Vintage cars are still a feature at the Philadelphia Auto Show. This 1948 Lincoln Continental cabriolet was featured at the 1998 event.

The car that had been found in a barn the previous year, and not run in more than 25 years, was now the tool for the pair to begin organizing a club. They got the single-cylinder vehicle in operational condition during a quick restoration and realized what fun it was. They planned to participate in the fun of more antique automobile derbies and were especially motivated to meet other enthusiasts of vintage vehicles.

There they were, and, as it turned out, the fun was sitting half frozen with a bunch of other disgruntled car owners in Rayburn Plaza. On September 20, 1935, Abramson and Fiala, along with Jack Dlugish, sent a letter to each derby entrant and queried the participants on the idea of forming a club to promote the appreciation of antique automobiles and to build a cohesive front to get better derby recognition. They enclosed a reply card and received mostly positive responses. On October 28, 1935, a second letter was sent announcing a meeting at the Philadelphia Automobile Club. The fifth running of the Antique Automobile Derby was scheduled to help launch the new 1936 cars. Participants were going to be prepared with their new organization. The group was not unlike a newly organized labor union wanting better pay and working conditions.

Thirty-five people showed up for that first meeting on November 4, 1935, and the name Antique Automobile Club of America was coined. Fourteen of the thirty-five paid the whopping $1 dues on-the-spot to form the first treasury. Abramson and Fiala would admit in a later interview they did not pick the name with any great insight as to the vast future the club would enjoy nationwide, let alone worldwide. The choice was a chance stroke of genius and an amazingly appropriate one.

The original fourteen founding members were:

Frank Abramson	*Philadelphia, Pennsylvania*
Theodore B. Brooks	*Wayne, Pennsylvania*
Earl S. Eckel	*Washington, New Jersey*
John J. Eichorn	*Philadelphia, Pennsylvania*
Theodore J. Fiala	*Havertown, Pennsylvania*
Joseph M. Kern	*Media, Pennsylvania*
Clarence W. Letts	*Glenside, Pennsylvania*
Paul Marvel	*Lancaster, Pennsylvania*
Walter Matter	*Hawley, Pennsylvania*
Fred Parsons	*Bryn Mawr, Pennsylvania*
Anton Schuck	*Stockton, New Jersey*
D. Spagnolia	*Philadelphia, Pennsylvania*
Noah Swartley	*Souderton, Pennsylvania*
Joseph C. Williams	*Franklinville, New Jersey*

Frank Abramson became the club's first president, and remains with us today as the only survivor from this original group of pioneers.

Ted Fiala was elected secretary-treasurer. It seemed only fitting that he and Abramson would be two of the officers of the club. Earl S. Eckel was elected vice-president.

The group did not vote to take any rash action against the auto derby, but the organization was the first step in promoting automotive history and the hobby of antique car collecting worldwide. The club attracted hobbyists dedicated to collecting, preserving, driving, and restoring America's great automotive heritage. That first meeting launched what would become the first club of this kind in the United States and would dominate the hobby to this day. Only the Veteran Car Club of Great Britain was older, having been formed in 1930.

Not many meetings were held the first year. Members, however, did participate in the following events: the 1936 Trenton Antique Auto Derby; the Cavalcade of Transportation in Washington, DC; the Philadelphia Antique Automobile Derby; and the Philadelphia Mummers Parade.

A typical early meeting of the group might include a talk by P.M. Heldt, a well-known engineer at that time, and by Fred Nicholson. Nicholson remained the AACA chief judge and a popular speaker on the subject of early motoring.

The 1948 New York Auto Show at the 71st Regiment Armory in New York held March 8-14, 1948. Note the incredible display of roadsters and race cars in the foreground including "Old 16." (Philadelphia Auto Show Program)

Other meetings late in 1936 and 1937 included only officers showing enough interest to attend. From the first $14 dues, the club ended 1936 with $1.30 in the treasury. In 1937, the club published its first publication, a forerunner to *Antique Automobile* titled *The Bulletin*. The first mimeographed issue was only a hint of what was to become one of the AACA's strongest benefits: professional publications. (An in-depth look at club publications is featured in a chapter later in the book.)

The club constitution had been drawn up and submitted for approval in 1936 and was mailed out with an early 1937 edition of *The Bulletin*. The main thrust of the document stated:

"The purpose of this organization is to perpetuate the memories of pioneer days of automobiling by furthering interest in and preserving antique cars, and to promote sportsmanship and good fellowship among its members."

The club truly lived up to the constitution's promise. The love of old cars came first on the priority list of members. Individual backgrounds and persuasions were of little consequence. While the car hobby has been perceived by many as a rich man's preoccupation, the AACA has never promoted it to that end.

Remembering AACA Founding Member Anton Schuck

Stockton, New Jersey, a small community along the Delaware River, was the home of AACA founding member Anton "Tony" Schuck, and the site of his auto repair garage. The area during the 1940s and 1950s was quiet, slow moving and basically agricultural. It was a pleasant place for me to grow up. At the time in nearby Lambertville, George Green of curved dash Oldsmobile fame operated a machine shop and Fred Parsons, another AACA founding member, had a small auto parts and motorcycle store. It was an area rich in antique auto pioneers and elderly citizens hanging onto and driving cars such as a '25 Model T Ford and '26 Chevy to a '38 Oldsmobile and '41 Lincoln Continental throughout that period. Adding to this was bandleader Paul "Pops" Whiteman, who had a beef farm near Stockton. He was always buzzing up and down the road in a European sports car of one make or another. With this background, it is no surprise that I was fascinated with old cars at an early age. I started my old car and truck collection at the age of 13.

On one occasion in high school, some classmates told of their hazardous adventures along the rock cliffs and bottomless pond at the stone quarry attached to Tony Schuck's vacant farm adjacent to the village of Raven Rock where the missing link of Route 29 turned into a dirt road. What really piqued my interest was their description of an old Chevy roadster and an empty office trailer at the quarry. Upon investigating the property, I immediately fell in love with the '29 Chevy, which turned out to be a badly deteriorated coupe or cabriolet, but mechanically complete. I had to have it. To complicate things, I was a quiet country boy and the owner of the car was German born Anton Schuck who had a stern no-nonsense manner. Much so, that local folklore at the time claimed that he would chain the car of a customer with a bad reputation for paying bills to a pole on the small parking lot across the road from his garage.

After weeks of building up courage, I finally went to Schuck's Garage. On asking Tony about buying the Chevy, he answered with his serious eyes and unmistakable somewhat throaty voice, "What do you want that junk car for? I couldn't sell it if I wanted to. The whole quarry is tied up in a court order. Nobody can set foot on the land and nothing can be removed." It turns out that during the atomic energy boom of the late '40s, some slick operators from Philadelphia rented the quarry from Schuck and promptly sold stock for what turned out to be a bogus uranium mine located at Raven Rock, New

Jersey. The property was tied up in a legal tangle for years. I never saw the '29 Chevy again.

Tony was a capable and respected auto mechanic who had a collection of old cars from early Stanley Steamers to a late 1930s Packard coupe that his wife, Bertha, drove into the mid-1950s. Inclined to be a bit frugal, Tony used a 1936 Chevrolet wrecker until about 1960. I always admired his tow truck, and one day it was replaced by an early 1950s model Chevy tow rig. I was sure he would save the '36, and retire it to his farm. I didn't ask about it. Much to my distress, I learned from a friend that Schuck sold it to Schuster, the junk man from Sergeantsville, and it was cut up for scrap. I know that if I could have gotten my hands on the old tow truck, it would be parked next to my one-ton 1927 Chevy today.

Tony died in the mid- to late-1960s, and his son Richard now operates Schuck's Garage as a European car repair facility.

Anton Schuck's inspirational 1929 Chevrolet "coupe or cabriolet?"

Panoramic view

(Weintraub photo, donated to AACA by Charles Betts)
Cars and owners left to right include:
Buick—Brooks; Cadillac—Irvin Theis

of the Sixth

Jackson—Paul Marvel; Oldsmobile—George Green;

Annual Automobile

Waltham-Orient—Ted Fiala; Hupmobile—George and Grace Hughes;

Derby in Reyburn

Buick—Joseph Kern; Ford—Walter Matter;

Plaza, Philadelphia

Buick—Bert Mushkin; Hupmobile—Frank Abramson;
Pierce-Stanhope—Fred Parsons;

November 12, 1936

International—Sol Berman; Renault—(unidentified);
Oldsmobile—Clarence Letts

During the Great Depression, the club treasury was woefully inadequate, and the members could not make up the difference. Money was raised by using members' cars for commercial endeavors. The cars were not used in the name of the club, but funds from those endeavors seemed to find the club treasury anyway. Photographs of early cars and other items were sold by members as fund-raisers for the treasury as well.

By the 1940s, most commercial use of members' cars was no longer necessary. Increased membership and the sale of automotive jewelry and other items bolstered the treasury. Selling antique automobile merchandise has been a tradition AACA still continues today. The organization's current line of merchandise is still truly impressive. The retail arm offers members everything from model cars and trucks, to clothing items, jewelry, and even automotive-themed neckties. Chances are you bought this book from an AACA trade show booth.

Stepping back to the 1930s, we should note that most old cars were priced very low. Vehicles needing a lot of work went begging for new owners. Many cars went to the scrap heap due to hobbyists having a lack of storage space—a situation not so different from cars going to the scrap yards today due to environmental and legislative reasons. Speculation on old cars was as common in the 1930s as it is

Mabel Bailey, wife of Sam Bailey, at the wheel of the couple's 1914 Mercer in the spring of 1942. Scenes like this typified what the AACA was all about in the early days—committed hobbyists having fun in truly significant and exciting cars and not being afraid to drive them. (Chris Hannevig photo)

Press accounts of the 1959 New York Auto show and the emphasis on antique automobiles in participation.

today. Accounts of hobbyists doing a quick fix-up of an old car, then offering it for resale, were commonplace. One can only guess how many great "original" cars received devastating quickie restorations in those days. It might have been decades later before the auction circuit and paint jobs in "resale red" were common; nevertheless, the profit motive was there and just as damaging. Of course, as a result, the profit motive can also be credited to saving many of the cars we enjoy today and creating the aftermarket industry. Many cars and parts we enjoy today are a result of true hobbyists and their love of the motorcar over money.

Wartime scrap drives were even more catastrophic than public apathy for old cars. Many old cars were sold or donated to scrap drives to build weapons for World War II. Yet, pioneer collectors like Detroit's Barney J. Pollard virtually squirreled away some of the greatest cars to survive today. Pollard became known as an eccentric for hanging hundreds of vintage cars on end in his warehouses in Detroit. In reality, the cars were being hidden from the scrap drives to be saved later as his collections were dispersed. He and many other hobbyists saved a lot of our cars from the foundries; other hobbyists just did not save cars in such volume. They created large collections that helped preserve a big part of our automotive heritage today. Hobbyists such as Henry Austin Clark, William H. Harrah, James Melton, D. Cameron Peck, Barney Pollard, Joe van Sciver Jr., William E. Swigart, and many others did all of us today a real service.

As the hobby expanded, interest began to turn away from the reliability run type events and shifted toward appearance, authenticity, and judging of antique cars. The resulting cars were thoroughly and authentically restored as opposed to just being made functional again.

The public had a preconceived notion that all old cars were just old junkers, barely safe for the highways and public road hazards. Safety standards were not yet emphasized in events as they are today. Even tires during the Depression and war era were hard to come by and cause for safety concerns.

Tires for early hobbyists were definitely a major problem. The old sizes simply were not produced during World War II. Used tires and recaps were all that were available to hobbyists. In some sizes, even that was impossible. Only Model T tires were readily available. Bald tires were the rule of the day and early tours always included many tire repairs along the route.

In 1946, the AACA was invited to participate in the auto industry's Golden Jubilee celebrations. The biggest problem in getting members to participate in the Detroit celebration was the need to overcome the tire problem. New tires in the old sizes were needed and Firestone Tire and Rubber Company came forward to fill the need. The AACA committee for the tire project wanted "non-skid" style tire treads. Firestone advised against the design due to the short life and possible safety considerations of the "nonskid" tread design. The committee pressed the issue and Firestone produced the tires in spite of these concerns. The cars made it to the Jubilee on Firestone nonskids. By the time the club had its own 25th anniversary in 1960, Firestone was replacing the "nonskid" design with a more conventional tire design—one that would match the needs of the hobbyists traveling greater distances and at higher speeds. Today, we see Coker Tire reintroducing the Firestone "nonskid" pattern as history repeats itself. Firestone would later surrender the

AACA President Embarrasses Teenager

Accompanying my family on the 1946 and 1947 Glidden Tours™ was a key factor in interesting me in antique cars. As a recently licensed sixteen year old driver, anything resembling an automobile held my attention.

My dad, Sidney Strong, Atwater, Minnesota, was a longtime (1909) Ford Dealer and had acquired several early automobiles. In 1948, the previous Glidden Tour experience prompted him to contact a few other Minnesota people who had "old cars", with the idea of forming an autonomous Minnesota club.

The late D. Cameron Peck of Evanston, Illinois (a Chicago suburb), the soon to be elected 1949 president of AACA, requested a meeting of selected AACA members from five states. Dad was invited to represent Minnesota and I went along to keep him company.

On January 22, 1949, a small group of people met with Mr. Peck and the Chicago Region, comprising the states of Illinois, Indiana, Iowa, Minnesota and Wisconsin, was formed. George V. Campbell was elected Region Director and Dad was appointed Minnesota Director. On November 1, 1949, the Chicago Region was renamed the Midwest Region. I received my AACA Midwest Region membership card on March 18, 1950, personally signed by D. Cameron Peck.

The organizational dinner meeting was held in the banquet room of the Chicago Lake Shore Club. The "head table" was situated on a raised platform at the front of the room, with seat assignments arranged by President Peck for each state representative. I had seen my name next to Dad's but having noticed a charming young lady seated in the lower banquet room, this 18 year old secured a seat at the young lady's table. I was just getting settled when President Peck came up to me, asking that I take my seat at the head table. I thanked him but declined. A few moments later, President Peck announced over the microphone: "Would David Strong please take his assigned seat at the head table so we can began the dinner!" Needless to say, my ears glowed red all the way up to the head table and worse yet, I never did find out the name of that young lady!

In 1951, Dad petitioned the Midwest Region to permit the formation of the Minnesota-Iowa Region. On March 17, 1951, the new Minnesota-Iowa Region was chartered. A few years later, Iowa left Minnesota and the rest is history.

David K. Strong
AACA President, 1986

Death of Charles E. Duryea

The club made special note of the passing of Charles E. Duryea on Sept. 28, 1938. The club recognized Mr. Duryea not only as the organization's first honorary member, but for his contributions to the automobile industry.

'Father of the Auto' Dead at 76

antique tire market to specialty companies such as Coker, Denman, Kelsey, Lester, Lucas, Martin, and Universal. Some of the companies would eventually get permission to produce tires in the original styles and brands. Major manufacturers such as Firestone, Goodyear, Goodrich, Michelin, and U.S. Royal are available today for the purest in authentic designs. Tire availability was one of the factors that permitted the resurrection of great tours like the Glidden Tour™. We will talk more about tours in a later chapter.

With its publications, the AACA became well known for promoting automotive history. Industry pioneers such as Charles E. Duryea and Charles B. King were asked to speak at club functions. They would recount the great stories of the early auto industry. Honorary memberships were one of the first ways such dignified guests were rewarded, and Duryea was the first recipient of this membership.

★★★

In 1939, the club "logo" or emblem was designed by honorary member Herbert Van Haagen of Upper Darby, Pennsylvania. German by descent, Herbert was chief engineer at the same dental equipment company where Ted Fiala, Sr. and Ted Brooks were employed. He was interested in the club since its inception, often giving valuable assistance to the officers in the early months of organization. The club asked Van Haagen to design the club's logo, having already gotten permission to use the 1895 Duryea image from Charles E. Duryea.

Designed in 1937, the logo appeared in print for the first time in the April 1939 edition of *The Bulletin.* Herbert spent many patient months cutting the emblem master pattern in metal from a three-foot drawing with a power engraver. A beautiful one-pound brass emblem was created for the members at a whopping cost of $1.50.

Van Haagan was awarded an AACA honorary membership for his achievement in designing and producing the emblem that is still the basis for the AACA emblem. He was the second individual to receive such an award, following only Charles E. Duryea.

★★★

In 1937, President Frank Abramson began a letter-writing campaign to various magazines to promote the club and the hobby of antique auto collecting. He brought up non-existent controversies such as "whether or not to restore a car completely or only refurbish it as needed with contemporary parts just to get the car running." The result was letters from folks all over the country who did not know of a national old car club.

Some letter writers offered cars to the club. One White Steamer was offered if it would be given a full restoration. It was difficult to accommodate such gifts because the club had not yet even dreamed of having its own museum. Some replies from collectors who did not want the hobby promoted were even downright hostile; perhaps thwarting their own selfish efforts to amass hoards of cars. Remember, this was the era when some of the greatest collections were assembled.

★★★

The emblem was redesigned by Don McCray of Chicago in 1951 and has gone unchanged to this day, an important step in AACA development we will detail later as well.

The first design was an oval with the Duryea automobile in the center and the words "Antique Automobile Club of America" inscribed around the edge. By 1939, when the bronze medallions were made available to the membership, the logo had been changed to include the word "Duryea" under the car, and "Founded Nov, the year 1935" had also been added to the inscription around the edge of the emblem to designate the founding of the organization.

The basic format of the logo has remained constant throughout the years; however, there have been some subtle changes. The club name in the early design used a lettering style consistent with formal engraving of the period in which the letter "u" appeared to resemble the letter "v." The word "Antique" appeared as "Antiqve." In 1952, the logo was changed to show a more modern version of the lettering with the "u" appearing as a "u."

★★★

Competition among some of the great early collectors was at times intense. Abramson replied that the AACA was formed to promote the hobby and not ruin it. He felt that the more people who could join the club, the more all would benefit. He wanted to see as many old cars preserved as possible in collections or by individuals with only one car as possible.

★★

There has also been some controversy over the design of the Duryea automobile on the emblem relative to whether it was the 1895 Times-Herald race car or the 1896 production vehicle. In the 1939 initial announcement about the availability of the logo, Ted Fiala, editor of *The Bulletin,* stated that permission had been obtained from Duryea to use the likeness of the 1895 car for the logo.

In his 1985 interview, Fiala told the story of the logo choice a bit differently. He recalled that when the group was trying to decide what it wanted in the design, someone produced an old postcard that advertised the Duryea automobile. The first car made in America, it was on display at the Barnum & Bailey Circus during its forthcoming appearance in Philadelphia in 1896. Fiala said at the time, the club had never even heard of Duryea, but because it was the first American car (and who could dispute the word of the great P.T. Barnum), it had to be on the emblem. The car on display at the circus was indeed one of the thirteen 1896 production cars made by Charles E. and J. Frank Duryea. However, the car on the logo is an artist's rendering and has insufficient detail to absolutely conclude whether it is the 1895 or 1896 version. In any case, it is

★★

> *The club's first "official" event that year was a meet at Martin's Dam, described in more detail in the Events chapter of this book.*

★★

representative of the earliest automobiles produced in the United States and has certainly become recognized as the symbol of the AACA

The club's first life member, Thomas McKean, was recognized in 1943. He was shortly followed by J. B. van Sciver Jr. and S.E. Bailey to the status.

AACA membership had reached 413 members by 1944. With World War II over, activities really began to spring up all over the country. The first AACA Region, the Illinois Region, was formed in 1945 with the Cleveland Region following shortly thereafter.

1936 to 1944 membership count:

1936	14
1937	11
1938	no record
1939	28
1940	no record
1941	143
1942	no record
1943	109
1944	413

★★

Walter "Sparkie" Matter trying to talk his way out of a traffic ticket during the 1946 tour. (Dick Teeter photo)

A determined Walter Matter drove his 1910 Ford Model T to every possible event. (Dick Teeter photo)

Walter Matter in front of his Ford dealership in 1937 with "the car that won more prizes that any other car in the U.S.A." Exactly how Walter made that claim is up for debate, but no one will dispute that this 1910 Model T was driven more miles and to more events than any other car in the AACA's early days. Walter wrote on the back of this Dick Teeter photo:

"Ode to old Lizzie"...

The car that rides real smooth and fine
She takes you up and down the line
She goes no faster than "35"
She's safe and sure to keep you alive
So the OPA will never pursue
For she knows the laws thru and thru.
      Regards - SPARKY

Walter Matter in front of his Hawley, Pennsylvania, Ford dealership on Oct. 26, 1939. Judging from the banners in the showroom window, the '40 Fords had just arrived. (Dick Teeter photo)

The famous Walter Matter Model T as it appears today owned by Bill Tuthill of Binghamton, New York. He purchased the car from the Matter Estate. He states that Ford only listed the Torpedo roadster as a one-year model, 1911. The car was probably sold in

the 1910 calendar year even though it was a 1911 model year car. The car has been restored and still carries the dozens of dash plaques earned by the car's many miles traveling to events and on tours. (Bill Tuthill photo)

James Melton poses with Helen Mattson's Marmon roadster. Mattson had earlier teased Melton with an offer to trade the Marmon for his restored '07 Rolls-Royce Silver Ghost. The photo and note was his reply back. (Helen Mattson photo; by Duane White, Art Bragg collection)

James Melton's Museum was a congregating place for many a New England car enthusiast. The then-contemporary and now highly collectible cars in the parking lot would indicate the photo was around World War II era or slightly thereafter.

The National Trust for Historic Preservations invited the AACA to participate in its program in 1960. (The Antique Automobile)

The Other Historic Car Clubs

Just two years following the formation of the Antique Automobile Club of America, the Horseless Carriage Club of America was formed in Los Angeles on November 14, 1937. Westerners felt they needed a club based closer to California than Philadelphia.

The Veteran Motor Car Club of America was formed by twelve men at the Statler Hilton Hotel in Boston on December 2, 1938. Seventy-five cars turned out for the club's first event at the estate of John R. Macomber in Framingham, Massachusetts. Boston was only 315 miles from New York and 415 miles from Philadelphia, but members also felt that distance too far and their own club was needed. VMCCA began its publication, The Bulb Horn, in 1939. VMCCA actually beat the AACA to forming a region/chapter with the formation of its New York Region on March 9, 1940, and a Michigan Chapter in October 1944. The VMCCA and AACA shared in many events with great camaraderie in those early days. In 1949, the VMCCA acquired the entire auto collection of Larz Anderson and, for a time, used the coach house of the museum and estate as headquarters for the club.

The club's official colors were chosen in July 1945. The group selected "Packard blue" and gold to represent "brass." This was the first time regional chapters were discussed as well.

In April 1951, AACA President James Melton, presiding at the board meeting in Philadelphia, appointed Leslie R. Henry as the first vice-president in charge of regions. The first region had been established two years earlier and with interest shown in other areas of the country it was obvious that the position was needed. At this meeting, the number of board members was increased from fifteen to twenty-one.

The cover of the 1949 Philadelphia & National Antique Auto Show program shows co-sponsorships by the Philadelphia Automobile Trade Association and the Antique Automobile Club of America.

The 5,000th Member!

In 1954, Dwight D. Eisenhower was named the AACA's 5,000th member after receiving a complimentary life membership from both the national club and the Gettysburg Region.

The club has grown steadily ever since. Club publications, dues collection, and activities announcements had become a monumental job. The Tradesmen's Bank and Trust Company of Philadelphia, Pennsylvania, was hired to take over these duties. This consumed almost a full-time job at the bank. During Bill Pollack's presidency, a committee was formed to bring about a permanent full-time national office. The office would take over the bank's role and additional club functions.

In 1959, James Ladd helped obtain an invitation from Hershey Estates to use a part of the Hershey Museum as the national office. Bill Pollack and Bill Boden played an important role in the establishment of Hershey as the club's permanent address.

William Bomgardner, a local accountant, was contracted as business manager. Bomgardner was entrusted with the responsibility of directing and staffing the first permanent office of the AACA. He literally acted as an independent contractor in the position. Bomgardner hired his own staff and built the office into a fine unit.

First prize at the 1948 New York Auto Show went to Ralph R. Weeks in his 1903 Rambler. M.J. Duryea is shown presenting the award to Weeks in a staged photo at the "Nash" booth during the auto show. (Chilton News)

By this time, AACA membership was up to 9,000 members, pushing 10,000 by 1960. There were more than eighty regions and chapters by then in the United States and Canada. President George R. Norton and the National Board of Directors saw the need for more regional events. Six annual national meets were scheduled. Spring and fall meets were held annually in three different divisions of the country.

In 1960, the AACA was invited to become a participating member in the National Trust for Historic Preservation. The trust was the only non-governmental, educational organization chartered by Congress to safeguard America's historic heritage. Other groups also in the trust included: the American Historical Associations, American Association for State and Local History, Naval Historical Foundation, the Henry Ford Museum and Greenfield Village, and American Heritage, to name a few.

The club's Silver Jubilee was celebrated in 1960. Many special events included a tour of Europe. A special edition of *Antique Automobile* was created by editor L. Scott Bailey. The special edition had an excellent account of early club history by Henry Feinsinger, who was able to discuss the early days with a lot of the club founders at the time.

In 1960, the club, after much debate, set the eligibility rule for showing cars at 1935. Previously, the rule had been a sliding 25 years old for vehicles to be eligible. Now, go back earlier in this chapter to the list of contemporary cars from 1935 and think what prizes they would have been even in 1960.

But wait—1960 was a pretty great year for cars too. How about another one of the contemporary car lists? This time from 1960…think about taking any one of these cars to your next local car show: 1960 Corvair Monza coupe, 1960 Corvette Fuel Injection convertible, 1960 Buick Electra 225 convertible, 1960 Cadillac Eldorado convertible, 1960 Thunderbird coupe with a factory sun roof, 1960 Lincoln Continental convertible, 1960 Plymouth Sport Fury convertible, 1960 MGA, 1960 Mercedes-Benz 300SL, or a 1960 Studebaker Hawk—all pretty great cars today!

It wasn't until 1974 that the 25-year rule would be re-established permanently when forward-thinking members realized the future of the club's growth would be endangered if it did not move forward. Let's see, those cars would have been 1949 models, hmmmm? What would be your pick to take to a show?

AACA in the 1950s

by Willard J. Prentice
Timonium, Maryland

Although I had owned three different antique cars beginning in 1949 and had driven them around the Baltimore area where I then lived, it was strictly a personal hobby. I wasn't aware of any organized car club for antique vehicles or any group activities with the cars.

I had somehow met Lawrence Stilwell of Goodville, Pennsylvania, who was somewhat of a dealer in old cars, and I had bought a 1913 Ford Model T from him. Later, I sold him a 1928 Packard sedan that I had purchased from a local Packard agency. During one of our meetings, Mr. Stilwell asked me if I belonged to any old car club. I told him that I did not and, in fact, didn't know of any such clubs. He told me about the AACA and about the club's various activities and publications. I was very much interested and soon made out the application to join the club. This was in 1950 as I am listed in the 1950 roster. My membership certificate, however, was not issued until 1951. It is signed by the 1951 president, the nationally known tenor and entertainer, James Melton (1904-61). I don't know how long this type of certificate was used by the club.

Along with our club membership, all members of course learned of forthcoming car meets around the country. One such event scheduled for June 1950 was to be held on the Boardwalk at Atlantic City, New Jersey, which was some 140 miles from our home in Baltimore. This sounded like an interesting trip so my wife Agnes and children Warren (4) and Mary Lynn (2) and I loaded the 1913 Model T touring with essentials for an overnight trip and headed east about 8:30 a.m. on June 3. The car seemed to be running well, but at Aberdeen, Maryland, the fan belt broke and the engine overheated. Fortunately, there was a shoe repair shop nearby, and the cobbler was able to splice our ailing fan belt.

In those days there was no bridge across the Delaware River in that area so we had to wait our turn to get on the ferry. In spite of these delays, we made it to Atlantic City by 4:30 in the afternoon. We located a hotel room for $5.00, parked the car in the armory, and were looking forward to the Boardwalk parade the following morning.

While the weather had been good but quite windy on the trip, the morning was very different with almost steady rain. But now there was no turning back. We drove our Model T onto the Boardwalk and took our place in the lineup. There were no side curtains on the Model T, and we really weren't prepared for rain. We had a morning paper, and the kids wrapped themselves in that. There were about 60 cars in the parade. Few spectators were out, though, because of the heavy rain. After the Boardwalk parade we drove to the country club where the cars were judged. We received a second-place ribbon in our class, which delighted our kids. After breakfast at the club, we headed for home. Just about then I heard a sharp ping from the differential. I felt sure a tooth had broken from the ring gear. We continued on, however, but using extreme care not to accelerate too fast or apply the foot brake too hard. Fortunately there were no steep hills on the way, the rain let up, and we were able to make it home before dark. I heaved a sigh of relief, and the gears were replaced before the next event.

Many more recent club members think that Eastern Division Fall Meets have always been held at Hershey, but not so. The 1950 Fall Meet, for example, was at Devon, Pennsylvania, some 15 miles west of Philadelphia. We saw Mr. Stilwell there with his 1909 Schacht. Not only was the location different, but the scope of the meet was more limited. There were no venders, no flea market, no car corral, just an antique car show.

Owners of very early cars such as the Schacht, no doubt brought their cars to the shows on trailers. But nearly all members with multi-cylinder cars of the 1920s would not even have considered using a trailer. Cars, they said, were made to drive.

The 1952 AACA Eastern Spring Meet was held in Pottstown, Pennsylvania, in mid-June. At that time, we owned a 1924 Franklin four-door sedan. We decided to drive this to the meet. It was a nice trip with no problems, and the event personnel really treated us well. My wife, two children and myself were all given a free dinner at the country club and two nights lodging at the Hill School. There were two hundred cars registered. We all paraded through the city as part of its bicentennial celebration.

Other out-of-town events we attended during the 1950s included a trip to Lake Forest, Illinois, in June 1958 to attend a National Spring Meet sponsored by the Illinois Region, which claimed to be the oldest Regional Club in AACA. By now, we were driving a 1929 Franklin Sport Sedan that we had recently acquired. We had done some mechanical work on the car, and it drove beautifully, but we had made the mistake of trying to continue using some of the old tires. After two flats before reaching Chicago we were in real trouble. However, a visit to J.C. Whitney's store in Chicago rewarded us with a NOS (new old stock) 6.5 x 19-inch tire for the surprisingly low price of only $10.00. The tire problem, however, delayed us somewhat, and we didn't get to Lake Forest until 2 p.m.

Two years later (1960) we were again in the Midwest with the 1929 Franklin and attended the AACA Granville Rally at Kenyon, Ohio. We were awarded the Longest Distance trophy, which we still have on our mantle. By now, we had new tires and no car problems.

When I joined the AACA in 1950 there was still no AACA chapter or region in the Baltimore or Washington area. Several old car enthusiasts in the Washington area including Edgar Rohr (later an AACA National President) were talking of organizing a region there. They invited me to join them, and together we applied for a charter, which was granted as the National Capital Region about 1952. We usually held our meetings at the home of W. Lynwood Cook in Bethesda, Maryland. Lynn is best known for his 1928 Phantom I gold-plated Rolls-Royce. We had lots of local activities right from the start. I recall playing host to the Glidden Tour as the participants spent a night in Washington and in putting on a show at the opening of a new branch of the Woodward & Lothrop department store.

Baltimore was now sandwiched between two active AACA Regions: National Capital to the south and Gettysburg to the north. A local Franklin enthusiast, Karl Feather, talked to me about forming a chapter or region here. We arranged a time and place for a meeting in Baltimore and invited all interested parties. The meeting was held on March 13, 1955, and a petition for a Chesapeake Region charter with 24 signatures was prepared. The charter was granted on April 30, 1955. Chesapeake Region now has approximately 500 members. The Region has taken an active part in various aspects of the hobby including sponsoring three National Eastern Spring meets in 1978, 1982, and 1989. In addition, we have had an early spring flea market (or swap meet, as they say in the West) for several years, which have proved to be popular with hobbyists throughout the Mid-Atlantic area. Also two of our longtime outstanding members advanced to the presidency of AACA: J. Leonard Rhinehart in 1962 and Howard V. Scotland Jr. in 1988.

The Executive Directors

William E. Bomgardner, Executive Director 1955-1986

William E. Bomgardner had his own accounting business in 1955 that he continued after serving as business manager for the AACA until 1962. At that time he sold his business and devoted himself to the AACA full-time. In 1970, he took on the added responsibility of editing the club publication the *Antique Automobile*. He served in both capacities until his retirement in 1986. During his 28 year service to the club, Mr. Bomgardner aided the organization in growing from 7,000 members to over 50,000. He was instrumental in obtaining the National Headquarters building in 1970 and was active in the development of the Library & Research Center.

At a December 5, 1986, testimonial dinner, Bomgardner and his wife Jean, who served as the AACA office manager, heard many stories of their dedication and hard work. They received a beautiful clock inscribed with the names of the 1986 AACA board members. In addition, the AACA Library building was named "Bomgardner Hall" in recognition of Bill's service. The plaque was presented to Library & Research Center President Richard H. Taylor by Bill Smith. That plaque now hangs in the facility.

Also during the same testimonial for the Bomgardners, Vice President of National Awards Ed Baines announced a new national award to be known as the Bomgardner Award. The award would be given annually to the best restoration of a post-1942 vehicle. The award had been donated by Ed Marion.

President Ken Stouffer directed the unveiling of a portrait of Mr. Bomgardner to be displayed in the Library. The painting, commissioned by AACA, was painted by artist Karl Foster. The evening was topped off with 1987 President Al Edmond informing the Bomgardners that the AACA membership was sending them on the London-to-Brighton Run, in England, in November of 1987.

William H. Smith, Executive Director, 1986 to present

After an extensive six month training period, William H. Smith took over the Executive Directorship of the AACA from Bill Bomgardner on January 1, 1987. Bill Smith is a life member of the club and served on the National Board of Directors beginning in 1975. He was National President in 1979 and 1980 in addition to being the first President of the Library & Research Center in 1981.

Bill was the founding president and a life member of the Scranton Region, past president of the Northeastern Pennsylvania Region and a member of the Hershey Region. In 1980, he received the Charles E. Duryea Cup for outstanding contribution to the general welfare of the club. He was also the winner of the 1982 Founder's Award for contributing notably to the guidance of AACA toward its founding principles. He also received recognition for his outstanding service to the Library and Research Center.

Bill came to AACA as president of his family owned business, Keystone Burial Vault Co., Inc., in Scranton, Pennsylvania. He had been a civic leader throughout his career, which he continued after resettling in Manada Hill, Pennsylvania.

In recent years, he has been instrumental in helping to develop and act as the local liaison in the pursuit and goal of building an AACA Museum in the Hershey area. Through Bill's efforts, many political and financial barriers were hurdled during development of the project. Under his guidance, business relationships with programs such as the MBNA / AACA Credit Card program have also served to benefit the club. Bill travels exhaustively around the country pursuing his duties and extending the hand of the AACA National Headquarters throughout the hobby. Jeanne Smith, Bill's wife, plays a more than competent role in the operation of the club and especially in the production of the *Antique Automobile.*

As this book is written at the near end of the 20th century, we can only presume the AACA and William H. Smith will see many years and many more accomplishments together.

Incoming Executive Director Bill Smith reads the Bomgardner Hall plaque as Richard Taylor makes the presentation to Bill and Jean Bomgardner.

1957 Ford Thunderbird Restoration

by Joe Sims

The history of our Thunderbird really started almost two years before it was built. I had been driving Fords since my first job out of college and one weekend in the late spring of 1955 I was in Birmingham and visited one of the Ford dealers who happened to have a new Thunderbird in stock. After some conversation with a salesman, I was invited to take the little 'Bird out for a test drive. It was wonderful. However, I had a 1954 Ford sedan that was less than a year old and I did not feel that I could afford to trade. My time would come later.

About six weeks after the 1957 models made their debut, I decided it was time and went to visit my friendly Ford dealer in Huntsville, Ray Motor Company. With the help of a salesman, the sales manager, and all of the Ford literature in the building, we put together an order for my Thunderbird. It was to be Colonial White with a red hardtop and a black

Joe Sims' 1957 Ford Thunderbird when purchased new, posed on the sands of Daytona Beach, Fla., in February 1957.

canvas convertible top. Since performance was really what I was looking for, I ordered the 312 cubic inch engine with the two four-barrel carbure-tor option that included a special high-performance camshaft. This com-bination was backed up by a standard three-speed transmission and an overdrive. Delivery was promised in about six weeks so my Christmas present would be here.

After numerous calls to the factory, my car finally arrived on Wednes-day, February 6, 1957. The following Saturday I was on my way to Day-tona Beach, Fla., for SpeedWeek 1957 for some sun and fun and to show off my new Thunderbird. Back to work, the most often asked ques-tion was, "How much did you pay for it?" The usual reply to my answer was, "You could have bought a Cadillac for that much." My rebuttal was, "I did not want one."

A few weeks after I got my car I met Camille. After a pleasant sum-mer and fall, the T-bird got to go back to Florida again, this time to take Camille and me on our honeymoon.

Joe Sims' T-bird after undergoing a restoration in 1983.

The Thunderbird provided us with good reliable transportation as well as maintaining what I considered to be a unique air of elegance. Homes were bought, children were born, and station wagons were bought for the family, but the T-bird always carried me to work. Now the question most often asked me was, "When are you going to trade?" Eventually, even this question stopped because my co-workers learned that my answer was always, "If anyone ever builds another car, I will buy one."

Time and use took its toll, however, and in 1972 I bought a Sunbeam Tiger to drive to work while I restored (I didn't know the meaning of the word) the T-bird. The project never got off the ground and the T-bird saw limited use until 1976 when it was stored away after approximately 115,000 miles.

Finally the big day arrived. After inspecting several Thunderbirds that had been restored by Ed Robbins of Tuscaloosa, I had decided to have him do the restoration. During the course of several conversations with Ed, including a visit he made to evaluate the condition of our 'Bird, we decided upon the extent of the restoration work. Basically, we decided to do a ground up, complete restoration of show quality. Ed picked up our car in his trailer for the trip to strip tank and electrolytic tank in Jackson, Mississippi.

Our first trip to Tuscaloosa was timed to enable us to see and photograph the results of this operation being unloaded from Ed's trailer. All of this bare metal was an awesome sight and we found the body sheet metal to be in much better shape than I had believed it to be. This was the first of the series of visits we paid to Ed and the car during the course of the restoration. During each of these visits, Camille took a number of pictures so that we have a rather extensive photographic record of the work.

Since the restoration, my car has won the following area awards:
1st Junior
Senior
Grand National 1st Place
2 Grand National Senior Awards
Postwar Car Award - 1990 (National Award)
25 Preservation Awards

Membership

Life Membership

The club's first life member, Thomas McKean, was recognized in 1943. He was soon followed by J.B. Van Sciver Jr. and S.E. Bailey.

Honorary Membership

Based on great automotive and hobby contributions, the AACA has awarded periodic Honorary Memberships to a number of worthy individuals. Charles M. Duryea was the first to receive such an honorarium in 1937.

Complimentary Membership

The AACA exchanges publications with a wide variety of related organizations through the Complimentary Membership Program. This is not really a "membership" in the true sense of the word; it is more of a communication method for staying in touch with organizations that share mutual interests and missions. Antique Automobile is mailed to most of the major organizations including the Veteran Motor Car Club of America, Horseless Carriage Club of America, Classic Car Club of America, Society for the Preservation and Appreciation of Antique Motorized Fire Apparatus in America (SPAAMFAA), American Truck Historical Association, the Smithsonian Institute, and the Automotive Hall of Fame.

Publications from these organizations are retained in the AACA Library and Research Center as a valuable reference resource for AACA members. Ease of access to these publications has proven valuable to countless members performing research on vehicles and for automotive research in general.

One of the most successful examples of these complimentary exchanges is the relationship between the AACA and SPAAMFAA. SPAAMFAA's archives are physically maintained by the AACA Library and Research Center. This has created an enormously valuable asset for fire fighting apparatus enthusiasts, plus it has given SPAAMFAA a place to keep its literature collection.

Membership in the '90s

Late in 1990, members of the Membership Committee, along with several other National Directors, met to review some membership growth concerns. One of these concerns related to the fact that the AACA did not have a program to recognize members who actively recruited new memberships. Another area of concern was that, except for routine correspondence, an occasional letter of complaint from some member, and the open forum agenda at the President's Dinner during the Annual Meeting, the AACA did not have an effective procedure to encourage feedback from its members.

Numerous other clubs had special recognition programs for members who were active recruiters. In one organization, these individuals were inducted into the President's Club. Other clubs recognized the recruiters in their magazines.

The membership application form at that time had a section that required the name and signature of a sponsor who was currently an active member. An obvious question was, how do individuals who are interested in the hobby join the AACA if they don't know another member to sponsor them? The answer to this question was simple: If a membership application was received at headquarters without a sponsor's signature, the stated requirement was ignored and the application was accepted.

A decision was made to eliminate the requirement of a sponsor, but to retain the section of the form to identify the AACA member who recruited the new member. An "I Got a Member" pin was designed and distributed to each recruiter starting in 1991. The program was announced in The Antique Automobile and The Rummage Box and became an instant success. The pins became a badge of distinction and were proudly worn at all kinds of AACA activities.

The program was continued in 1992 with a pin that indicated the year that a member signed up at least one individual. A special "I Got a Member" name tag was designed in 1993 and presented to members who had recruited others for each of the first three years of the program. Small year tabs were distributed to people who continued to be active in recruitment activities and, after five years, the participants were awarded a blue briefcase with the "I Got a Member" and AACA logos.

During the above-mentioned meeting in 1990, several ideas were discussed about how to improve feedback from members. The one that seemed to have the most potential was to host a "roundtable" discussion in conjunction with a National Meet. There would be no formal agenda. National Directors would be there and respond to questions or concerns voiced by any member who wished to attend.

The first Roundtable Discussion was held in Sunnyvale, California, at the 1990 Western Division National Fall Meet. Participation at the Western Meet is relatively small compared to other divisions. Because this was the first attempt to hold a roundtable, the advance notice was somewhat limited, but a funny thing happened: seventy-five AACA members came loaded with some interesting questions.

While the National Directors who attended were surprised by the participation, they were not necessarily unprepared. They had chosen several things that were crucial to make this an effective process. The meeting was to be moderated by the vice-president of membership, but there would not be a specific agenda. Prompting questions such as "How do you like Antique Automobile?" could be used to encourage participation. Questions about any subject, except comments or questions on Class Judging, would be accepted and recorded. There is also a Judging School at each meet where questions about judging procedures are common. The intent of these roundtables was to generate discussion focused on other AACA concerns.

The directors who were present were asked to sit in the audience as opposed to being behind the head table. This was to make the process more informal and preclude any "them-against-us" appearance. The directors were also cautioned about becoming defensive. They were instructed, "If there is an obvious answer to a stated concern, record the statement and provide a simple answer."

The first Roundtable Discussion was an enormous success. Feedback from the audience covered a wide range of topics and indeed confirmed that there was a need to continue the program. A decision was made to continue these meetings at each National Meet and maintain a detailed list of questions as a guide to improving operations and developing new programs.

One of the most frequently asked questions was why the organization always holds its Annual Meeting in Philadelphia and why in February each year. The standard response was always that this date and location were dictated by the Constitution of the AACA and that the logistics for putting on a meeting of this type is most favorable in Philadelphia. As discussion of the subject continued, it was revealed that what the members who could not attend really longed for was the wonderful seminars held during the Annual Meeting each year. There was not nearly as much interest in missing out on the annual business meeting. This led to the concept of "exporting the seminars" and holding similar learning opportunities in conjunction with National Meets throughout the country. The club is now looking to expand the concept to Regions and Chapters offshore from the mainland United States.

The first such exported seminar was held at the Southeastern Division Spring Meet in 1992 at Montgomery, Alabama. The seminars were well received by the participants. Because eastern members can attend the events in Philadelphia, it was decided to hold these seminars on a rotating basis. They would be staged annually between the Southeastern, Central, and Western Divisions.

The impact of the Roundtable Discussions has exceeded all expectations. The comments have resulted in policy and procedure changes and implementation of several new programs. These discussions were held at the National Meet through 1996. Recognizing that some members only participate in tours and not meets, they were extended to the AACA tours. By 1996, many of the roundtables had become fairly routine and repetitious, and they were limited to one of the National Meets in each division instead of every National Meet. The program still remains one of the most essential methods to encourage members to let the National Directors know their concerns.

At the end of 1997, the exact membership count for the AACA was 56,241. Junior membership grew to 148 members with eighteen young people participating in the 2nd Annual Junior Hobby Display at the Hershey Fall Meet in October. The organization's "I Got a Member" program continued with a high number of sponsors, many of them new members themselves.

Current membership seems to grow for the AACA, but at a slower pace than in early years. It is one of few clubs in the hobby that, in fact, is growing. Efforts to attract younger members and staying current on keeping the "25-year rule" in effect, hence bringing in younger members and later model cars, seem to help.

For 1999, the club approved a modest increase in membership dues to $26 for a single or joint membership eliminating the difference; plus life and honorary. It was noted that in some cases, members, in an attempt to save several dollars, would not list their spouses as well. In an effort to include the spouses more, the board elected to make the fee the same for single or couples.

An ironic twist to the membership subject is that a surprising number of AACA members do not hold joint memberships in the Region or Chapter in their areas. Because this is where the best grass roots activities for AACA exist, it is a wonder why members do not spend the small extra dues for the local memberships.

Because one cannot obtain flea market, car corral, or car show entry at major events like Hershey without an AACA membership, it is suggested that some members only belong to fill this need in their hobby activities.

That, of course, is the key; the hobby and the AACA mean a lot of different things to a lot of people. From the most active hobbyist who tours, restores cars, competes in shows, and vends at meets, the AACA provides automotive fun and fulfillment at many levels of membership.

Application for New Membership

ANTIQUE AUTOMOBILE CLUB OF AMERICA, 501 W. Governor Road, P.O. Box 417, Hershey, PA 17033. Phone (717) 534-1910.

Name of Applicant

Date of Application

Sponsor's Name (optional)

Address

Make of Car

Sponsor's Signature

City   State   Zip

Year   Cyls.

Sponsor's Address

First Name of Spouse

Body Style

Sponsor's Membership Number

INDIVIDUAL MEMBER **$24.00**
Enjoys voting privileges, receives the bi-monthly issues of ANTIQUE AUTOMOBILE magazine, is eligible to join an AACA region and/or chapter and is eligible to exhibit cars and compete for national prizes and annual awards.

JOINT MEMBERSHIP (Member and Spouse) **$26.00**
This membership is for both husband and wife. Both enjoy voting privileges, are eligible to join an AACA region and/or chapter and are eligible to exhibit cars and compete for national prizes and annual awards. This membership will receive one copy of each bi-monthly issue of ANTIQUE AUTOMOBILE.

LIFE MEMBERSHIP **$600.00**
Enjoys the same privileges as Individual Membership. Spouse is also included and is entitled to the same privileges as Joint Membership. The surviving spouse of a Life Member shall remain a Life Member at no additional cost.

Make your check payable (U.S. Funds) to AACA.

ANY CHECK DISHONORED BY A BANK AND RETURNED TO AACA WILL BE SUBJECT TO A CHARGE OF $15.00.

Authorized Signature

Charge to: Visa Acct. No. _____   MasterCard No. _____
Expiration Date: Mo. _____ Yr. _____ **VISA** **MasterCard**   Applicant's Phone No. _____
Required

A membership application.

Member Cars
A Sampler

AACA Member Cars Sampler

The cars of the AACA are as diverse and unique as the members who lavishly pamper these wonderful vehicles. From the ancient horseless carriages that the club was founded on, to the muscle cars that frequent today's meets, member cars represent every automotive taste.

We have witnessed trends in which trucks and commercial vehicles have become popular. Motorcycles to mini-bikes are represented in the two-wheeled circle, and race cars, which can be just about anything that has passed under a checkered flag, from Mercers to "funny cars." It is almost ironic that in recent years, under the title of "dry lakes" racers, a pair of beautiful '32 Ford highboy hot rod roadsters graced the back cover of *Antique Automobile*.

The following cars have been selected to show the great diversity and tolerance for each other's interest that has made the AACA the greatest car club on earth. Each member may have his or her own likes and dislikes, but, nonetheless, we have a format in which to show our cars, share in the excitement, and honor our automotive past.

It is with that perspective and respect to the hundreds of thousands of cars our members have labored over that we present this small sample of the club's interests. The photos are taken from the pages of *Antique Automobile* and fellow members' scrapbooks.

1931 Buick roadster, Frank R. Langer, 1993.

1922 Brockway-LaFrance, William Lawlor, 1997.

1910 Ford Model T runabout, Walter Matter, 1948.

1913 Buick touring, Fred Kamprath, 1991.

1949 Buick Roadmaster convertible, Bob and Reba Vogel, 1995.

1962 Chevrolet Corvette, G. Van Vechten, 1997.

1966 Ford Mustang GT 2+2, Robert C. Lichty, 1982.

1953 Chevrolet Bel Air convertible, Jack R. Robinson, 1997.

1956 Chevrolet Bel Air Nomad station wagon, Richard and Pat Chappell, 1982.

1953 Cunningham coupe, Melvin Olshansky, 1993.

1901 Columbia, Henry Austin Clark, 1959.

1931 Cord L-29 convertible coupe, S. Ray Miller, 1990.

1931 Chrysler Imperial convertible coupe, Irv Davis, 1982.

1963 Chevrolet Corvair convertible, AACA Library, 1993.

1929 Duesenberg coupe, Joseph B. Folladori, 1989.

1947 Dreyer race car, Fred Sherk, 1991.

1931 Ford AA Wayne school bus, Bruce and Bunny Palmer, 1993.

1948 Ford cab-over-engine truck with trailer, Robert J. Malley, 1991.

1953 Ford F-100 pickup, Monroe K. Bryant, 1993.

1955 Ford Thunderbird, James P. Connolly, 1991.

1955 Chevrolet 210
Sport Coupe,
Charles H. Potts,
1991.

1923 Cadillac V63
phaeton, Dr. F.
Marvin Edwards,
1957.

1931 Citroen Asian
Expedition half track,
Reynolds Museum,
1982.

1936 International Harvester telephone truck, Edward Wilson, 1993.

1954 Jaguar XK-120 roadster, Pat F. McGarity, 1993.

1925 Locomobile touring, Lynn D. Curry, 1981.

1940 LaSalle convertible coupe, Harold B. Carpenter, 1991.

1929 Lincoln Imperial Victoria, Jack Dunning, 1990.

1923 Oldsmobile touring, William R. Lock, 1990.

1932 B.S.A. Scout Twin roadster, Larry W. Ayres, 1977.

1912 Pope Hartford touring, Ray Salentine, 1965.

1955 MG-TF roadster, Luther Carden, 1990.

1964 King Midget roadster, Ernest V. Freestone, 1991.

1933 Marmon 16 sedan, Allan Schmidt, 1984.

1935 Harley-Davidson, Timothy Uziel, 1998.

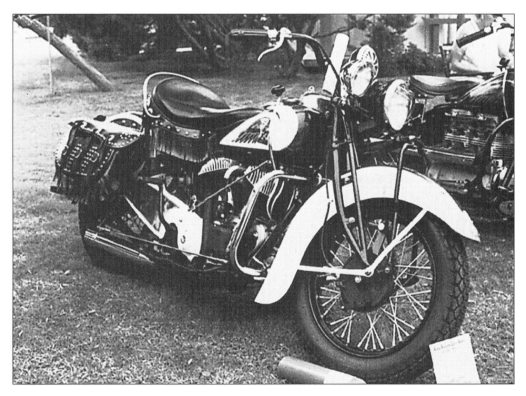

1938 Indian motorcycle, Norman Gamblin, 1984.

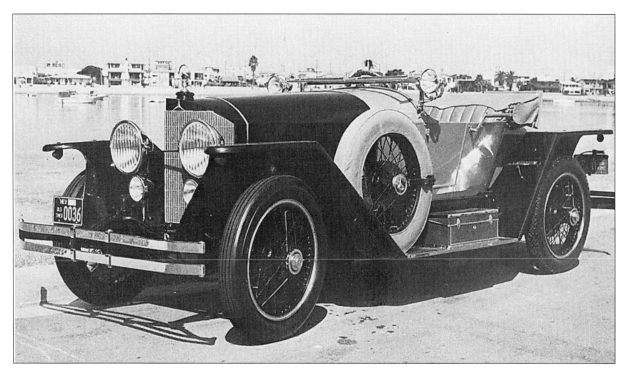

1923 Mercedes roadster, Harry B. Johnson, 1981.

1923 Rickenbacker sedan, Willis Selle, 1980.

1929 Oakland sedan, Norman E. Hutton, 1997.

1959 Lincoln Continental four-door hardtop, Kenneth M. Hohe, 1994.

1956 Oldsmobile 98 convertible, Seeber Bodine, 1988.

1941 Cadillac convertible coupe, Lou Freda, 1996.

1956 Ford Fairlane Crown Victoria Skyliner, John F. Godfread, 1990.

1959 Goggomobile van, Norman Bradford, 1988.

1909 Huselton touring, B.C. Huselton, 1988.

1931 Packard, Ralph Marano, 1997.

1954 Plymouth Belvedere convertible, Merv Afflebock, 1996.

1947 Plymouth coupe, Dennis L. Haak, 1981.

1903 Pope-Tribune, Paul E. Poe, 1993.

1957 Pontiac Bonneville convertible, George W. Weaver, 1984.

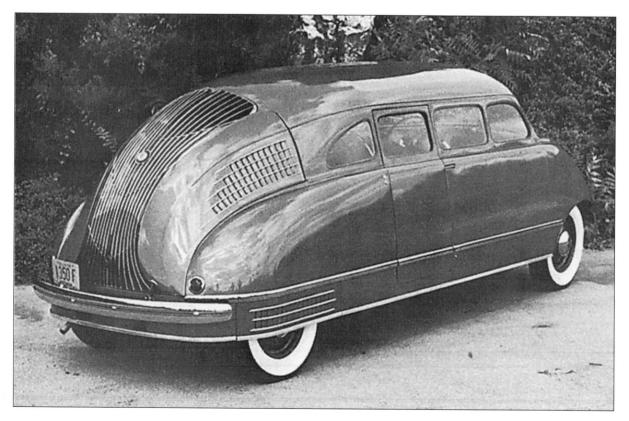

1936 Stout-Scarab, Ronald N. Schnieder, 1989.

1917 Reo touring, Ele Chesney, 1993.

1913 Simplex touring, Robert and Annie Hayes, 1985.

1970 Oldsmobile 442 two-door hardtop, Anthony Cerami, 1997.

1922 Rolls-Royce tourer, Karl F. Zoller, 1993.

1941 Studebaker Commander Skyway coupe, Wes Millenberger, 1981.

1918 Stanley Steamer touring, T. Clarence Marshall, 1961.

1907 Stanley Steamer Gentleman's Speedy Roadster, James Melton, 1957.

1951 Studebaker Champion coupe, Vern Balliet, 1991.

1963 Studebaker Daytona two-door hardtop, Harold C. Lichty, 1988.

1957 Volkswagen convertible, Larry Holbert, 1988.

1909 Waverly Electric roadster, Turner Kirkland, 1961.

1968 Skat-Kitty, Glenn G. Rand, 1997.

1909 Pullman touring, Paul Jones, 1965.

1934 Pierce-Arrow "production" Silver Arrow coupe, John D. Lebold, 1997.

Regions
and
Chapters

Regions and Chapters

From the first Region in Illinois to specialized chapters catering to specific automotive interests, AACA Regions and Chapters represent what the car hobby is all about on a grass roots level. The local level is where the real hands-on activities take place. Sometimes the names of chapters belie their real location, but you can rest assured that no matter where you live, you will find a local region or chapter of AACA to serve your hobby needs. There are also groups which are national in scope but focus on one specific interest or specialty.

Regions and Chapters formed much the same way the national group did; small bands of auto enthusiasts gathering together to share a like purpose and fun. Oftentimes these groups began as a local car club and then became an AACA region or chapter. In other cases, the group may have been from a chapter of another national car club and decided that the AACA fit its needs better.

The discussion of divisional groups started around July 1945. There does seem to be some confusion as to what constituted a region or chapter in the early days. In some cases you will even see us refer to these groups as regional chapters.

A New Club Organizes in Pennsylvania

The Historical Car Club of Pennsylvania was formed in 1949. The founders include several prominent AACA members as well as some of the AACA Founding Members. They were concerned that the activities of AACA were stretching well beyond the boundaries of the original club, in other words it was becoming too big. It was becoming a truly national club in character and the group was afraid the needs of the local area, particularly around Philadelphia were not being addressed. The group wanted to participate in meets and tours on a more local basis.

Ironically, this was at the time the regions concept was formed, but the initial emphasis was being placed on areas in the central part of the nation, not in Pennsylvania. Regions and Chapters were chartered throughout the state within the next few years. However, the Historical Car Club of Pennsylvania continued to thrive and will celebrates its 50th Anniversary in 1999.

It is interesting, from a historical point of view, to wonder if the Founding Members had anticipated the ultimate impact of selecting the name Antique Automobile Club of America and had they selected a more local name in the first place, would the national organization ever have been developed?

The September 1951 issue of Antique Automobile defined a club as a local group while a region was part of a larger national organization. The AACA encouraged the formation of new regions.

The first original charter was voted upon by the national directors and issued to a group in northern Illinois on November 29, 1945. It came about by petition of members principally in the Rockford, Illinois, area. This group was referred to as the first "regional/chapter." Other resources we checked show this group chartered on January 15, 1946, as the Northern Illinois Region after having been informally organized for two years.

The Cleveland Regional Chapter followed on May 21, 1946. The group had clearly-defined boundaries and is considered the club's first "region." The March 1949 issue of The Antique Automobile listed the group as the "Cleveland Region." This group would become what is known as The Ohio Region and has several chapters today. The Dayton Chapter later changed to the Southern Ohio Chapter and was the AACA's first chapter.

In 1950, five more chapters were formed. Antique Automobile began running a listing of Regions and Chapters in the April issue of 1959.

The Minnesota Region received the first actual charter at a formal ceremony in Minneapolis in 1951. The charter served as a model that had been approved by the National AACA board. All previously organized chapters received similar documents in June 1951.

By 1967 the March-April issue of Antique Automobile listed 112 Regions and 58 Chapters.

Today the club hosts 405 Regions and Chapters. The AACA developed a Region and Chapter training video, which sold out in its first printing and continues to sell well. There is a speakers bureau with a representative in each division. It can be arranged to have these representatives speak at local club meetings. The AACA also offers an extensive list of movies and videos available on loan from National. An updated list is accessible on the AACA Internet site: www.aaca.com.

It would be impossible to list every activity or significant event that was ever held across the country. Through Antique

Automobile and additional mailings, we asked regions and chapters to submit what they felt was a special bit of history, event account, or illustration from their area to share in this book. What follows is but a sampling of what the AACA is all about—local regions and chapters are where the "nonskids" hit the pavement, and the fun really begins. Not all regions and chapters responded, but this is a good sampling of the vast number of AACA Regions and Chapters. We at least tried to recognize each group and indicate what part of their state is serviced by each body.

A.A.C.M.E. Region

The A.A.C.M.E. (Arizona Antique & Classic Motorcycle Enthusiast) Region is based in Phoenix, Arizona. Karen Rodgers has been serving as the group's president since 1997.

Accomac-Northampton Region

The Accomac-Northampton Region is based in Cape Charles, Virginia. The group elected Emmett H. Bailey president in 1997 and Franklin A. Russell, Jr. from Parksley, Virginia, in 1998.

Alamance Chapter

The Alamance Chapter is from the Graham, North Carolina, area. Sylvia Smith served as president in 1997, followed by Earl Ewing in 1998.

Algonquin Region

The Algonquin Region of AACA services the area in and around Sydney, New York, with William F. Deering as president for 1998.

Allegheny Mountain Region

The Allegheny Mountain Region was recognized on February 2, 1951, as the AACA's ninth region. It is currently based in Boalsburg area. Stanley B. Smith was the 1998 president.

Aloha Region

Ever beautiful—but distant—Hawaii has a region based in Kaneohe. The president of this group for 1998 is Art Medeiros.

Amarillo Region

Texan David N. Patterson was elected as president of the Amarillo Region for 1998.

Ancient City Region

St. Augustine, Florida, is one of the state's most ancient cities and is home to a number of ancient vehicles owned by the Ancient City Region members. Of course, that does not mean the members are ancient by any means! A. Frank Phillips is the president of this group for 1998.

Ankokas Region

The Ankokas Region deals with AACA matters and good times in the West Berlin, New Jersey, area. Robert Schuman was elected president for 1998. The region hosted the 18th Annual AACA Grand National Meet at Garden State Park in Cherry Hill, in July 1998.

Antelope Valley Region

The Antelope Valley Region is based in Lancaster, California. David F. Floyd was president in 1998.

Anthracite Region

Anthracite is just one more mineral that the rich state of Pennsylvania is famous for. This region is located in the McDoo area and enjoyed Joseph S. Forish as its 1998 president.

Antique Auto Mushers of Alaska Region

The Antique Auto Mushers of Alaska Region is the organization's most northern group of stalwart enthusiasts. The group frequently wins awards for its outstanding newsletter. One has to wonder if the makers of antique car tires make snow treads? Richard D. Allen of Fort Richardson, Alaska, was president for 1998.

Appalachian Region

You will find 1997–98 president George F. Helms III and the members of the Appalachian Region touring the roads around the Bluff City, Tennessee, area.

Apple Country of North Georgia Region

Looks like Georgia is known for more fruit than just peaches. The Apple Country of North Georgia Region is from the Ellijay area. Roy W. Smith was president of the region.

Arrowhead Chapter of the Minnesota Region

The Arrowhead Chapter of the Minnesota Region serves the area around Carlton, Minnesota, and enjoyed Stephen W. Blaede as its 1998 president.

Artesian City Region

Albany, Georgia, is home to the Artesian City Region. The group elected Lillian Law as its president in 1997 and John B. Kelly, Jr. took over in 1998.

Athens, Georgia Region

The Athens, Georgia Region enjoyed Thomas E. Cothran as its president in 1997 and 1998.

Azalea Region

Palatka, Florida, is home to the Azalea Region and 1998 president Arthur B. Hall.

Batavia Region

Brockport, New York, is home area to the Batavia Region of the AACA and 1998 president Charles Marshall.

Baton Rouge Chapter

You can bet if we ever get down to the Baton Rouge Chapter in Louisiana, we'll ask 1998 president Jim McDaniel for some pointers on great Cajun food in addition to old car advice.

Battlefield Region

The Battlefield Region covers the area not that far south of Nashville, Tennessee. Mike T. Tschida from Thompsons Station, Tennessee, was president for 1997 and 1998.

Bay Country Region

The Bay Country Region is located in the Queenstown, Maryland, area and the Chesapeake Bay area with Albert G. Miner as 1998 president.

Big Horn Mountain Region

The Big Horn Mountain Region from Sheridan, Wyoming, elected Jacquelyn Dygert, president for 1997 and 1998.

Big Spring Region

The Big Spring Region enjoyed having Steve Barrington as president in 1997 for the activities the group held in the Lamesa, Texas, area. E.L. Hendon serves as 1998 president.

Blackhawk Region

The Blackhawk Region is more than 2,000 miles from the California auto museum of the same name. This group of AACA fans are in the Belvidere, Illinois, area and Robert G. Meline is the group's president for 1998.

Black River Valley Region

If you are ever touring way up in the St. Lawrence Seaway part of New York state near Watertown, you will find the Black River Valley Region hard at work expounding the virtues of the AACA. Frederick J. Killian III is the Region's 1998 president.

Blue Grass Region

Who says horses and horse power don't mix? The Blue Grass Region from the heart of Kentucky horse country is living proof they do. James N. Fettig was the 1998 president.

Blue Water Region

Port Huron is a pleasant Michigan coastal town and certainly inspiration for the name of this AACA Region. Brian C. Campbell was the group's president in 1998.

Bluestone Region

Princeton, West Virginia, is home to the Bluestone Region, which elected Christopher Ziemnowicz as president in 1998.

Boll Weevil Region

The Boll Weevil Region, based in Phoenix City, Alabama, is a lot more interested in cars than the cotton eating bug used as its namesake. Allen F. Kahl was president in 1997 and 1998.

Boyne Country Region

Boyne City, Michigan, is the area covered by this AACA group. Samuel M. Chipman was the 1998 president.

Brandywine Region

The Brandywine Region is based in Wilmington, Delaware, home of the famous DuPont family and car. Walter Clifton was elected president of this group in 1998. 1998 saw the region hold its 30th Annual Swap Meet at the Delaware Technical & Community College in Stanton.

Brass-Nickel Touring Chapter of the North Carolina Region

The Brass-Nickel Touring Chapter of the North Carolina Region is based in Clayton, North Carolina, with G. Barker Edwards, Jr. as chapter president.

Brunswick-Golden Isles Region

James F. Simpson was the 1997 president of the Brunswick-Golden Isles Region in St. Simons Island, Georgia. 1998 saw Brian J. Mallon become president of the group.

Bull Run Region

The Bull Run Region elected Gene E. Welch as president for 1997 and 1998 for the Manassas, Virginia, based group. The region hosted its 23rd Annual Edgar Rohr Memorial Antique Car Meet at the Northern Virginia Community College in Manassas in September 1998.

The First AACA Divisional Tour

by Bill Peugh

(Excerpted from the July-August, 1995 *Antique Automobile*)

The Bull Run Region hosted the first AACA Eastern Divisional Tour on May 4-6, 1995. The new, short, two or more day Divisional Tours had been announced by the AACA Board of Directors in May 1994.

Sixty cars, covering the model years of 1935 to 1970 participated in the two days of touring. The first day covered 165 miles and visited the White Post Restoration Facility, the Blue Ridge Parkway, the Luray Caverns and Museum. It finished up on the way back to the hub, Manassas, Virginia with a stop at the Sperryville, Virginia antique emporium.

With the evening free, many took advantage of the open house at the Rohr Museum, operated by Walser Rohr, a founding member of the Bull Run Region and the widow of the late Edgar Rohr, president of the AACA, 1963-1964.

The second day covered 100 miles, visiting the Great Falls Park, skirting the Potomac River and on to Alexandria, visiting Mount Vernon, the plantation home of George Washington and enjoying lunch in the visitors center. Then the final drive on the Prince William Parkway, bordered by magnificent flowering dogwood and azaleas.

A banquet in the evening completed the festivities where AACA President Benny Bottle was presented a tour trophy. Seven AACA National Directors attended the tour: Roy Graden, Sterling Walsh, Harold Henry, Benny Bottle (AACA National President), Doc Stratton (Tour Liaison Director) Earl Beauchamp and Earl Muir.

Bus Transportation Region (non-geographic)

The Bus Transportation Region may be based in Lemoyne, Pennsylvania, but welcomes AACA members from all over the country who are interested in collecting, restoring, showing, and documenting antique buses and motor coaches. 1998 president Richard J. Maguire and his group would "rather take the bus!"

Butler-Old Stone House Region

Butler, Pennsylvania, home of the Butler-Old Stone House Region, is in the western part of the state. The group's 1998 president was Edwin J. Wilbert.

Buzzards Breath Touring Region (non-geographic)

This region is focused less on geography than on a specialty. In this case the Buzzards Breath Touring Region likes to...tour! Daniel Binger was the 1997–98 president. This group sponsored the First Southeastern Divisional Tour in Arab, Alabama, in 1998.

Cabrillo Region

The Watsonville-based Cabrillo Region enjoys the balmy ocean breezes and moderate climate of the central California coastline. "K" and "KB" Lincoln expert Jack Passey, Jr. was the group's president for 1997 and 1998.

California Region

The AACA's first West Coast-based region was the California Region recognized on June 16, 1951. The group was also the organization's thirteenth region. The group is based in Walnut Creek, California, with Lloyd D. Riggs as the 1998 president. Members come from all over California, but especially communities such as Walnut Creek, Lafayette, Pleasanton, Dublin, San Ramon, Danville, and Blackhawk, among others.

Canton Chapter, Ohio Region

The Canton Chapter of the Ohio Region is one of the region's oldest and most active chapters. The Canton Chapter Charter was issued at the AACA Annual meeting held on February 6-7, 1965. Ray Odds was the first director. Clarence Moesle began the first newsletter in 1966. Canton Chapter members who have reached National President status include Ray Henry, Richard Taylor and Edward Baines.

A touring group by nature, any given weekend will find this active group with up to eighty cars traveling the central Ohio countryside, from Cleveland to Holmes county and Amish country. This group loves to eat and it is common to find seventy-five or eighty antique cars parked in front of one of the many family style restaurants in the region. The area is home to the Professional Football Hall of Fame, the National McKinley Monument and Museum, and The Canton Classic Car Museum, which won the 1998 "The AACA Plaque" award at the national winter meeting in Philadelphia, Pennsylvania. While not directly linked, the Canton Chapter is highly supportive of the car museum.

The group hosted the 1996 Founders Tour as it came through the Canton area, working hard to assure a fun time for all participants.

1996 National President Ed Baines and the author of this book, Bob Lichty, are also active members of this chapter. 1997 president was Gene Rannigan with Tim Mast following in the position for 1998. Roadsters on any given local tour can range from "Doc" Presler's early Chalmers to Ray Dodds' Dodge Wayfarer.

The group hosted the best "Dam" tour of 1998, circling Ohio's conservancy district in antique automobiles as their spring event. In August 1998, Bob Lichty, also on the board of the Lincoln Highway Association, took the group on a short tour east over the historic highway to Bedford, Pennsylvania, and the Swigart Museum in Huntingdon.

Cape Canaveral Region

You can bet the activities for the Cape Canaveral Region, even though based in Melbourne Beach, Florida, are "out of this world." Arthur G. Griffin, Jr. was the 1998 president of the region.

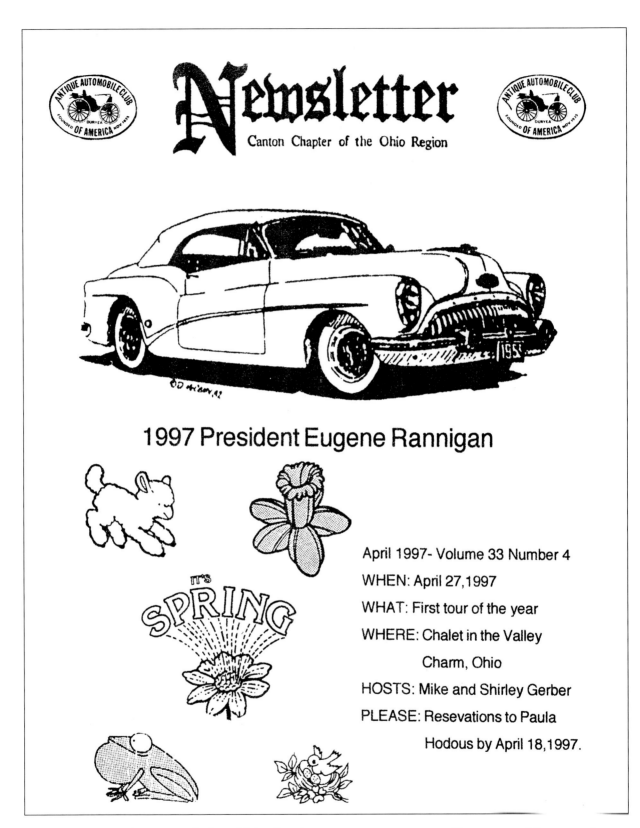

Newsletter

Canton Chapter of the Ohio Region

1997 President Eugene Rannigan

IT'S SPRING

April 1997- Volume 33 Number 4

WHEN: April 27,1997

WHAT: First tour of the year

WHERE: Chalet in the Valley

Charm, Ohio

HOSTS: Mike and Shirley Gerber

PLEASE: Resevations to Paula

Hodous by April 18,1997.

The Canton Chapter of the Ohio Region puts out an excellent monthly newsletter edited by Darlene Sutton. This 1997 edition shows Chapter President Gene Rannigan's '53 Buick Skylark. (Canton Chapter files)

Cape Fear Chapter of North Carolina

No not the movie, the Chapter! The Cape Fear Chapter is from Wilmington, North Carolina. George J. Weidenhammer stars as chapter president for 1998.

Capitol City Chapter

The Capitol City Chapter of the Minnesota Region is from St. Paul. Dale E. Ives was president for 1998.

Catahoula Junque Collections Association Region

Based in southern Mississippi, this group certainly has one of the AACA's most creative names for a chapter. Paula Gould of Monroeville, Alabama, was elected president for 1998.

Catskill Region

The Catskill Region has some scenic New York countryside to call home and enjoy antique cars in. John DeCastro was president for 1998.

Cedar Rapids Region

Cedar Rapids and Amana, Iowa, are just two of the towns serviced by this region of antique auto enthusiasts. William F. Ackermann was the 1998 president.

Cedar Valley Region

The Cedar Valley Region is in and around the Denver, Iowa, area with Steven M. Walker as president.

Celebration City Region

The Celebration City Region works out of the Shelbyville, Tennessee, area. Jimmy L. Taylor was the group's president in 1997 and 1998.

Central Alabama Region

The Central Alabama region hosted the Southern National Spring Meet in Montgomery, Alabama, in 1992. As Vice-President of National Activities, Janet Ricketts, organized the first National Meet Seminar Program at this event in which over six hundred members attended. Marsha Killian was elected president for 1998.

Central Chapter of the Minnesota Region

The Central Chapter of the Minnesota Region covers the Bloomington area, with Duane C. Shuck as 1998 president.

Central Chapter of the Ohio Region

This Central Chapter is part of the Ohio Region and covers the central part of the state. William E. Thomas was elected president for 1998.

Central Connecticut Region

The Central Connecticut Region is located in Newington, in the central part of this New England state. The 1998 president was George Scheyd.

Central Louisiana Chapter of the Louisiana Region

Roger Peters was president of this Pineville, Louisiana, group in 1997 with Dwight Rashal following in the position for 1998.

Central Mountains Region

Clearfield and the folks in the Central Mountains Region can be found in the same part of Pennsylvania. Roger O. Menard was president for 1998.

Central Texas Region

The Central Texas Region is from the Austin area. Greg Herbert is the president for 1998.

Charleston-Lowcountry Region

The Charleston-Summerville area of South Carolina is home to the Charleston-Lowcountry Region. Peter L. Theofield was the president in 1997 and 1998.

Chautauqua Lake Region

The Chautauqua Lake Region has the scenic Jamestown, New York, area to call home and tour in antique cars. Raemon E. Williams was president for 1998.

Chemung Valley Region

Hornell, New York, is the home area for the Chemung Valley Region with Lucciano Brundu elected the 1998 president.

Cherokee Region

The Georgia-based Cherokee Region enjoys having Curtis Martin as president in 1998.

Cherokee Strip Region

Another Region named for the famous Native American tribe, the Cherokee Strip Region is from the area around Arkansas City, Kansas. Stephen W. Smith was president for this group in 1998.

Cherokee Valley Region

Another group that took the name of the Cherokee, but this time located in Tennessee near Cleveland, home of John H. Karnes, 1997 president. He was followed by Harold Miller in the position for 1998.

Chesapeake Region

When Willard Prentice, a pioneer Baltimore car collector, witnessed the activities going on under the auspices of the AACA in Philadelphia in 1950, he was inspired to start a series of events that would lead to the formation of the Chesapeake Region. After seeing the activities in Fairmont Park, Prentice joined the National Capital Region in 1952. He would meet Karl Feather who suggested the idea of forming the chapter. With help of Dr. Mark L. Redding, director of the Gettysburg Region, a charter was drafted with twenty-four signatures. The document was approved on April 30, 1955, by the national board.

Ed Hook led the 1955 Easter Parade with his 1909 Hupmobile in what was to become the region's first official event. The group accompanied "The March of Dimes Massachusetts to California Motorcade" through the geographic region in 1956.

The Chesapeake Bulletin is the newsletter for the region it is named for. The publication frequently features historic region photos such as this photo of Agnes Prentice with the family's 1928 Pierce-Arrow model 81. (Chesapeake Region files)

The Chesapeake Region 1966 installation banquet featured AACA past president George Norton, Jr. as guest speaker. Visiting with Norton was outgoing Region President Earl D. Beauchamp, Jr. and his wife Judy. (AACA photo)

The club's first newsletter was published in March 1957. In that same year, a procession of club members and their cars led the parade to open the new Baltimore Harbor Tunnel. In 1959, William Miller was elected Regional Director, and Maryland initiated antique auto license tags at the urging of the club. The Reistertown Road Plaza Meet was established in 1963 and was carried on for many years as the facility became an enclosed mall.

In 1976, Earl D. Beauchamp was elected Regional Director for the second time and was General Chairperson for the National Spring Meet in 1978. In 1977, at the region's annual dinner, F. Ports and Willard J. Prentice were given awards for their early work in the club. The National Spring Meet came off beautifully at the Timonium Maryland Fairgrounds with 575 cars in attendance on a rainy Saturday. The meet was so successful the club hosted another in 1982.

An annual Winter Swap Meet was established at Norris Ford in Dundalk. The swap meet would continue through 1986 when the facilities at the Ford dealership would no longer be available—parking had been the main logistical problem. The event would move to Thompson Lincoln-Mercury but parking would remain a problem to plague the event.

In 1983, the Glidden Tour™ was held in the Baltimore area with many region members participating. Member Lou Fritz won best Chevrolet with his 1926 touring car. A bus trip to the Edgar Rohr Museum in Manassas, Virginia, was also enjoyed by the region that year.

For economic and equipment reasons, the region's newsletter, The Bulletin, went to a commercial printing in 1985. In 1986, member Rector R. Seal was given credit for writing the book Maryland Automotive History 1900–42.

The region hosted the Eastern National Spring Meet for the third time in 1989. The Catonsville Community College, site of the event, created a parking nightmare by scheduling State Real Estate Exams and Insurance Broker Exams on the same day for a total of 1,500 people. The event came off successfully through good planning, though.

In 1990, the group organized the cars for the anniversary of the Maryland MVA with a display of cars from 1910 to 1990.

It is of note that early members of the Chesapeake Region included AACA past presidents Howard Scotland, Les Henry, Edgar Rohr, and J. Leonard Rhinehart, one of the earliest to officiate. Harry Wilhelm Jr., from Baltimore, was president in 1997 and 1998.

The group's 25th Annual Antique Auto Parts Flea Market was held on March 14, 1998, at the Howard County Fairgrounds in West Friendship, Maryland.

Chickamauga Region

W. Hunter Byington was listed as the 1997 president of this group of Georgians living in the Lookout Mountain/Chichamauga area. The presidency went to Jack Daugherty for 1998.

Chicora Region

Gus H. Hardee from Conway, South Carolina, was the 1998 president of the Chicora Region.

Cimmaron Region

No, these folks don't all collect the diminutive Cadillacs from the early '80s. Their name indicates they are from the central part of Oklahoma just east of Oklahoma City. The 1997–98 president was John Pollock of Harrah, Oklahoma.

Clinton Region

The Clinton Region covers the area just north of Knoxville, Tennessee. William N. Arnold Jr., of Powell was president in 1997, followed by Forrest Walter, Jr. in 1998.

Clocktower Region

Dennis O'Shea was president of the Clocktower Region in Silver Creek, Georgia, in 1997 and is followed by Terry Maloney in 1998.

Club de Autos Antiquos de Costa Rica Region

The Club de Autos Antiquos de Costa Rica Region is located in San Jose, Central America. Gaspar Ortuno Sr. was president for 1997 and 1998. The region hosted an antique auto meet in 1998 that included an AACA sanctioned judging school with representative instructors coming from the United States for the sessions.

Coastal Carolina Region

The South Carolina coast is home to this region. Sharon Monheit was president in 1997 and Bill Gray will serve in this capacity in 1998.

Coastal Georgia of Savannah Region

Raymond Daiss was elected 1998 president.

Coastal Plains Chapter

The Coastal Plains Chapter of the North Carolina Region elected Tommy Elks president in 1997 and he was followed in the position by Preston Turner in 1998. The group is based in Choco-winity.

Coke Center Region

The Coke Center Region from Connellsville, Pennsylvania, is in the historic heart of coal country. Joseph Roy, Jr. was 1998 president for this region.

Colombia South America Region

This stalwart group hales from Medellin, Colombia, South America. Victor Valencia was the president for 1997 followed by Arturo Vayda in 1998. Watch for more and more interaction with distant chapters like this one in the future; the AACA has truly become global in scope.

Commodore Perry Chapter of the Ohio Region

The Commodore Perry Chapter of the Ohio Region enjoys the warm summers along the western shore of Lake Erie between Cleveland and Toledo. Commodore Perry is a famous part of Lake Erie history. Raymond Dellefield was president of the chapter for 1998.

Connecticut Valley Region

On April 23, 1949, a joint region of the AACA and VMCCA was chartered in Springfield, Massachusetts, as the Springfield Region. In September 1950, the name was changed to the "Connecticut Valley Region." This would become the club's third official "region." Roland A. Corbeil, from nearby Wilbraham, was president in 1997 and 1998.

Contraband Chapter

The Contraband Chapter is from Sulphur, Louisiana. Lee Roy Meaux was president in 1997 and 1998.

Cooper's Cave Auto Enthusiasts Club Region

The South Glens Falls, Pennsylvania, area is home to the Cooper's Cave Auto Enthusiasts Club Region. Martin Lemmo from Fort Edward, New York, was elected president for 1998.

Covered Bridge Region

Just how many covered bridges still remain in the Washington, Pennsylvania, area for this group to tour over? Andrew C. Tumicki, Sr. would know; he was club president for 1998.

Crater Antique Auto Club Region

The Crater Antique Auto Club Region covers the Chesterfield, Virginia, area and elected Frederick J. Fann president in 1997 and Douglas R. Strother president in 1998.

Crescent City Chapter of the Louisiana Region

The Crescent City Chapter is from the Crescent City/Gretna area of Louisiana. Melvin F. Durr was elected president for 1998.

Curved Dash Olds Owners Club Region (non-geographic)

This non-geographic region focuses on those wonderfully simple and dependable early Oldsmobiles from the "curved dash" era. Members who share an interest in these fine cars from all over the nation participate in this region. 1998 president was Robert Giuliani from Demarest, New Jersey.

Dairyland Chapter of the Minnesota Region

It is only reasonable that "America's Dairyland" would include a Dairyland Chapter of AACA, but this group, from the Turtle Lake area of Wisconsin, is actually part of the Minnesota Region. The group has thirty-nine members and sixty cars and likes to participate in area parades. The group has attended the St. Croix River Car Show and Swap Meet for eleven years. Willis H. Selle was the 1997 president, and is currently president of the Minnesota

Region. Henry Selle from Turtle Lake, Wisconsin, was president for 1998.

Members of the 1996 Dairyland Chapter pose for the camera in Wisconsin. (Dairyland Chapter photo)

Dan'l Boone Region

Named for a famous Tennesseean, the Dan'l Boone Region is located in the Kingsport, Tennessee, area. Donald E. Cox was the 1997 president followed by Wallace G. Vest.

Davy Crockett Region

It is pretty doubtful that Davy Crockett ever saw an antique car, but the Greeneville, Tennessee, area that is home to this region is rich with history honoring this famous American hero. Robert Laxton, not quite as famous as Davy, was president to the region in 1997. Ralph Safriet became president for the region in 1998.

Deep East Texas Region

Wendell N. Spreadbury, from Nocogdoches, was elected president of the Deep East Texas Region in 1998.

Deep South Region

The Deep South Region began with twenty-nine Mobile, Alabama, enthusiasts meeting on January 19, 1967. A charter was granted on March 7, 1967, and Pierre Fontana was elected as the group's first president. The group actually had organized as early as 1962 as the independent Old South Antique Car Club. Initially a lot of Old South members joined the VMCCA to participate in the Glidden Tour™ that was in the region at the time. In 1972, the Deep South Region of the VMCCA and the Old South Antique Car Clubs were disbanded; members from these groups joined the Deep South Region of AACA.

By 1983, the region had grown so large that it had difficulty finding a meeting place, so it was decided to develop a clubhouse for the organization. With a limited budget, the group decided to seek "lost or abandoned" city property. The group found a 2.2 acre tract for a twenty-year $1 lease from the Garden Club next door. After the membership enthusiastically cleared the land, the group found an old kindergarten building for $500 and moved it 3-1/2 miles to the lot. With constant hard work and many dollars of investment, the building is hardly recognizable today. In 1996 the building was dedicated as the "Lloyd Crowdus Memorial Club House."

Charles Paquet was president for 1998.

Delaware Valley Region

Landsdale, Pennsylvania, is home to the group which comprises the Delaware Valley Region. Fred C. Schempp was elected president for 1998.

Denver Chapter of the Rocky Mountain Region

Based in the high mountains of Colorado, this Denver-based AACA chapter holds a host of varied events and activities for members. Ted G. Rossi was the 1998 president.

Depression Vehicles Region

It is a safe bet that the members of this New Jersey Region are fond of cars built in the 1930s! Doris M. Werndly was president for 1998.

Des Moines Region

The Des Moines Region hosted the first Divisional Tour in the Central Division. Gerald Christensen was president in 1997 and Donald Newby was president for 1998.

Des Plaines Valley Chapter of the Illinois Region

The Des Plaines Valley Chapter of the Illinois Region is based in Lockport with Lee Nelson as its president in 1998.

Devils Lake Chapter of the North Dakota Region

Long winters don't stop this group from having old car fun! The Devils Lake Chapter is part of the North Dakota Region. The group calls Devils Lake, North Dakota, home. The 1998 president was Glenn Lannoye.

Dixie Region

The Dixie Region is based out of Birmingham, Alabama, with Janice L. Hyche as its president in 1997 and 1998.

East Carolina Chapter

The East Carolina Chapter of the North Carolina Region is located in the Angier area with Jeff Breton as its 1998 president.

Eastern New Mexico Region

The Portales area is home to the Eastern New Mexico Region. Douglas Walker was the group's president for 1998.

Eastern Shore Region

The Eastern Shore Region is based in Maryland. The club told AACA members "U Auto Meet Us" for the 1998 Eastern Division AACA National Spring Meet in Salisbury, Maryland.

Jack Wood was the 1998 president.

East Tennessee Region

Eastern Tennessee, around the Seymour area, is home to this region and 1998 president Len Royston. This group hosted the Southeastern Division National Fall Meet in September 1998 in Oak Ridge, Tennessee.

Edison Region

Joseph L. Uher was president of the Lehigh Acres, Florida, area Edison Region of the AACA in 1997 and followed by John M. Scoville in 1998.

El Camino Region

The El Camino Region was not named for the Chevrolet pickup truck/car, but for the famous El Camino Real, a trail linking the historic missions of California from Mexico to San Francisco. The group is based in San Jose, California, at the tip of San Francisco Bay. Ron Tinkey was elected president of this group for 1998.

Emerald City Region

No, Toto, it's not Oz, or Kansas—it's Greenwood, South Carolina, home of the Emerald City Region of the AACA and W. Earl Davenport, 1997 and 1998 president.

Endless Mountains Region

The Endless Mountains Region takes in the hill country around Tonawanda, Pennsylvania, with Howard Crain as its president for 1998.

Enid, Oklahoma Region

The Enid Oklahoma Region enjoyed Gordon C. Smith Jr. as president in 1997 and 1998.

Evangeline Chapter of the Louisiana Region

The Evangeline Chapter is from the Carencro, Louisiana, area. JoAnn Guilbeaux was the 1998 president.

Evergreen Region

The AACA Region servicing the beautiful area around Seattle, Washington, is appropriately named the Evergreen Region. Richard E. Dotson was president in 1997 and Dean R. Lee assuming the post in 1998.

F.R. Porter Region

The Raymondville, New York, region honors F. R. Porter. Janice L. Sauter from Selden was president for 1998.

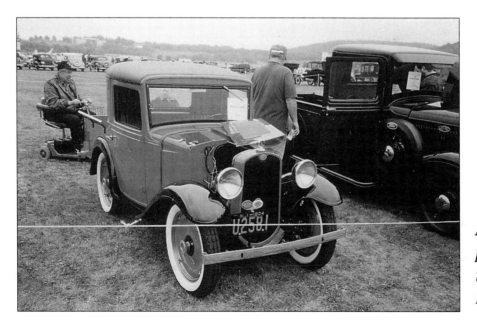

An Austin Bantam pickup attending a typical F.R. Porter Region event.

Fairfield County Connecticut Region

The Fairfield County Connecticut Region is headquartered in Norwalk, with William Seuch as President.

Fallbrook Vintage Car Chapter of the San Diego Region

The Fallbrook Vintage Car Chapter of the San Diego Region is one of California's most active, producing a wonderful car show annually in the desert community just east of Orange County. The Fallbrook Meet is one looked forward to by many and has been immortalized in the artwork of famed automotive illustrator Ken Eberts. Eberts' Fallbrook poster is in full-color in the color section of this book. Don Kramer is this chapter's 1998 president.

Fingerlakes Region

James Vitale from Auburn, New York, was the 1998 Fingerlakes Region president. The Fingerlakes are among some of southwestern New York's most scenic areas and home to Watkins Glen race track among other attractions.

First Capital Antique Car Club Chapter of the North Carolina

The North Carolina Region hosts the First Capital Antique Car Club Chapter from the New Bern area with Larry Rucker as the 1998 president.

Flint Region

The Flint and Grand Blanc areas of central Michigan area are serviced by this hardy group of AACA members. Mary Ann Steele was the group's president for 1998.

Flood City Region

The Flood City Auto Club, so named for the nickname given to Johnstown after the famous flood that nearly washed the town away, was organized on May 24, 1968, at the home of its first president, Ray Leach, in Johnstown, Pennsylvania. The group applied for an AACA charter the same year with twenty-three members.

Approval came in February 1969, and the club adopted the name Spark Plug for its newsletter.

The club's first national endeavor came in 1989 when it hosted the Centennial Tour at the University of Pittsburgh at Johnstown. Four hundred guests with 170 cars joined in a parade commemorating the 100th anniversary of the famous Johnstown flood.

The Flood City Region hosted the Eastern Division National Spring Meet at the University of Pittsburgh at Johnstown in 1996. Region members pose with the club's banner, a 1938 Chrysler Custom Imperial, and a 1928 Ford Model A roadster pickup. (Flood City Region files)

SPARK PLUG

NEWSLETTER

Oct., Nov., Dec. 1989 Quarterly Newsletter of Flood City Region AACA — Johnstown, PA   Vol. 7 No. 4

HIGH PRAISE FOR CENTENNIAL TOUR

Centennial Tour Notes

"On July 21, 22 and 23 the Flood City Region AACA hosted their tour with a success that I don't think could be topped. Our compliments to each and every member!"

—Hank Wackenhuth
Secretary, Fort Bedford Region AACA

"The Johnstown Flood Centennial Celebration Tour turned out to be a terrific weekend ... very exciting, educational, and packed full of food, fun and fellowship. The Flood City Region were perfect hosts. Everything was so well-planned and ran smoothly."

—Jane Armstrong
Editor, Harford Region AACA

"Thank you so much for the best, by far, "antique auto weekend" we have ever had —and we have had many! Your tremendous amount of planning and organizing was very evident and certainly made for an interesting, informative, "scary" (elevator ride), and most memorable time for us. If you do it every year, we will come!"

—Dot and Ray Montgomery
National Capital Region AACA

"...Personally, I feel it was one of the finest Regional AACA affairs I have ever had the pleasure to attend. I was simply stunned by the overall operation, and the attention to detail, which was evident at all times. Having been an AACA member in excess of 30 years, I have attended my share of AACA Regional events, but I cannot recall any past events I attended that could challenge the quality of your event."

—Lynn Zettlemoyer
Orefield, PA

"This was, without a doubt, one of the most exciting and rewarding tours we have ever attended. It was a great pleasure to have the opportunity to celebrate this once-in-a-lifetime event with you!"

—Charles Blevins
President, Harford Region AACA

"All of you are to be commended for such a successful event."
—Nancy Tryon
Secretary, Chester County Antique Car Club

"I know that I speak for all of us who attended from our region in expressing our thanks for the invitation and for the grand hospitality and fellowship shown to us by everyone in Johnstown."
—Ed Rogers
Treasurer, 3 River Region Model A Club

"Congratulations to, what seemed, a "cast of thousands" members for putting together, what most certainly was a **perfect score** AACA event! In many years in this hobby, I have attended many a fine event, and I am happy to say, this was the first I would describe as **perfection.** Perfection cannot be improved upon! National AACA can be very proud of the Flood City Region and its members!!!"

—George Norton
Past National President AACA

"Thanks again for showing us a very enjoyable time. You thought of everything that we might need."
—Dorothy R. Feiser
Gettysburg Region AACA

"Everyone had a great time. Your club members did a super job."
—Chet Whiting
Chester County Antique Car Club

"We are still telling our friends about the tour. The accommodations were great, the food delicious and the tour outstanding!"
—John and Catherine Cremers

"You folks didn't leave out a thing. You all did a fantastic job and we had a great time as a result of it. Thanks again!"
—Ed and Betty O'Leary

"Everything we did from beginning to end was most interesting!"
—Irene and Gene Poole

"Everything was well planned and organized from Registration thru to the Breakfast Buffet. Thanks again."
—Dale and Mary Kersehner
Hershey Region AACA

"The tour was truly fantastic. Everyone we met were just wonderful and we had a wonderful time."
—Charlie and Alverta Moore
Rothsville, PA

"You thought of everything and you made it a most enjoyable weekend. I speak for all the Western Pennsylvania Region members who attended when I say, "Well done!" Thanks for a wonderful tour."
—Marge and Bill Salvatora
Western Pennsylvania Region AACA

And thanks again to our entire Region for their willingness to give to others. George Norton said it best in his letter to all of you ... "I am sure you must be pleased that you brought so much enjoyment to others. It is this spirit of **giving** that has made our club the world's largest and finest!!"

—Terry and Lois

In Memoriam

Meredith Berkebile (died September 9, 1989) — a native Hooversville resident and faithful member of our Region. We extend our deepest sympathy to Thelma and their children.

The Spark Plug is the pulse of the Flood City Region. This is the December 1989 edition, which praises the just-completed Centennial Tour. (Flood City Region Files)

Attractions included the Flood Museum, Incline Plane, National Dam Site, the Grandview Cemetery, and a '50s theme dance.

The group hosted the Eastern Division National Spring Meet in June 1996 at the same location. The Learning and Living Center and area hotels hosted over 700 cars, ranging from a 1901 Duryea to muscle cars of the '70s. A special feature was a gaslight tour for the early cars.

The Flood City Region hosted the first AACA Vintage Tour for cars 1927 and older in the Johnstown, Pennsylvania, area. The event premiered in August 1997, and was held at the University of Pittsburgh at Johnstown campus.

The region now boasts 125 members and claims National Director Earl Muir as past president. Meade I. Bailey was elected president in 1998.

Florida Region

The state of Florida is a very prolific state for regions. This group, based in Ocoee, Florida, had Dena Holt as its president for 1997 and 1998.

Florida West Coast Region

Covering the western edge of the Sunshine State is the Florida West Coast Region from Largo. This group hosted its first national event in the form of the 1989 Winter National Meet in Clearwater, Florida. Packed with beautiful vehicles, the event was highly successful. Frank Brown was the group's 1998 president.

FoMoCo Collector Club of America Region (non-geographic)

A new region was formed in 1998 for the enjoyment of Ford products. Bill White was elected the group's first president.

Foothills Region (California)

The Foothills Region serves the communities and enthusiasts in the rolling hills south of the San Francisco Bay area in Los Altos. This Bay Area group hosted the 1998 Founders Tour from the town of Milpitas. Richard Eckert was the 1998 president.

Foothills Region (North Carolina)

This Foothills Region is from the Hickory, North Carolina, area. Russell L. Maynard Jr. was this group's 1998 president.

Fort Bedford Region

The Fort Bedford Region is located in a rich, historic section of central Pennsylvania near Manns Choice and Bedford. When visiting the area on the old Lincoln Highway, Rt. 30, now a Pennsylvania Historic Byway, don't miss old Fort Bedford. Stop for lunch in the historic Jean Bonnett Tavern and then do a little shopping in the antique shops of Shellsburg. Many other AACA regions and chapters plan tours into this part of Pennsylvania because it is so rich in things to do and see. Manns Choice resident Clifford B Nicodemus Jr. was the president of the region for 1998.

Fort Lauderdale Region

Florida's eastern beach area is served well by the Fort Lauderdale Region with Russell Gagliano, Jr. as president in 1997 and 1998.

412 Lakes Chapter of the Minnesota Region

There are plenty of lakes in the Detroit Lakes, Minnesota, area for this group to cruise around in antique cars. Duane P. Wething was its president for 1998.

Fox Valley Chapter of the Illinois Region

Elgin, Illinois, home of the historic "Elgin Road Races," is host to the Fox Valley Chapter of the Illinois Region. Wm. Dale Woosley was president for 1998.

French Creek Valley Chapter of the Presque Isle Region

The French Creek Valley Chapter of the Presque Isle Region is from the Erie, Pennsylvania, area in the furthest northwestern part of the state. Edward L. Mengel was president of the chapter for 1998.

Freshwater Chapter, North Carolina Region

The Freshwater Chapter of the North Carolina Region was formed in 1994. From the group's beginnings, meetings have usually been held at the National Guard Armory in Edenton. Activities in the first two years included barbecues, parades, car shows, and many other regional events. Walter R. Linhardt was president in 1997 followed by William H. Manke in 1998.

Furnitureland Chapter of the North Carolina Region

North Carolina is certainly well known as a producer of fine furniture, and this Thomasville chapter of the North Carolina Region logically selected this name. The group elected Arnold Gallimore as chapter president for 1998.

Garden State Half Century Region

Franklin Lakes, New Jersey, is but one Garden State community serviced by the Garden State Half Century Region. Clyde W. Sorrell, Jr. was the group's 1998 president.

Garden State Model A Region

Put a bunch of Model A Ford buffs together in New Jersey and you have the Garden State Model A Region of the AACA. Charles B. Epley from Runnemede, New Jersey, was president for 1998.

Gas & Brass Chapter of the Illinois Region

The Gas & Brass Chapter of the Illinois Region is from the Beecher area. Donald H. Sonichsen was its 1998 president.

Gascar Region

Frank Folino was the 1997 president of the Gascar Region from the Martincz, Georgia, area. Gerald Melchiors of Appling, Georgia, took the position for 1998.

Freshwater News

N C Region * Freshwater Chapter * AACA

ANTIQUE AUTOMOBILE CLUB
DURYEA
FOUNDED OF AMERICA NOV. 1935

January - March 1996	Volume 2 Number 1

1937 Chrysler Airflow
In one demonstration, an Airflow was sent over a 110 foot cliff. The car fell end over end down the side of the cliff and landed on its wheels when it reached the bottom. The car was then driven away under its own power.

The Freshwater News is the newsletter for the North Carolina Region, Freshwater Chapter of the AACA. This is Volume 2, Number 1, from January-March 1996. (Freshwater Region files)

129

Gateway Antique Auto Club Region

The Gateway Antique Auto Club Region from the Stamford, Connecticut area derived its roots from a local auto club. Peter A. Cavanna was the group's president for 1998.

Gateway City Region

St. Louis, Missouri, the "Gateway to the West" and home of the famous "St. Louis Arch," is also home to the Gateway City Region of AACA. Will Wack was the president for 1998.

General Green Chapter of the North Carlolina Region

The General Green Chapter is part of the North Carolina Region and formed around the Greensboro area. Ronald Stanley was its president for 1998.

Genesee Valley Antique Car Society Region

Bonnie Franko reported to us from a brief region history earlier compiled by Sue Thomann, one of the club's earliest historians. The Genesee Valley Antique Car Society was founded in October 1950 by Warren Perrins and four others. The first event was at Medon Ponds Park with fourteen cars present. The dues where $2, and twenty-one members were garnered from the event. The club logo was created by Fred German and artist Dean Reynolds. The club publication, The Brass Lamp, quickly followed.

The club was incorporated in 1953 and affiliated with AACA in 1958. Speakers at early events included George Schuster, one of the two drivers from the famous Thomas Flyer race car, Henry and George Selden, Charles Pope of Pope-Tribune fame, and race driver Billy Knipper.

Current events include a winter picnic, overnight tours, garage tours, brunch runs, and the group hosts a bi-annual 1000 Mile Tour. The group held its 37th annual Antique Car Show at the RIT Campus in 1997.

The region was host club for the 1963 and 1975 Glidden Tours™. The group hosted the 1980 Eastern Division National

Spring Meet. For its forty-year anniversary, the group celebrated by holding the 10th Annual Grand National Meet.

The club annually presents trophies to deserving individuals. At the 20th anniversary party, L. Scott Bailey presented the club with the "Billy Knipper" trophy which has since been awarded to a GVACS member annually.

In 1984, the club donated the "I.C. Kirkham" trophy to AACA in memory of Elmer Bassage. The trophy is awarded in Philadelphia every year to the region showing the greatest increase in membership.

Edward L. Franko was elected the 1998 president of the Genesse Valley Antique Car Society.

Georgia - Alabama Region

Pine Mountain, Georgia, is home to 1997 president Brennon D. Williams and the Georgia-Alabama Region. Willis R. Ball of Grange, Georgia, assumed the duties in 1998.

Gettysburg Region

Early in 1952, a small group formed the Brass Age Car Club in Gettysburg, Pennsylvania. In about a year the organization had one hundred members. It was about at that time the group voted to become an official AACA Region. The Gettysburg Region was first listed in Antique Automobile in the Spring 1954 edition.

The organization staged its first "Battlefield Tour" on May 17, 1954, with twenty-nine cars in attendance, including a 1906 Sears, 1909 Maxwell, and a 1914 Buick.

On June 11, 1954, the region voted United States President Dwight D. Eisenhower a life member in the group. The national AACA followed shortly with a lifetime membership to the AACA and named the President the 5000th member. The group purchased a gold wallet card for him. Members preserved his gold card at the Eisenhower Museum in Abilene, Kansas.

The region hosted the National Spring Meet at the Carlisle, Pennsylvania, Fairgrounds in 1990. A huge turn-out and well-run event was complemented by the superb facilities. The Carlisle Fairgrounds hosts the many events run by Carlisle Productions throughout the year and are designed for car shows and swap meets. The location was a natural choice for the nearby Gettysburg Region.

May 23 saw the region host its 23rd Antique Auto Show and Flea Market at the New Oxford, Pennsylvania, Social Grounds.

Gerald D. Black was president of the region for 1997 followed by Arthur Rutledge in 1998.

Golden Crescent Region

The Golden Crescent Region is located in the Victoria, Texas, area. Gordon O. Smith was president in 1997, followed by B.J. Cornstubble in 1998.

Golden Gate Region

Just as the name implies, the Golden Gate Region serves hobbyists in and around the bridge of the same name. Based in San Rafael, the group enjoys many Bay Area activities with their vehicles. Randall W. Sanders was president for 1998.

Golden Triangle Chapter of the Gulf Coast Region

The Golden Triangle Chapter is part of the Gulf Coast Region in Port Arthur, Texas. Charles E. Howard was president in 1997. Kenneth Smith served the post in 1998.

Governor's Chapter of the Allegheny Region

The Governor's Chapter of the Allegheny Region is from the State College, Pennsylvania, area, home to Penn State, the "state college." The 1998 president for this chapter was Scott Deno.

Greater New York Region

The Freeport, New York, area is home to the gallant group in the Greater New York Region, with William Ragona as the 1998 president. The region hosted its 32nd Annual Spring Meet on June 7 at the Old Westbury Gardens Historical Mansion & Gardens. Chevrolets through 1942 were spotlighted at the event.

Greenbriar Valley Region

The Greenbriar Valley hosts the AACA region of the same name based in Rainelle and the famous hotel that has housed presidents and heads-of-state from all over the world. Raleigh L. Sanford was president of this region in 1997 and David Hutsenpillar became president in 1998.

Greenwood Lake Region

The Monroe, New York, area is host to the Greenwood Lake Region. John F. Kerwan, Jr. was 1998 president.

Griffin Piedmont Region

The Griffin Piedmont Region represents the Griffin, Georgia, area. Ken Youngblood was listed as president in 1997 and 1998.

Gulf Coast Region

The Gulf Coast and Bellaire, Texas, are home to this group of Lone Star State enthusiasts. James Bartlett was the 1998 president.

Harford Region

The BelAir, Maryland area is home to this AACA Region. William L. Pritchett was elected president for 1998.

Hershey Region

You are treated to a huge Hershey car show section in this book, so you will find very little mention of it here. In this space we will honor the Region that is responsible for the event. The Hershey Region is a viable and vibrant group, participating in the typical activities you will find in any other AACA group.

To form the region, a meeting was held in the James W. Ladd home in Mount Gretna. The Hershey Region received its charter in 1955 with Ladd as Director. The group met the first Friday in the Green Room of the Hershey Community Center. The first meeting as a region included movies of the 1954 Glidden Tour by Director Ladd. Ruth Shonk pushed activities and attendance in those days.

In 1955, the Pottstown Region was planning a tour to the Zimmerman museum in Harrisburg. The Hershey group thought it would be nice to provide coffee. Jim Ladd discovered that Ben and Ruth Shonk had a 1915 Ford Model T depot hack and the vehicle was used to dispense refreshments. This vehicle would become the symbol of the Region and known the world over as "The Chuck Wagon." The Shonks agreed to sell it to the region for a mere $500, bought in installments as the region could not come up with the entire $500 in one lump sum. The truck performs the same duties for the Region today.

The club newsletter reported in 1956 that antique car license plates would soon be available in Pennsylvania. All cars except Model As would be eligible if over 25 years old. The Model As were left out because so many were still registered in Pennsylvania at the time.

In 1957, the Glidden Tour™ was to start in Roanoke, Virginia, and end in Hershey, Pennsylvania, at the Fall Meet. The combination of the two events culminating at Hershey Stadium would truly give birth to the "World's Largest Antique Auto Meet." 1958 was the first official year the eighty-member Hershey Region would host the Fall Meet, and the year the national headquarters would locate in Hershey.

In a humorous account by George Norton, it is told that at a meeting in 1958, it was heatedly discussed as to whether the club should furnish coffee and donuts after the business meetings. Mahlon Patton felt that each person should pay for their own because it would set the club back $2.50 per meeting. As the discussion followed in the next meeting, Patton worried that it took the club months to raise $19.60 from selling greeting cards and that donuts represented a squandering of club assets. In the excitement of the meeting, Patton ate four donuts and drank three cups of coffee, DeRay Miller dropped a cream filled donut on the floor, and Mike Kingsley stepped on it, squirting cream into Paul Stern's eye, causing concern over not having enough liability insurance to cover dangerous situations like having donuts. Paul Stern said he would not sue because he was now rich from selling a 1932 Chrysler Imperial touring for $400. Of course the club had just spent $100 to rebuild the engine and wooden body on "The Chuck Wagon" making for conservative financial concerns.

As years passed, the Hershey Region members participated in Glidden™, Founders, Reliability, and European tours. The Hershey Region celebrated its 15th anniversary in 1969 with a gala event at the Hershey Hotel.

In 1970, the Hershey Region voted to spend $7,000 on the renovation of the reception hall at National Headquarters and another $10,000 was proposed to establish a library facility.

"Bob" Ladd was the Hershey Region's first director. (Hershey Region files)

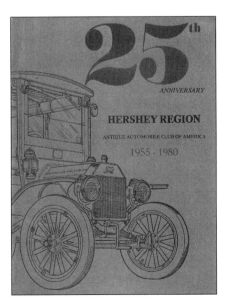

The Hershey Region celebrated its 25th anniversary with this special edition of the club publication. "The Chuck Wagon" was featured prominently on the cover. (Hershey Region files)

The Chuck Wagon Lodge, the nerve center for all Hershey Region business and activities, is located in nearby Palmyra. (Hershey Region files)

In 1973, AACA General Manager William E. Bomgardner was elected President of the Hershey Region. He was a very capable manager and Region President, but when hired into his national position, he did not even own an antique car—he was hired for his business professionalism. His love for antique cars came later and he grew to become an active member of the Hershey Region.

The Hershey Region became one of the first AACA regions to have its own headquarters building, "The Chuck Wagon Lodge," in nearby Palmyra. The building would house meetings, business affairs for the Fall Meet, and even provide garage space for "The Chuck Wagon."

By 1976, the membership of the Hershey Region was up to 602 members. By the mid-1970s, the Fall Meet required expansion. The Hershey Region did so reluctantly due to limited manpower and dwindling profits due to huge stone and tractor bills from several years of "extreme mud." New fields were added and restrictions were created to combat "black marketing" of flea market spaces.

1980 marked the region's 25th anniversary, and a special edition of the club publication was full of rich history, wonderful photographs, and had a silver cover.

The region is still hosting the Fall Meet and now plans for a new region headquarters to be located on the new AACA Museum property just north of Hershey on Rt. 39. The president of the region for 1998 was Gene W. Weaber of Lebanon, Pennsylvania.

Hiawatha Chapter

Rochester, Minnesota, is home to the famous Mayo Clinic and this very active AACA Chapter. Lydia Hanson, from Chatfield, was elected president for 1998.

Highland Lakes Region

The Highland Lakes Region is based in Sebring, Florida, home to sports car racing for more than 40 years. David H. Root was president in 1997 and 1998 president was Robert H. Hartford.

High Plains Region

The Cheyenne, Wyoming, based High Plains Region elected Neil Whitehead president for 1997. Chapters in this region include the Laramie Hi Wheelers and the Oak Spokes. Bob Routson from Laramie became president for 1998.

Hill Country Region

The Hill Country Region is located around the Kerrville, Texas, area. Julius Neunhoffer was 1997–98 president.

Hillbilly Chapter

There is nothing unsophisticated about the Hillbilly Chapter of North Carolina—one look at this group's cars is living proof. Done Lewis Sprinkle was president for 1998.

Hillsborough Region

The Tampa Bay area of Florida is home to the members and officers of the Hillsborough Region. William Fernandez was the group's president for 1998.

Historic Fredericksburg Region

The historic region around Fredericksburg, Virginia, is home to this region of AACA enthusiasts. J. Gordon Brown was president in 1997 and 1998.

Historic Virginia Peninsula Region

The Virginia Peninsula is a historic area, and there is no doubt the Historic Virginia Peninsula Region contains some pretty interesting "historic" cars as well. Lloyd W. Williams was president of this group for 1997 followed by Walter A. Porter in 1998.

Hornet's Nest Region

The Hornet's Nest Region has been one of AACA's biggest and most visible regions in the club. Mel Carson and the many other committee members have been responsible for the giant Charlotte Auto Fair, a festival held each spring at the Charlotte Motor Speedway. "Charlotte" has become one of the top swap meet/car show/auction events in the world, with participants traveling from all over to attend. While in Charlotte, participants can buy a car in the car corral, or visit the Dennis Carpenter operations nearby, one of the country's largest purveyors of Ford and Cushman parts. Rodney Hawkins, Jr. was elected to the presidency of the region in 1998.

Housatonic Valley Region

Bethal, Connecticut, is home to the Housatonic Valley Region of the AACA. Albert T. Yankowski was its president for 1998.

Huntington Region

The Huntington Region covers the beautiful hill county surrounding that city in West Virginia. Julian D. Hensley was the 1997–98 president.

Illinois Brass Touring Region

This group's name tells a lot about what it likes to do around Illinois in brass-era cars. David G. Weishaar was elected president for 1998.

Illinois Region

Talk about your regional identity crises! This group was chartered on January 15, 1946, as the Northern Illinois Region, changed to the Chicago Region in 1949, then to the Midwest Region, and then the Illinois-Indiana Region. Finally, in December 1953, the organization became the three present Illinois Regions.

The name changes actually are a significant portrayal of the region and charter system. In the early 1940s, members were spread far and wide. Robert and Ruth There of Rockford, Illinois, knew it was important to associate with the national AACA.

D. Cameron Peck was one the other early active members. Being from Chicago, he and others broadened the scope of the club and hence the change to the Chicago Region was enacted. Later the name was again changed, resulting in the Midwest Region taking in five states.

As the group grew and expanded, the region was split into three separate regions: Illinois-Indiana, Minnesota-Iowa, and Wisconsin. All of these groups eventually subdivided into separate regions and added many chapters. It was in this way the Illinois Region mirrored the way the club grew nationwide.

The First AACA Region

by Bob Thayer

During a recent conversation with old time friends Connie Nydam and Gail Manz, questions arose of how, why, and when the very first Region of any of the antique car clubs happened to originate here in Rockford, Illinois.

I will go back fifty years or more, and recount the facts as I remember them. Two ladies figure prominently in this epic. First, we have my dear wife and companion Ruth, and her mother Marjory Jordan; both are deceased. These women helped form the first region. Ruthie contributed with seemingly endless correspondence, and her mother helped with her feeling and enthusiasm.

Ruthie's mother was born in a small town in New England, near Boston. Her parents, Mr. and Mrs. Daw, named her Emma. This was, of course, changed to See Saw Margery Daw by her school mates in grade school. It was then changed to See Saw, and then to just Margery, which she kept, but spelled Marjory.

Soon after completing high school, Marjory's parents died, and she lived with various aunts and uncles while furthering her education. It so happened that one of her uncles was a telegrapher for the railroad and one of the fastest on the line. Marjory, being exceptionally alert and eager to learn, had him teach her the ins-and-outs of the telegraph procedure. Soon she was as fast and accurate as he was. He often let her sit at his key and transmit railroad business to give her experience.

In the course of more studies, and while living with other relatives, Marjory lived next door to Fred Marriott of Stanley Steamer fame. He, being highly impressed with her abilities at the telegraph key, suggested to the Stanleys that she be recommended to the national news services covering the world record speed trials at Daytona and Ormond Beaches. The Stanleys did, indeed, endorse the idea. Marjory was given the job and stayed with it for quite a number of years.

Just think of it, she was right in the center of the world's record racing scene, and she knew them all personally, such as R.E. Olds, Henry Ford, Willie K. Vanderbilt, the Stanleys, and many others, some of whom set records, and many who tried and failed.

Sometime later, while still with the wire service, she was covering an automobile convention in Cleveland and met a Studebaker executive named George W. Jordan (no relation to Ned), and they were married soon after. Later, G.W. Jordan left Studebaker and moved to the West Coast where he represented Hupp-Yeats and Croxton-Keeton.

It was there, in California, that my future wife Ruthie was born in 1912. After the dismal demise of these two ill-fated examples of hundreds of automobile companies that fell by the wayside, the Jordans moved to Chicago, where George became associated with the Michelin Tire Co. He remained there until a heart attack finished him a few years later.

The next move came when Marjory and her two children, Ruth and Bill, relocated to Rockford. She was appointed to the State Welfare Department as a supervisor for the state of Illinois, except for Cook County. This was in 1936, and when I met Ruthie later on, I wooed her in a variety of used cars such as a Ruxton roadster, a 1928 Stutz BB Black Hawk boattail speedster—which was, in fact, the very one that raced the Hispano-Suiza Boulogne at the Indianapolis Speedway on April 18, 1928. I also courted her in a few Pierce-Arrows, a Packard dual cowl, and a little old 38-horsepower Simplex roadster that was built circa 1911, and was one of 100 made to test out shaft drive against the former chain drive that was used on the larger Simplexes. I don't know if these and other interesting specimens of automotive rarity influenced Ruthie or not, but it must have impressed Marjory. Ruthie told me shortly after we were married that Marjory had said any guy who liked cars like that couldn't be all that bad, and to go for it.

But enough of this digression, and so back to the original questions of how, why, when, and where. Late one evening sometime in 1943, Ruthie, her mother, and I were returning from visiting friends in Chicago. We paused in front of the Simon Buick Agency in Belvidere, captivated by a little 1909 model 10 Buick displayed therein. Fascinated by the novelty of seeing such a rare and pretty sight, we sat there very much impressed and pleased by what we saw. After a few minutes, Marjory said, wouldn't it be fun to get something like that and fix it up to go on picnics and little rides in the country. That's what started it all, as every once in a while from then on, we talked about the little Buick, or something like it to play with.

So with this thought uppermost in our minds, when we journeyed to Juda, Wisconsin, to replenish our sausage supply, we asked if there were any old cars in the area. We were told that there was a 1911 Maxwell two-cylinder Model AB in the shed across the street from the store, and was for sale for $50. Needless to say, we brought it home the next weekend and had it running in half an hour. This was lots of fun, but as it was strictly a car for two people, we sold it to our next door neighbor. We then found a little white Buick just like the one in the Buick agency window. We had it fixed up, and went on our little trips and picnics.

We found a lot of people who were interested in the idea of resurrecting an old-timer like ours, and the fact was, there were a lot of old cars lying around in barns and sheds, etc.
As a result of getting acquainted with Harold Simon, of the aforementioned Simon Buick Agency, we found out there were three old car clubs, but they were located in California, New York, and Pennsylvania. This precluded any chance of our local car enthusiasts from joining in on any of their activities. Ruthie, Marjory, and I talked it over and came to the conclusion that, as the AACA was the largest and most active of the three clubs, why not write them and see if we could establish a regional group here in the Midwest under their rules and regulations. In other words, hitch our wagon to a star, rather than try to get something going on our own.

This gave the AACA a cause for thought, and after much, much correspondence, we received our regional charter just over fifty years ago, after being initially approved by the AACA in November 1945. So, my fellow hobbyists, credit my two ladies with a great deal of inspiration and perspiration. I just hope you have enjoyed the hobby as much as I have.

May 21, 1949, saw the group stage its first Region Meet in Skokie, Illinois, with sixty-eight cars from eight states.

The June 1949 issue of The Antique Automobile shows the Chicago Region. On November 1, 1949, the Chicago Region became the Midwest Region.

The attached sidebar is yet another account of the first region story by member Bob Thayer as published in the July-August edition of Sidelights, the Illinois Region newsletter.

1998 president was Arthur Swanson.

Current chapters include: Des Plaines Valley, Fox Valley, Gas & Brass, Momence, North Shore, Silver Springs, and Waukegan.

Illinois Valley Region

In addition to the Illinois Region, there is an Illinois Valley Region based in Princeton. The 1998 president was Jim Saal.

Indian River Region

A.C. Bowser was president of the Indian River Region in 1998. The region covers the Vero Beach, Florida, area.

Inland Lakes Region

The Inland Lakes Region in the central Michigan/Houghton area surrounds some of the state's most scenic bodies of water, apart from the Great Lakes. Paul S. Goodell was president for 1998. The region hosted its 21st Annual Car Show and Swap Meet in June 1998.

Iowa Great Lakes Region

The Iowa Great Lakes Region is from around the Spencer, Iowa, area as is 1998 president Everett Amis.

Iowa Valley Region

The Iowa Valley Region is from the West Liberty, Iowa, area and saw James J. Conery as president in 1997 and Richard F. Vitosh in 1998.

Irish Hills Region

The Irish Hills Region is a Michigan group. The 1998 president was Charles M. Manley, who lives in Tecumseh, Michigan.

Iroquois Region

The Iroquois Region was acknowledged on April 7, 1951, as the AACA's twelfth region. Gary Muehlbauer was president of this Johnson City, New York, group for 1997–98.

Jersey Cape Region

The Jersey Cape Region serves the part of coastal New Jersey, near Sea Isle City. Gerald A. Desiderio was president for 1998.

Kanawha Valley Region

Charleston, West Virginia, is home to the Kanawha Region. Glenn L. Howard was the 1998 president.

KC Metro Region

Metropolitan Kansas City, Kansas, and the surrounding parts of Missouri are the area serviced by this AACA Region. Janet Clyde from Kansas City, Kansas, was elected president for 1998.

Kern County Region

The Kern County Region of AACA serves the hot and dry central part of California. Arthur Teesdale was president for 1998.

Keystone Region

The Keystone Region is located in the Upper Darby area. The northern Philadelphia suburb is also home to J.C. Taylor Insurance, a pioneer in the insuring of antique and classic cars and an even bigger supporter of AACA activities. The 1998 Keystone Region president was Adam W. Anderson.

Iroquois Region, The Early Years

by Bruce Bruckner

Having collected early auto ads since sixth grade or so, I was excited to hear of an announcement in the Ithaca Journal inviting anyone interested in early automobiles to meet in the Red Room of the Ithaca Hotel to see if there was enough interest for a club. This was the fall of 1950, and I was sixteen years old. About twelve people attended. Only three are still living: Ted Stafford now of Largo, Florida; Elmer Stickler of Ithaca; and myself.

The three people who called this first meeting were Floyd Parke, an Ithaca printer; Ted Stafford, a store owner; and Myron Miller, a funeral director and furniture store owner from Candor, New York. The organization was named the Iroquois Car Club. The club emblem was an arrowhead pointing to the right, with the letters ICC on it. A number of bronze emblems with this logo are still in existence.

During the winter of 1950-1951, we applied to AACA for a regional charter. This was granted in February 1951. Ted Stafford was director, Bill Summers was assistant, L.J. VanMarter was Secretary/Treasurer. (His father reportedly owned the first car in Ithaca, a Curved Dash Olds.) We had twenty-six members and were the twelfth or thirteenth Region of AACA. At that time, regions were protected. We were given a fifty mile radius around Ithaca.

I recall an early meeting when we were introducing ourselves around the table. I stated that I didn't have a real antique, but was driving a 1928 Ford. Myron Miller said "That's all right son; someday they'll be collecting those."

The region's first tour was on April 22, 1951 to Taughannock State Park for a ham and chicken picnic. Forty people attended in thirteen cars, led by the Miller's Sears.

The first show was held in July, 1951 outside Comell's Barton Hall. There were over fifty cars, including sports cars.

Three interesting cars were purchased that year by members: a 1907 Dragon speedster, a 1910 Franklin touring, and a 1913 Case touring.

Meetings continued to be held monthly, sometimes in Candor. In March of 1952, a meeting was held in Binghamton to accommodate some of our members in that area; Mihran Melkonian, Fowler Wilson, Bill Tuthill, George Ferell, Gordon Matthews, and Ed Stolarcyk. Yordon Fenner, an early member, now has an auto museum in Longview, Texas.

The second show was held in August of 1952, again at Barton Hall. Les Henry was in charge of judging. He was well known in the hobby even before he was with the Ford museum. Trophies, utilizing two sprockets and a timing chain, made by the Morse Chain Company, were awarded at the evening banquet, held in the Statler Hotel. Les Henry gave a talk on the history of AACA. The winning cars were a 1905 REO of Walt Benedict from Canistes, a 1910 Flanders from Rochester, a 1921 Mercer from New York, a 1908 Sears and 1927 Mercedes of Ed McFarland from Binghamton. Best air-cooled was Fowler Wilson's 1914 Franklin from Binghamton. At this time, the total AACA membership was about 400.

We planned our third show for 1954, but I can't remember the show; unless we awarded silver sugar and creamer sets. Hmm.

Nationally, the annual meet was moved to Hershey, Pennsylvania. The entire show, including a flea market, was held inside the stadium. Five or six of us from the Iroquois Region attended that year and the next.

In the spring of 1955, we participated in the Binghamton Sports Car Show with our antiques: 1929 Cadillac phaeton, 1928 Ford phaeton, 1903 Pierce, 1906 Ford, K Mercedes, and 1912 Cadillac. Mihran Melkonian was club program chairman and provided films of the Watkins Glen races and Concours D'Elegance, and had photo identification contests.

In July of 1955, we had a picnic in Owego. Members attended from Brewerton, Syracuse, Ithaca, Binghamton, Elmira, and Corning. Some of the cars present were: 1910 Franklin, Auburn, 1915 Ford, 1934 SSI, 1908 Maxwell, Model As and Melkonian's Locomobile. Remember, this was before trailers were in fashion! We had tours as far as Syracuse when a Model T was not the slowest car on the tour.

One project we were working on was pressing the New York State Legislature for special antique plates.

Our fall tour was to Hammondsport with the New York-Pennsylvania Antique and Classics Car Club. In 1956, this became the Chemung Valley Region, AACA. About thirty cars were present. A 1931 Pierce, on its way from Buffalo via the thruway, lost its bearings and had to be towed home.

The big one for the region was the 1956 National Spring Meet, held in Ithaca. All the big names in AACA were there: Les Henry, Bill Pollack, Herb Singe Jr., Earl Eckel, Scott Bailey, Oakley Sumter, Dave Tumick, and Morris Kunkle. There were cars from as far away as Philadelphia and Connecticut. Due to rain, the show was moved from the field, to the 3-1/2 acre Barton Hall.

Club activities continued but slowed down for several years. Gordon Matthews was elected director in 1964. More members became active in the Binghamton area and the meetings gradually moved to the Triple Cities area. Some of the members from the Ithaca and Elmira areas continued active membership for some years, but other clubs came into being which required less travel.

Iroquois Region, The Later Years

a collaboration by: Steven Boettger, Mihran Melkonian, Emery Rose, Bill Tuthill, and Gary Muehlbauer

In 1965, a combined Iroquois Region/Classic Car Club parade of 150 cars traveled from the Sheraton Hotel on Front Street in Binghamton down, Riverside Drive to Westover and returned by way of Main St., Johnson City and Binghamton. The car show was held the following day in the hotel parking lot.

In 1967, the show was held at MacArthur School field. After that, the Iroquois Region's Annual Antique Car Meet was moved to Ty Cobb Stadium at Union Endicott High School for five years; Greensfield, Johnson City for ten years; Singer/Link, Kirkwood for two years; Johnson City High School for one year. In 1987, the show was moved to the Apalachin Fireman's Field where it is still held.

In 1970, Mrs. Myron Miller donated a Model T Acetylene Generator that was polished and mounted to become the Myron Miller Memorial Trophy in memory of her husband, a founding member of the Iroquois Region. Each year, the trophy is awarded to the best of the show and returned to the club in exchange for a permanent momento of the recipient's achievement.

1974 saw the change in title for the region's chief officer from Director to President, and the addition of Vice-President, Secretary, and Treasurer.

The Iroquois Region incorporated as a nonprofit corporation in 1992 and is now known as Iroquois Region, AACA Inc.

The region has held monthly meetings since the mid-sixties, and has toured to various sites in the New York State area, such as Lake Placid, for a Fall National Meet; Sonnenburg Gardens for a Grand National Meet; and many other locations with particular themes for our members' enjoyment. We have hosted events such as "Great Gatsby" parties, Halloween and Valentine's Day celebrations, and even a "Gong Show" for an evening of fun.

In 1994, we hosted the Shine Time America Car Show in conjunction with the Great North American Race's stop in Binghamton. Two teams in the race represented the Iroquois Region. Frank Whitney drove his 1914 Overland Speedster. Elliott and Judy Reitz drove their 1929 Model A Speedway Racer in the event from Ottawa Canada to Mexico City.

Members of the Iroquois Region own and enjoy automobiles from almost every era of automobile from 1912 through the newest "antiques." We meet once every month usually on the third Wednesday at various locations in the area to conduct club business, share good-natured fun, and enjoy programs geared toward the old car hobby. Additionally, the Iroquois Region hosts an annual Father's Antique Car Show and Swap Meet at Apalachin Fireman's Field. 1997 will be our thirty-second annual. Some of the other annual activities we enjoy are: a family picnic in August complete, with car games and lots of good food; a tour usually in the fall; and a Holiday Family Dinner in December.

Kingdom of the Sun Region

Appropriately named, the Kingdom of the Sun Region covers the part of the "Sunshine State" near Ocala, Florida. Carol A. Scoglio was the group's president in 1998.

Kinzua Valley Region

Warren, Pennsylvania, is home to the Kinzua Region of AACA and David Jenkins, 1998 the president.

Kiski Valley Region

The Kiski Valley Region hosts AACA events and meetings in the Pittsburgh suburb area of New Kensington. Jerry R. Sheets was president of the group for 1998.

Kissimmee-St. Cloud Region

The Kissimmee, Florida, area is home to the Kissimmee-St. Cloud Region. C. Gordon Matthews was elected president in 1998.

Kit-Han-Ne Region

The Kit-Han-Ne Region is from the Worthington, Pennsylvania, area. Matthew O. Bowser was president in 1997 and 1998.

Korean Antique Automobile Region

The Korean Antique Automobile Region is one of AACA's most unique regions. Jchoo S. Kimm of Seoul, Korea, was president of the region for 1997 and 1998.

Kyana Region

The Kyana Region is famous for its excellent annual events held in Kentucky. July 17–19th saw the club host the 1997 National Fall Meet in Louisville at the Kentucky Fair and Exposition Center. Two hundred and seventy-six cars competed for judging awards. Jim Hicks was the president in 1998.

Lake Erie Region

West Seneca, on the far western edge of New York, is home to the Lake Erie Region. The region hosted the 1998 Special Fall Meet at the University of Buffalo Amherst Campus. This group enjoyed Thomas Koziol as 1998 president.

Lakelands Region

Listed as a Pennsylvania region, the Lakelands Region of AACA covers the area in and around Fowler, Ohio. Daryl R. Timko was the group's 1998 president.

Lanchester Region

The Lanchester Region of the AACA is located in the Coatesville/Lanchester area and enjoyed having Albert E. Storrs, Jr. as its president for 1998.

Laramie Hi Wheelers Chapter

The Laramie Hi Wheelers Chapter is part of the High Plains Region. Based in Laramie, Wyoming, the group elected Robert D. Smith president in 1998.

Laurel Highlands Region

The Laurel Highlands Region elected Dennis J. Rising as president in 1998 for the group's activities in and around the Derry, Pennsylvania, area.

Lawrence Region

The Lawrence Region is from the Lawrence/Topeka, Kansas, area. Michael Cormack was the 1998 president.

Lehigh Valley Region

Roland W. Hoffman was the 1997 president of the Lehigh Valley Region, located in the Bangor, Pennsylvania, area. Joseph M. Pokojni, Sr. served as president in 1998.

Lemon Bay Region

Let's hope there are not any automotive lemons in the Lemon Bay Region, from Englewood, Florida. Chapters of this citrus-themed region include Royal Palm and Venice. The 1998 president was Sandy M. Keefer.

Lincoln Trail Region

The folks that named this Elizabethtown, Kentucky, region didn't have a string of luxury cars in mind when they picked this name honoring President Lincoln. Jerry T. Mills was 1998 president.

Little Crow Chapter

The Little Crow Chapter is based in the Atwater, Minnesota, area with Russell N. Johnson as president.

Livingston Region

The Livingston Region is located in the Livonia, New York, area. Donald Biggs was the group's 1998 president.

Lord Selkirk Region

The Lord Selkirk Region is from the Winnipeg region of Manitoba, Canada's heartland. Cold winters and summer tours over the flat countryside are just some of the things this group looks forward to each year. T.R. Turner was the 1998 president for the group.

Louisiana Region

The Louisiana Region elected Karen Kleinman as president for 1998. Chapters include: Baton Rouge, Central Louisiana, Countraband, Crescent City, Evangeline, St. Bernard, and Slidell Antique Car Chapter.

Lower Bucks Region

The Lower Bucks Region is from the southern part of Pennsylvania's Bucks County near Bensalem. James Cunningham was president in 1997 and 1998.

Lynchburg Region

Welcome to historic Lynchburg, Virginia, home of the Lynchburg Region of the AACA and Lennis P. Wade, 1997–98 president.

Magic City Region

The Magic City Region is located in the Minot, North Dakota, area. The group enjoyed Allen Larson as president in 1998.

Maine Region

We bet this group in Maine wishes for a longer season to enjoy antique auto driving. Of course it does give a hobbyist those long Maine winters to spend in a toasty heated garage doing special restoration. Carl Barker, from Falmouth, Maine, was president for 1998.

Maple Leaf Region

The Maple Leaf Region calls Richmond, in south central Ontario, home. David J. Gurney was its president for 1998.

Marshalltown Area Restorers Region

Based in Marshalltown, Iowa, this group elected James C. Willey as its 1998 president.

Martinsville-Danville Region

Another group in and near the Danville, Virginia, area is the Martinsville-Danville Region. Lillard O. Shelton was president in 1997, and Ronald T. Poteat took over as president in 1998.

Mason-Dixon Region

With members covering both sides of the Mason-Dixon line, this Chambersburg, Pennsylvania, region covers events in Maryland and Pennsylvania just to the west and south of the Gettysburg Region. Chambersburg is only a short drive from Carlisle, Pennsylvania, home of the U.S. Army War College and some real big old car events. The region hosted its annual Antique Car Show at the Williamsport Redman Grounds on June 27, 1998. The 1997 region president was J. Stanley Stratton, who is a former (1990) AACA national president. Paul J. Rose assumed presidential duties in 1998.

Massachusetts Region

Paul Lehtola was elected president of the Massachusetts Region for 1998.

Meander Chapter

The Meander Chapter of the Ohio Region is from the Canfield area in Northeast Ohio. Frank Rehlinger was the group's 1998 president.

Metro Phoenix Region

The Metro Phoenix Region covers the greater Phoenix, Arizona, area. Edwin T. Cain, Jr. was president during 1997 and followed by Kathi Waterman in 1998.

Middle Georgia Region

The town of Perry, Georgia, is in the middle of the "Peach State" and the heart of activities for the Middle Georgia Region. Richard Whitlemore was the 1998 president.

Middle Tennessee Region

Franklin, Tennessee, is home to 1997 president Ronald Brice and the Middle Tennessee Region. James L. Page took the presidency over in 1998.

Mid-Hudson Region

About midway up the eastern part of New York state, in Poughkeepsie, you will find the Mid-Hudson Region and Carol Ann Champion, the 1998 president.

Mid-Jersey Region

The Mid-Jersey Region is from the Lawrenceville area. The group elected Raymond Bouchard as 1998 president.

Mid-Ohio Valley Region

The Mid-Ohio Valley Region covers the part of West Virginia in and around Sistersville. John B. Barnard was the 1997–98 president.

Mid-South Region

The Memphis, Tennessee, area is home to the Mid-South Region. Joyce S. Gray was president in 1997, and Bob Watkins from Cordova took over in 1998.

Mille Lacs Lake Chapter

This Minnesota Region chapter is located in the Isle, Minnesota, area. Lawrence Bremer was elected president for 1998.

Minnesota Region

The Minnesota Region started with just a few hardy auto buffs getting together for the sharing of mutual interests. These roots were very much like the origins of the national organization. On October 8–9, 1949, thirty-six people and twelve cars gathered for the First Fall Foliage Run at Green Lake, Minnesota. This group would be the nucleus of the Minnesota Region. The group had also participated in the Minnesota Aqua-Centennial Tour with eighty cars July 26–28, 1949.

On July 28–31, 1950, many members participated in the Minnesota-Iowa Mid-Century Tour at Douglas Lodge and Itaska Park.

The second Fall Foliage Run was held September 30–October 1, 1950, and took place through the beautiful St. Croix River Valley, headquartered out of Stillwaters' Lowell Inn. Demonstrating the fast growth of the region, ninety enthusiasts showed up in forty-two cars, generating even more enthusiasm and membership.

On March 17, 1951, the formal inauguration of the Minnesota-Iowa Region took place at a banquet in Minneapolis' Leamington Hotel. AACA President Cameron Peck awarded the group its first Charter. In June 1951 all previously organized regions received a similar charter.

Minnesota President Sid Strong was mailed one of the additional charters in June as well. This caused some confusion as to the exact date of the charter for Minnesota. Because both documents are dated 1951 there is at least little doubt of the year the Minnesota Region received its charter. Sid Strong stated in 1988 that, in his opinion, if the original charter that was presented by D. Cameron Peck still existed at that time, it should be the one recognized.

Minnesota Region chapters include: Arrowhead, Capitol City, Central, Dairyland, 412 Lakes, Hiawatha, Little Crow, Mille Lacs Lake, Pioneer, Prairieland, River Bend, and Viking.

Thomas H. Leafgren was the 1997 president, giving the group a Stillwater address for that year. Turtle Lake resident Gerald Brown took over the presidency in 1998.

Miracle Strip Region

The Miracle Strip Region enjoyed Joseph A. Lynn as president of the Lynn Haven, Florida, AACA group.

Mississippi Valley Region

AACA enthusiasts in the Port Byron, Illinois, area call the Mississippi Valley Region home to many events. Jim Scott was the 1998 president.

Model A Ford Foundation Region (non-geographic)

The Model A Ford Foundation Region is another example of a group dedicated to a specific interest over a non-geographic area. This group's fascination is with those ever popular Model A Fords built in 1928 through 1931. Howard A. Minners from Bethesda, Maryland, was elected president for 1998.

Momence Chapter

Robert Salm, 1998 president of the Momence Chapter of the Illinois Region, and the group are from the Bourbonnais area.

Mon Valley Region

The Monongahela, Pennsylvania, area is home to the Mon Valley Region. Myron L. Shaaf was the group's president in 1997, followed by James P. McCune in 1998.

Monterey Bay Classic European Motorcycle Region

Here is a unique band of Californians from the Monterey Bay area: they focus on European motorcycles as a basis for their region. Members do not necessarily have to live in Monterey to share in the group's interest of these classic bikes. The president for 1998 was Jay Whyte.

Morehead City Chapter

The Beaufort, North Carolina, area is serviced by the Morehead City Chapter, with Larry B. Crowder as president.

Mother Load Region

The Gold Country of Soulsbyville is the home of this central California group. Ron Smith was the 1998 president.

Mountain Empire Region

Elmer D. Mottesheard was president of the Dublin, Virginia, based group known as the Mountain Empire Region for 1997 and 1998.

Mountaineer Region

The Mountaineer Region is from the Waynesville area of North Carolina. Robert M. Brown was its president in 1997 followed by Timothy Shook in 1998.

Muddy T Region (non-geographic)

The name of this group certainly brings visions of early motoring to mind, or at least a trip to Hershey in October. This is another non-geographic region with members from all over getting together to enjoy the Ford Model T (1909–1927). Lyle Sheley was president of this "T" region for 1998.

Muscle Shoals Region

Bryant Hester was the 1997 president of the Muscle Shoals Region, based in Florence, Alabama, and was followed by Billy D. Hendrix in 1998.

Naples-Marco Island Region

The Naples-Marco Island, Florida, area is a great place to live, enjoy cars in the sun, and belong to the AACA. Dominic DiSarro was president for 1998.

National Capital Region

The National Capital Region was founded on November 19, 1950, as the AACA's seventh region. The region is based just outside of the District of Columbia in Alexandria, Virginia. President William R. Thomas was president in 1998. The group hosted the AACA Eastern Divisional Tour, May 21–23, 1998.

National Capital Region

by Bill Peugh

The following item appeared in the March, 1951 *Antique Automobile*.

"The National Capital Region of the AACA was organized at a meeting held on November 19, 1950, at the Bethesda, Maryland, home of member William L. Cook.

The elected officers of the Region are C.E. Simmons, director, and Howard B. Grubb, secretary-treasurer. The activities committee consists of chairman W.L. Cook, assisted by Don Arminger, J.W. Bonnell, E.W. Goodwin, C.R. Lewis, and E.A. Spellacy. With 26 cars owned by the members of this Region, to say nothing of the size of the activities committee, there should be a lot going on in this group next summer.

In addition to the officers and the members of the activities committee, the following attended the organizational meeting: George A. Barker, Paul W. Burke, Jr., Mr. and Mrs. Jack Carroll, William G. Collier, W. Fred Dowell, Jr., C.E. Henley, A.D. Hooks, Mr. and Mrs. Roscoe J. Lancaster, Clarence G. Lintz, Charles R. Miller, S.H. Oliver, Willard J. Prentice, Mr. and Mrs. Edgar E. Rohr, Thomas G. Shipley and Charles C. Wells".

Edgar E. Rohr went on to become President of the AACA in 1963-1964 Of the original members, only Charles C. Wells is still a member of the National Capital Region, although several are members of other Regions.

The charter for the National Capital Region was issued by the AACA on February 16, 1951, and was signed by James Melton, president.

In its original application, the National Capital Region indicated that it would cover the District of Columbia, all of the State of Maryland and all of the State of Virginia, not already covered by the Waynesboro-Staunton Region. Since that time, seven additional Regions have been formed in Maryland and seventeen additional in Virginia (1996).

The National Capital Region hosted the Eastern Division National Spring meet in 1985 at College Park, Maryland. Today (1996) with 141 family members, the National Capital Region is the AACA approved host for the 1998 Eastern Divisional Tour to be held in Southern Maryland.

New Jersey Region

The New Jersey Region, the AACA's fourteenth recognized region, was listed in Antique Automobile for the first time in January 1951. The group's first meet was held at the General Motors Plant in Linden, New Jersey, on October 6, 1951. Edward Klotzburger was the first meet director. The group held its first meeting at the Wiss Brothers showroom in Morristown, New Jersey. Earle Eckel, Sr. was elected temporary chair.

In 1954, a meet was proposed and held at Beaker's Farm on October 31st. The meet would continue for a number of years and tie in with the Eagle Rock Hill Climb, held on November 3, 1956.

In 1957, the group voted to develop a permanent memorial to Jerry Duryea and restore an early Duryea Motor Wagon owned by Earl Eckle, to be trailered to national events. Franklin Tucker designed the club logo, utilizing the outline of the state of New Jersey in 1958. The group hosted the First Annual Spring Meeting in Jockey Hollow in 1959. The Watching Mountain Chapter was

The New Jersey Region Charter is typical of what most AACA regions and chapters have received over the years. (New Jersey Region files)

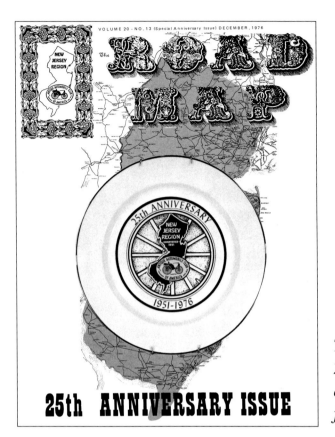

The New Jersey Region celebrated its 25th Anniversary with a special edition of the Road Map. (New Jersey Region files)

Eagle Rock Hill Climb, November 1952

Once again the New Jersey Region celebrated an anniversary with a special edition of the club publication. The 40th Anniversary Issue featured a dramatic photo of the 1952 Eagle Road Hill Climb on the cover. (New Jersey Region files)

also incorporated on March 27 of the same year.

Member Franklin Tucker was instrumental in getting antique auto license plates for vintage cars issued by the state of New Jersey. Franklin received the first set for his 1913 Metz, number "QQ A1." The plates would be permanent until 1986 when they would go to a three-year renewal policy.

A vintage airplane and MG-TF at the Pittstown Airport Fly-in/Drive-in on August 4, 1974. (New Jersey Region files)

In 1968, the New Jersey region hosted the National Spring Meet at the Mennen Company property, only to face seas of mud after torrential rain. In 1974 the Pittstown Fly-in/Drive-in came off successfully with the help of Bob Graham. The 1976 Eagle Road Hill Climb Revivial and Car Show took place on September 5, with 204 people in attendance. It was also the region's 25th birthday.

The New Jersey Region donated ten bricks to the AACA Library and Research fund in 1981 and one brick per deceased member the following year. By the late '80s many members were writing their congressmen to protest the demise of leaded gasoline, fearing that the loss would harm old cars.

Henry "Gene" Becker's 1917 Pierce-Arrow and several region members are shown at the First Annual Spring Meet in Jockey Hollow in 1959. (New Jersey Region files)

ANTIQUE AUTOMOBILE CLUB
FOUNDED NOV. 1935
DURYEA
OF AMERICA

EASTERN NATIONAL SPRING MEET

Morristown, N. J.

June 14, 15, 16, 1968

New Jersey Region - Host

NEW JERSEY REGION

WATCHUNG MOUNTAIN CHAPTER
CHARTERED 1959

NEW JERSEY PIONEERS CHAPTER
N.J.R. CHARTERED A.A.C.A. 1964

DONATION 25¢

June 14–16, 1968, saw the New Jersey Region host the Eastern National Spring Meet. This was the program for the event in which the Watchung Mountain Chapter and the New Jersey Pioneers Chapters were given equal billing on the cover. (New Jersey Region files)

The New Jersey Region, one of the largest in the AACA, and its chapters remain active. Chapters include: Depression Vehicles and the Watchung Mountain Chapter.

The president for the region in 1998 was Bernard F. Cooney.

New River Chapter

Another group from North Carolina is the New River Chapter from the Jacksonville area with Jeff Emery as president.

New York State Allegheny Region

This group of New Yorkers are from the Allegheny area with Francis Ford as the 1998 president.

Niapra Region

The Niapra Region is from the Kanawha, Iowa, area as is its 1998 president Vicki Anderson.

Niva Region

The Mason City, Iowa, area-based Niva Region enjoyed having H.W. Montgomery as its president in 1997 and Dan Swann in 1998.

North Alabama Region

The North Alabama Region has hosted several national meets including the Southeastern Division Golden Jubilee National Meeting in 1985. The group also hosted the Premiere Founders Tour in 1988. It was via this group's planning and innovations that the Founders Tours would be modeled for many years. The group also hosted the Centennial Annual Grand National Meet in 1996. A Huntsville, Alabama, group, the North Alabama Region of AACA had Bob Larrabee as 1997 and 1998 president.

North Carolina Region

The North Carolina Region chapters include: Almanac, Brass-Nickel Touring, Cape Fear, Coastal Plains, East Carolina, First

Capital Antique Car Club, Fresh Water, Furniture Land, General Greene, Hillbilly, Morehead City, New River, North Central, Old Salem, San-Lee, Triangle, Uwharrie, and Zooland. Ernie Stoffel, Jr. was president in 1997, and Herb Oaks followed as president for 1998.

North Central Chapter

The North Central Chapter enjoyed Jimmy C. Lawson as the 1997–98 president of the Danville, Virginia, area group.

North Central Florida Region

The North Central Florida Region is based around the city of Gainesville, Florida. Sherwin N. Karsh was its president for 1998.

North Dakota Region

The cold North Dakota winters must make it hard for this region to enjoy year-round car fun. The Devil's Lake Chapter is part of this region. Ronald Moen was president of this stalwart group in 1998.

North Idaho-Phans Region

Ernie Booth was president of the North Idaho-Phans Region in 1997. Harold Cunningham from Sagle, Idaho, took over the position in 1998.

North Shore Chapter

The North Shore Chapter of the Illinois Region is from the Highland Park area. James M. Rubenstein was president for the club in 1998.

Northeast Alabama Region

The Northeast Alabama Region is based in Gadsden, Alabama. Kitta Vanpelt was the group's president in 1997 and 1998.

Northeast Florida Region

The Northeast Florida Region covers the upper corner of the state near Orange Park.

Northeast Georgia Antique Auto Region

The Northeast Georgia Antique Auto Region of the AACA is based in the Mount Airy area. Randell Green was elected its 1998 president.

Northeast Texas Region

Dwayne Adams was the 1997 president of the Northeast Texas Region and Clifford W. Riggins served the post in 1998. The group covers the Celeste area.

Northeastern Pennsylvania Region

The first meeting of this group, then known as the Greater Wilkes-Barre Antique Car Club, was held on October 25, 1957. This group would constitute the founding members of the Northeastern Pennsylvania Region. After March 1958, all members would be called charter members.

The Northeastern Pennsylvania Region was formed in 1960. The group's first formal function was the Side Curtain Tour to Windy Valley Inn on Sunday, December 4, 1960, with seven cars and twenty-eight people. Popular vote selected the three top cars of the day with the following winners:

Tiny Gold	1931 Chrysler
Bernie Boack	1931 Ford Model A roadster
Jack Sardoni	1939 Packard

Events in the following months included a meeting at Dr. Gardner's home, a movie night, and tours to Benton and Montrose with the latter awarding first place to Leonard Wilcox in his 1917 Standard. The Glidden Tour took place in the Scranton area in 1961 and the region hosted the awards dinner.

In June 1961, the chapter motored from Kingston to Berwick and met up with the Berwick group for the 175th annual parade. In the June edition of the region's newsletter Lanbert Swingle from

Yestergears, *Volume 1, Number 1, illustrated two Stutz, Tiny Gould's Black Hawk Speedster, and Tony Koveleski's Bear Cat. (North Eastern Pennsylvania Region files)*

Dallas, Pennsylvania, offered for sale a 1933 Auburn convertible sedan in restorable condition for $750—don't we all wish we could turn back the clock?

In the Winter 1963 edition of the club magazine, a visit to William Pollock's museum was reported. In addition, found in the classified section, "Tiny" Gold offered a '37 Ford phaeton, '18 Stutz Bulldog touring, and a '13 Paige-Detroit touring.

To this day, the Northeastern Pennsylvania Region is an active one with tours and events occurring almost monthly. Karen A. Wolfe served as the group's president in 1998.

The group held its 37th Annual Car Show and Flea Market at Ralston Field, Kirby Park, in Wilkes-Barre, June 7, 1998. The group called the show the "area's oldest" and it featured more than forty classes for competition.

Northern California Antique Motorcycle Region

Lloyd Riggs was both the region president and president of this unique group interested in motorcycles in the northern California area.

Northern Chapter

The Northern Chapter of the Ohio Region covers the area in the northeastern part of the state in and surrounding Chagrin Falls. Paul S. Hornik was its president for 1998.

Northern Kentucky Region

This region services members from Kentucky as well as a number from the Cincinnati, Ohio, area. David G. Fangman from Covington, Kentucky, was president for 1998.

Northern Lakes Region

Not too far north of Iola, Wisconsin, the home of Krause Publications, is Rhinelander, Wisconsin, home of the Northern Lakes Region of AACA. Long, cold Wisconsin winters guarantee lots of time to work on restorations for this group. Gerald C. Larson was elected president for 1997–98.

The Northern Neck Region of Virginia was founded in 1993. (Earl D. Beauchamp, Jr. file)

Northern Neck Region

The Northern Neck Region of Virginia was founded in 1993. Servicing the White Stone, Virginia, area, the group elected Jackie B. Ashburn as its 1997–98 president.

Northern Nevada Region

Fallen, Nevada, and a whole lot of surrounding area is home to the members of the Northern Nevada Region. Merlin T. Sayre was president in 1998.

Northern Panhandle Region

The Northern Panhandle Region elected Al Robrecht from White Stone, West Virginia, president for 1998.

Northwest Georgia Region

Dalton, Georgia, is home to 1998 Northwest Georgia Region president Sue Caylor.

Northwestern Michigan Region

The Traverse City, Michigan, area is the geographic region covered by this group of AACA members. Clarance V. Smith was elected president for 1998.

Northwestern Pennsylvania Region

Based in the Erie, Pennsylvania, area, the Northwestern Pennsylvania Region elected Sidney P. Lewis as its 1998 president.

Oak Spokes Chapter

The Oak Spokes Chapter of the High Plains Region elected Curtis Wright president for 1998.

Ohio Region

This group formed as the Cleveland Regional Chapter on May 21, 1946, and chartered on June 26, 1946. It was the first group to be given specific boundaries. The organization was to form from 100 miles west of the Pennsylvania state line, west to Toledo, and 100 miles south of Cleveland. In December 1949 the Cleveland Regional Chapter was recognized as the "Ohio Region."

The Ohio Region celebrated the 1960 Jubilee with a Fall Foliage Tour. Tom Wilson is shown in his 1922 Cadillac touring with Irv Steele in his 1924 Cadillac emerging from a covered bridge. (Antique Automobile)

The Ohio Region is yet another region to put out a top-quality publication. This is the Summer 1996 edition celebrating a successful Founders Tour. (Ohio Region files)

The Ohio Region has to get the news of its activities and many chapters out. The Spark Plug, edited by Charlotte "Charlie" Britcher, does an admirable job of doing just that. (Ohio Region files)

The Ohio Region celebrated the 1960 Silver Jubilee with a Fall Foliage Tour, concluded by a dinner featuring George Schuster as guest speaker. Schuster presented a slide show on the 1908 New York to Paris Race, in which he was the driver of the winning Thomas Flyer. As part of the tour, the group ended up at the Thompson Products Museum (later changed to the Frederick C. Crawford Auto Aviation Museum) in Cleveland. Ruth F. Sommerlad was then the curator of the museum.

June 1979 saw the region host the AACA Central Division Spring Meet in Wooster.

More than 200 members pitched in a lot of hard work as the Ohio Region hosted the 1996 Founders Tour. The event traveled the byways of northern Ohio from Cleveland South to the Amish country of Holmes County. One of many highlights was a rare tour of the spectacular W.K. Haines car collection.

Glen E. Jugenheimer served as Region president in 1998. The club newsletter, The Spark Plug, and editor Charlie (Charlotte) Britcher, won an Award of Excellence in 1997.

Chapters include: Canton, Central, Commodore Perry, Meander, and the Northern, Southern, and Western Reserve.

Reminiscing on the Early Cleveland Region

by Franklin B. Tucker

Shortly after moving to Akron, Ohio in 1947, I was driving through Ravenna and spotted an early Cadillac parked in a garage at a used car location. I stopped and investigated, and met W.S. (Bill) Richardson the owner of the establishment and the Cadillac, which I found to be a 1906. He had recently purchased it, sight unseen, from somewhere down south. It had been loaded into a freight car and transported to this area so he could get it to his place. It was covered with hay and chicken droppings!

Bill told me about the AACA, gave me an application blank, sponsored me, along with his father, and I sent in my $3.50 dues for an associate membership. (The active membership was $6.00 at that time.) He also invited me to attend one of the Cleveland Region meetings, which I did. This group met at various restaurants in the area, drove their antique cars to the location, enjoyed a good meal, then a short meeting, then outside to look over the cars and talk about them.

At that time there were only two regions in AACA, the Cleveland Region and the Chicago Region Joseph F. (Joe) Kerns was the president of the Cleveland Region and D. Cameron Peck of the Chicago. The AACA membership was then under 1,000.

By 1949, the Cleveland Region had become the Ohio Region; the Chicago Region the Mid-West Region; and a third Region had been formed, the Springfield Region, in Massachusetts under the direction of M.J. (Jerry) Duryea. By 1951, there were 13 regions.

One of the Ohio Region members was Charles G. Jackson of Delaware, Ohio, who operated an insurance business. He also had an unusual car, a Brewster touring with a folding jump seat located on the right running-board. He had purchased this car from a museum.

Around 1949, the Maumee Valley Oil Association sponsored a get together in Dayton. They contacted one of the AACA Board members, James (Jimmy) Melton, the opera star and active in the AACA, to see if he could gather a group of the members with their cars to show at their meeting. Of course Jimmy contacted the Ohio Region and offered a free sit down dinner to each member and guest who would attend with their car. Several accepted and I rode down there with Bill Richardson and his father, F.F. Most of the antique cars were parked in front of the hotel for public display. This event was covered by television and one of the TV crew asked a gentlemen who was standing on the curb to make believe he was cranking one of the old cars so they could obtain an action shot. Ironically, that gentleman was Charles Kettering, the inventor of the self starter.

Some weeks after this event, it was discovered that although the Maumee Valley Oil Association had paid for our dinners, Jimmy Melton had been given a sizable amount of money for getting the old cars to Dayton. (He and flown his early IHC to Dayton). This, of course, irked quite a few of the Ohio Region members, so they passed a resolution that was sent to the National AACA asking that Melton be removed from the AACA Board for conduct unbecoming an AACA Club Member. No action was taken by the Board, and Melton became AACA President in 1951.

Also in 1949, a meeting of cars was held at Shoenbraun Village. I drove my 1913 Metz there and was disheartened to find that it was one of the newest cars in attendance This same year another meet was held in Canton celebrating the 50th anniversary of Timken. Each owner who brought an old car was presented with a Parker 51 pen desk set on which was mounted a handmade replica of an early Maxwell, which had been bronzed.

There was also an Ohio Region member by the name of Harry Bennett of Norwalk, Ohio. Harry worked on cars and had done so since before World War I. One wall in his place of business contained many shelves filled with Mason jars, each containing a small part for magnetos, carburetors, electrical items, etc. He had about most anything you would need. Down below there was also an early Cadillac which he had "souped" up prior to the first World War. Harry helped design the Norwalk automobile, which was made in that town. The former owner of the Norwalk Automobile Company had one of the first cars to come off the assembly line, and later years he had promised it to Harry. This gentleman died, and unfortunately did not leave anything in writing as to his desire to let Harry have the Norwalk. So, his widow sold it to a gas station owner who then attempted to clean up the grease that had accumulated under the body from the drive chain. He used a blow torch to burn it off. You guessed it, the body caught fire and burned. Harry never did get any part of that car. The Ohio Region publication, *The Spark Plug*, was without a masthead for some years. A contest was started asking the members to suggest a suitable masthead. Harry won it by submitting the drawing of a spark plug laying at a slight angle, which was used for many years.

Another member, name unknown, was in the U.S. Air Force stationed in Germany and participated as a pilot in the Berlin Airlift. On one of his trips he spotted a beautiful Horsch touring and negotiated with the owner. Berliners being short of food made a deal for a quantity of food in exchange for the car. The pilot then flew the car out of Berlin on the U.S. Air Force cargo plane. He later placed it on board a ship for shipment back to the United States and it was seen around the Ohio Region gatherings for some time.

My position with Firestone entailed traveling, so each time I located an antique I reported it to the members via the newsletter. One time, in a junkyard just outside of Indianapolis, I found six or seven early electrics with the curved glass intact. Another time I located a Cord ambulance with leaded glass windows, but since AACA did not then recognize ambulances or hearses, I guess it was scrapped, unless one of the Ohio Region members obtained it. AACA now recognizes these vehicles as I pushed for this recognition.

In 1950, I was transferred by Firestone to Jacksonville, Florida, and gradually lost contact with the members of the Ohio Region.

Another member, name unknown, was in the U.S. Air Force stationed in Germany and participated as a pilot in the Berlin Airlift. On one of his trips he spotted a beautiful Horsch touring and negotiated with the owner. Berliners being short of food made a deal for a quantity of food in exchange for the car. The pilot then flew the car out of Berlin on the U.S. Air Force cargo plane. He later placed it on board a ship for shipment back to the United States and it was seen around the Ohio Region gatherings for some time.

My position with Firestone entailed traveling, so each time I located an antique I reported it to the members via the newsletter. One time, in a junkyard just outside of Indianapolis, I found six or seven early electrics with the curved glass intact. Another time I located a Cord ambulance with leaded glass windows, but since AACA did not then recognize ambulances or hearses, I guess it was scrapped, unless one of the Ohio Region members obtained it. AACA now recognizes these vehicles as I pushed for this recognition.

In 1950, I was transferred by Firestone to Jacksonville, Florida, and gradually lost contact with the members of the Ohio Region.

The
Antique Automobile

OFFICIAL PUBLICATION OF THE ANTIQUE AUTOMOBILE CLUB OF AMERICA

VOL. 10 NO. 2   PHILADELPHIA, PENNSYLVANIA   2ND QUARTER 1946

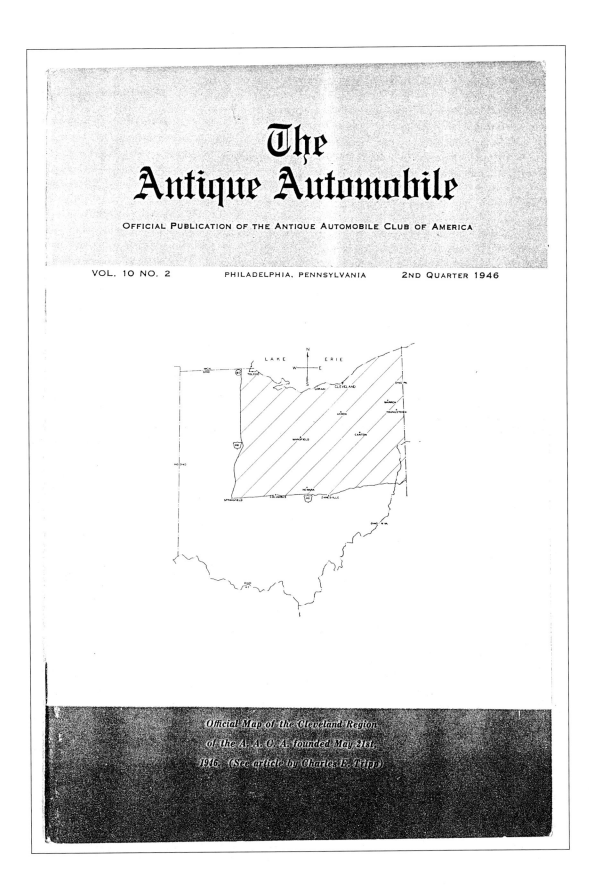

Official Map of the Cleveland Region of the A. A. C. A. founded May 21st, 1946. (See article by Charles E. Tripp)

Okie Region

The Okie Region covers the area around Chickasha, Oklahoma. Everett R. Andrus was president for 1998.

Old Salem Chapter

The Old Salem Chapter of the North Carolina Region covers the area around Rural Hall and Salem. Larry C. Shore was its president in 1997 and 1998.

Omaha Region

Larry Rader was president of the Omaha Region in 1997 and 1998. The group serves the great state of Nebraska.

Onaquaga Region

The Onaquaga Region is located in and around Windsor, New York, with Douglas Tucker as 1998 president.

Oneida Lake Region

Cicero and the surrounding areas of scenic New York state are home to the Oneida Lake Region. John F. Perkis was the 1998 president.

Ontario Region

The AACA has several regions based in Canada. The Ontario Region, from the areas surrounding Port Hope and Port Perry, is one. Arnold Kerry was the club's 1998 president.

Ontelanie Region

Donald Haines, of Whitehall, Pennsylvania, was elected president of this group for 1998.

A great looking Chevrolet wood-bodied screen side delivery at an Ontelanie Region meet.

Orange County Region

Hobbyists to the south of Los Angeles enjoy many activities put together by the Orange County Region. Kenneth A. Brody from Rowland Heights was elected president for 1998.

Palm Springs Region

Sun, sand, and plenty of heat guarantee warm weather events for the Banning, California-based, Palms Spring Region. Charles E. Chappel from Banning was president for 1998.

Peace River Region

The Peace River Region covers the area of Florida in and around Punta Gorda. Phyllis J. Smith was president of this group in 1998.

Peach Blossom Region

The Peach Blossom Region calls Spartanburg, South Carolina, home. Lewis Painter was president in 1997 and Mildred Mason performed those duties in 1998.

Pecan Region

The group hales from the Thomasville, Georgia, area famous for furniture and tasty pecans. Harry C. Jayne III was elected president for 1998. This group hosted the 1997 Glidden Tour™.

Peconic Bay Region

Another New York state region is the Lake Grove-based Peconic Bay Region. Peter K. Stokke was elected president for 1998.

Pennsylvania Dutch Region

The Pennsylvania Dutch Region, based in Lebanon, would seem on the doorstep of the Hershey Region, but both groups are quite healthy. Hershey may be famous for chocolate, but Lebanon holds its own with Pennsylvania Dutch cooking and world famous "Lebanon Bologna." In 1999, the group will host the AACA Eastern Division Tour in Myerstown. The president for this group in 1998 was Norman Risser.

Pennsylvania Dutch Region AACA

The Pennsylvania Dutch Region Antique Automobile Club of America was created by antique car lovers who were not able to get into the Hershey Region because of a membership ceiling and were not close to any of the other regions located in Pennsylvania.

This group of individuals formed and had some runs, just for fun, and then applied for their charter with the Antique Automobile Club of America. They received their charter in October 1984. The purpose of this club is to have a lot of family car runs and to not conflict with the projects of the larger regions in the area, yet benefit from being a part of the AACA.

They elected their first president, James Shirk, in 1985. The region has an official board with an activities chairperson to run the annual events and a newsletter, Upton Motor News. This publication covers events of the region, members' cars, and National AACA information. It also has a following who read the section by pen name, Amos Stoltzfus, who gives advice, which nobody can live with or without, about car restoration.

The founding members are William R. Miller, James Shirk, Nelson Neff, and Stanton Shilling. Charter members include these and Dennis Shirk, John Stalnecker, Donald Hickernell, William Jones, Jeff Lesher, Warren Hess, Alvin Hinks, Jr. Martin Shuey, Robert Gallo, William Crumbine, Bill Jones, Jr. Adam Lesher, Robert Hoffman, Marlan Heller, and Aaron Kaylor.

Current president of the region is Adam Lesher. He is the third in succession of Leshers who have been president of the region.

Events and meetings are held at different restaurants, and members always enjoy some of the good Pennsylvania Dutch cooking of the central Pennsylvania area.

The club has grown to 140 members at the end of 1996. Each year we take in some new members, who generally stay very active. The main event the club holds each year is the Annual Consignment Sale. In 1997, we marked the eleventh event, which is currently held in Jonestown, Pennsylvania. This gives the club members and outside vendors an opportunity to sell on consignment those car parts that they do not specialize in and want to get rid of, or those items that they are tired of carrying to regular flea markets. A car corral is also included with this event. The members of the Pennsylvania Dutch Region feel this event, held in late March, kicks off the beginning of the season for antique car flea markets and shows.

You can recognize members of the Pennsylvania Dutch Region by our distinctive logo, which is an Upton car parked by an antique gas pump. We used the Upton car because the first one was built by the Upton Motor Co. of Lebanon and was completed January 10, 1905. It was a five-passenger touring car with a thirty horsepower engine. The car was shipped to New York City for the Automobile Show at Madison Square Garden. The price was $2,500 with gas lights, horn, and tools. A top cost $200 extra. Total sales for 1905 were about fifteen cars.

The 1906 model was improved and enlarged with a forty horsepower engine and an increased price of $3,000. There was an Upton for 1907, and then production ended. In the spring of 1907, the Lebanon Motor Works "retired from business" and the Upton car became a part of the Lebanon area history. The members of the Pennsylvania Dutch Region have been in search of an Upton and to date have not been successful in finding one.

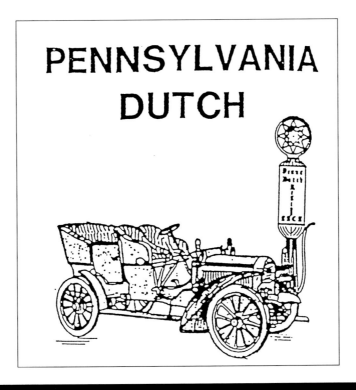

Pennsylvania Oil Region

Pennsylvania tourist bureaus will be glad to tell you of the many things the state is known for beyond Dutch cooking, shoofly pie, Amish cheese, steel and coal. Oil is one of the other things that makes this state great. The Pennsylvania Oil Region is from the Franklin area. Carl A. Hartle was president for 1998.

Piedmont Region

The Piedmont Region recently celebrated its 35th anniversary in 1998. As part of the celebration the region awarded lifetime memberships to three of the original founding members who are still active in the region: Tom Keith, Malcom Woodward, and Walter Hunt, Jr. Earl Beauchamp and his wife were guests of honor at the celebration. The Piedmont Region saw Richard D. McIninch from Nellysford, Virginia, become president for 1998.

Piedmont Carolina Region

The Piedmont area of South Carolina is home to this region. The group elected Craig A. Brooks for its president in 1997. Craig was followed in 1998 by Ricky Thompson from Gaffney, South Carolina.

Pioneer Chapter

The Pioneer Chapter is a Minneapolis-based chapter in the Minnesota Region. Paul L. Dudek was welcomed as president for this group in 1998.

Pittsburgh Golden Triangle Region

The Pittsburgh Golden Triangle Region plays host to AACA activities just to the north of the Pittsburgh, Pennsylvania, area, including Evans City. The 1998 president was William Ragona.

Pocono Region

Jake Mattenius, from Phillipsburg, New Jersey, was president of the Pocono Region in 1997. He was followed by Albert J. Smeraldo III in 1998.

Pottstown Region

The Pottstown Region was added to The Antique Automobile listing of regions in March 1952. The Pottstown Region cosponsors the annual Duryea Day Car Show and Flea Market in Boyertown with the Boyertown Museum of Historic Vehicles. The event is in its thirty-third year. Stephen R. Stastny was the group's president in 1997 and 1998.

Poudre Valley Region

Fort Collins, Colorado, is home to the Paudre Valley Region of the AACA. Larry K. Noller was its president for 1998.

Prairieland Chapter

The Prairieland Chapter is from the Comfrey area of Minnesota. Dennis A. Johnson was elected president for 1998.

Presque Isle Region

The Presque Isle Region is located in the Erie, Pennsylvania, area and hosts the French Creek Valley Chapter. Rodger Lawrence was elected president in 1998.

Punxsutawney Region

We have to wonder if 1998 president McClellan G. Blair and the members of the Pennsylvania-based Punxsutawney Region confer with "Phil," the famous groundhog, before getting their cars out of winter storage for another season of AACA events. The Shannock Valley Car Club Chapter is part of the Punxsutawney Region.

Queen City Region

The state of Maryland hosts the Queen City Region and 1998 president William Herbaugh, who is from Cumberland.

Ramapo Valley Region

The Spring Valley, New York, area is home to the members of the Ramapo Valley Region of the AACA. Dr. Stephen Lazar was the 1998 president.

Rare Birds of Florida Chapter

The Rare Birds of Florida Chapter, of the Sunshine Region, is a specialist group from the Sarasota area. Ann M. Bell was the group's president for 1998.

Red River Valley Honkers Region

The Red River Valley Honkers Region is from the Paris, Texas, area. David W. McKinney served as president in 1997 and 1998.

Redwood Empire Region

Santa Rosa, California, is in the heart of the famous old growth redwoods of northern California and home of the Redwood Empire Region. Margaret Bawden was president in 1998.

Richey Region

The Richey Region enjoys fun in the sun with old cars in the New Port Richey, Florida, area. Robert H. Stoehrer was the 1998 president.

Richmond Region

The Virginia state capital is home of the Richmond Region and 1997–98 president F.M. Fowlkes, Jr.

Rio Grande Valley Region

McAllen, Texas, is home to the Rio Grande Valley Region, named for the famous river. Tom Hellums was president in 1997, followed by Robert W. Doty, Jr. in 1998.

River Bend Chapter

Belle Plaine, Minnesota, is home to the River Bend Chapter of the Minnesota Region. Wayne Mediger was elected president for 1998.

Roanoke Valley Region

The Roanoke Valley Region of the AACA, with 1997–98 president Robert M. Pedigo, is located in Central Virginia near Vinton.

Rocky Mountain Region

The Rocky Mountain Region hosted a special meet to celebrate the Silver Jubilee at the Sylvan Dale Guest Ranch, near Denver,

Mountain Empire Region member, Eldon Neibling's early Maxwell is shown at the 1960 Rocky Mountain Region Silver Jubilee Meet at Sylvan Dale Guest Ranch near Denver, Colorado.

Colorado. Special placards were created and exhibited with each car. J.D. Bernard was president for 1997 and 1998. Chapters include Denver and Ye Old Auto Club.

Rolling Antiquers Old Car Club, Norwich Region

The Rolling Antiquers Old Car Club, Norwich Region, is from the Norwich, New York, area. Raymond C. Hart was elected president for 1998.

Royal Palm Chapter

Richard F. Ellsworth was president of the Royal Palm Chapter of the Lemon Bay Region in Murdock, Florida, during 1997 and 1998.

St. Bernard Chapter

The St. Bernard Chapter is from Chalmette, Louisiana. Patrick J. Lehrmann was president for 1998.

St. Joe Valley Region

The St. Joe Valley Region covers the Cassopolis, Michigan, area, which is located in the south-central part of the state, near the Indiana border. Richard W. Chandler was the 1998 president for the region.

St. Lawrence-Adirondack Region

"Upstate" New York members in the St. Lawrence-Adirondack Region enjoy the beautiful country side, lakes, rivers, and mountains with their antique cars. The 1998 president was James A. Tyler, Sr.

St. Lawrence Valley Region

The St. Lawrence Valley Region based in Spencerville, Ontario, Canada, with Steven W. Polite as the 1998 president.

Saginaw Valley Region

The Saginaw Valley Region is located in the town of the same name and has a rich past linked to General Motors during the company's heyday. Gerald F. Evans was elected president of the Saginaw group for 1998.

Salinas Valley Region

The Salinas Valley Region covers the beautiful area west of Monterey Peninsula. Edward A. McGlochlin, the 1997 president, gave the group a Carmel Valley address during his term of office. Thomas Huff from Salinas was elected the 1998 president.

San Diego Region

The San Diego Region is one of California's larger and certainly southern most groups of auto enthusiasts. Sheldon Jurist was its 1998 president. The Fallbrook Vintage Car Chapter is part of the San Diego Region.

San-Lee Chapter

The San-Lee Chapter of the North Carolina Region is from the Sanford area. Larry Wright was the chapter's 1998 president.

San Louis Obispo Region

The San Louis Obispo Region enjoys events and camaraderie along the central California coastline. The 1998 president was John Osborne.

Sandlapper Region

Edward F. Murphy of Lexington, South Carolina, was president of the Sandlapper Region for 1998. The Sandlapper Region is well known for putting on some good meets for auto enthusiasts.

Santa Barbara Region

The Santa Barbara Region is based in the picturesque community of the same name just north of Los Angeles. Michael N. McLaughlin was president in 1997 and 1998.

Santa Clarita Valley Region

Warren C. Russell was president of the Valencia, California, based Santa Clarita Valley Region during 1997 and 1998.

Schoharie Valley Region

Another beautiful section of "Upstate" New York hosts the Schoharie Valley Region of the AACA. Robert Addis was its 1998 president.

Scranton Region

The Scranton Region is an eastern Pennsylvania AACA region which is tied closely with the club's beginnings via its earliest members. Check this group's early rosters and you will find some well-known AACA names. The region hosted its 27th Annual Collector Car Show, Flea Market, and Car Corral, July 26 at the Salt Park Ground in Clarks Summit. A name to remember from 1998 will be James Lyons, the region's president.

Sedona Car Club Region

The Sedona Car Club Region is based in temperate Arizona. Vince Monaci was president for 1998. The club hosted the Western Red Rock Celebration Tour on April 13–15, 1998.

Shannock Valley Car Club Chapter

The Shannock Valley Car Club Chapter is part of the Punxsutawney Region. Wilmer P. Wingard of Rural Valley, Pennsylvania, was president of the chapter for 1998.

Shenandoah Region

The Shenandoah Region covers Winchester and the surrounding area in northwest Virginia. Robert L. Furgison was the 1997 president followed by Duane Catlett in 1998.

Shenango Valley Region

The Shenango Valley Region, based in Sharon, Pennsylvania, is in the northwestern section of the state. Sharon, Pennsylvania, is home to "Quaker Steak and Lube," the chain of restaurants featuring dining on the inside of a filling station that charms auto enthusiasts throughout the East Coast. Edward P. Bailey, Jr. was the 1998 president.

Shikellamy Region

In February 1956, fifty car enthusiasts gathered at Shamokin Dam, creating the Shikellamy Chapter of the Allegheny Mountain

Roy and Bertha Schell brought their 1953 Nash Healey to the 35th Anniversary celebration of the Shikellamy Region at Winfield, on June 24, 1990. (Shikellamy Region photo)

The Shikellamy Region on tour in Lycoming County as they stop for lunch at a steak house near Pennsdale, Pennsylvania. The tour took the group to the Williamsport Historical Museum. (Shikellamy Region photo)

Region of the AACA. Robert Reed was the first director of the group. Meetings were enjoyed from Bloomsberg to Gettysburg. The group's fifth anniversary picnic was held at the picnic grove of Mr. and Mrs. Lee Kauffman with over 145 participating. The groups fortieth anniversary was celebrated in 1990, and monthly meetings were held at the New Columbia Grange Hall. Covered-dish dinners are always a feature of this group's gatherings, with wonderful food brought and enjoyed by all. The group is now listed in Antique Automobile as a full region with George Campbell shown as president for 1997 and 1998.

The Shikellamy Region on tour in 1972—this time to Eagles Mere, Pennsylvania. Cars include: Russ Houseknecht's 1915 Buick touring, George Eroh's 1929 Ford Model A pickup, Russ Houseknecht's 1928 Ford Model A roadster, and Bill Rebuck's 1928 Chevrolet truck. (Shikellamy Region photo)

Shoreline Antique Auto Club Region

Michael A. Meir was president of the Shoreline Antique Auto Club Region of the AACA for 1997 and was followed by Larry Burridge in 1998.

Show Me Region

This group, from Missouri—the Show Me State—had Dennis Mertz of Cedar Hill as its president for 1998.

Silver Springs Chapter

The Silver Springs Chapter of the Illinois Region is from the Sandwich area. Herschel M. Cox was president for 1998.

Single Cylinder Cadillac Registry Region (non-geographic)

Paul Ianuario from Greer, South Carolina, has been registrar, in recent years, of this non-geographic AACA region. This region's interest lies in the early one-cylinder Cadillacs from 1903 to 1908.

Siouxland Region

The land around the Sioux City, Iowa, area makes up the Siouxland Region of the AACA. Vic C. Peterson was the group's president for 1998.

Slidell Antique Car Chapter of the Louisiana Region

The Slidell Antique Car Chapter is from the town of the same name in Louisiana. Walton M. Jones was elected president for 1998.

Snapper's Brass and Gas Touring Region

Not a bunch of turtles—this non-geographic region, established in Ripley, Ohio, in 1993, gets those old cars out and tours! The 1998 Snapper's Reliability Tour was held in Middletown, Ohio, August 2–7, 1998, with Fred Collett as Tour Chairman. Randall F. Hall Jr. was president of the group in 1998.

Snyder Wheels Region

David L. Cain was 1997 president for this Texas Region named for the group's hometown of Snyder, followed by Charlie Wilson in 1998.

South Alabama Region

The South Alabama Region's 1998 president was Wayne Thompson of Castleberry.

South Carolina Region

Rein Brueggeman served as president of the South Carolina Region in 1998.

South Dakota Region

The South Dakota Region elected Harry Tuttle president in 1997. He was followed by Vincent Swenson as president in 1998.

South Florida Region

The South Florida Region covers the Miami area. Bob B. Mayer was president for 1997 and 1998.

South Jersey Region

The South Jersey Region elected Gary M. Green president of the Pedricktown, New Jersey, based group for 1997 and 1998. The region hosted its 27th Annual Flea Market at "Cowtown" on March 8, 1998.

South Texas Region

On June 7–10, 1979, the South Texas Region of AACA hosted the 26th Texas Tour. The event was held in the San Antonio area with Earl T. Prade as the Tour Chair. John C. Mosley, of Garden

Ridge, Texas, was president in 1997 and 1998. This Region meets in San Antonio.

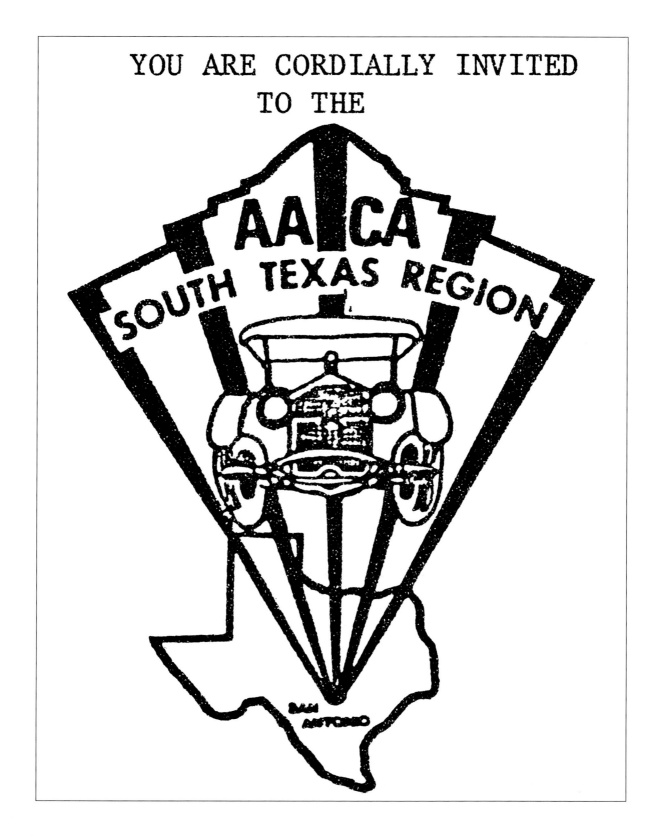

The 26th Texas Tour program featured an attractive adaptation of early motoring on the cover.

Southeastern New Mexico Region

Ralph and Ruth Trice share the presidency of the Southeastern New Mexico Region in the town of Hobbs.

Southeastern Region

From a small group of five car enthusiasts, including Leonard Guttride, Bert Harrington, Chester Martin, and Ben Webb, the Atlanta Antique Automobile Association was formed. The group had its first official meeting at "Mammy's Shanty Restaurant" in Atlanta, Georgia, in February 1953. The group immediately sought charter as a region in the AACA, and the presentation was made on July 18, 1953.

The Southeastern Region, the only club in Georgia and adjoining states at that time, saw membership increase rapidly. Many chapters and additional regions grew out of this group. The group participated in the 1956 cross-country tour organized by Henry Austin Clark, of the Long Island Auto Museum, for The March of Dimes. In 1963, the group helped organize the Gatlingberg National Meet.

Bob Garrison, Bert Harrington, and Charlie Adams from the Southeastern Region are shown presenting the Ford Trophy and check to Herman Smith. (Southeastern Region files)

In 1965, the group hosted the National Spring Meet at Stone Mountain Memorial Park, the first ever such meet in Georgia. By this time the group had 150 members. The club's official publication, Peachtree Parade, won the National Award of Distinction in 1965 and the Award of Excellence in 1966.

The "See Georgia First" Tour in 1968 and 1969 were led by Grady Minter. Lou Evans and Harold Dye headed a tour to the national meeting in Nashville in 1970.

The Southeastern Region has been an active one, participating in many Glidden™, Reliability, European, and Founders Tours. The group also helped raise money and donations for the AACA Library and Research Center and the AACA Museum.

The group elected Doug Hollandsworth as its president for 1998.

Inviting Governor Jimmy Carter to join in the Easter Parade are Southeastern Region members Dorothy Smith, Lu Harrington, Elizabeth Protsman, and Kay Bentley. (Lu Harrington photo)

190

The Peachtree Parade is the Southeastern Region's publication; the publication is so named because the group's parades always started downtown near the Coca-Cola sign on Peachtree Street. The Coca-Cola company made and presented the group with this illustration which it used for many years. The Hanson car featured was built in Atlanta and the Coca-Cola sign is in the Atlanta Historical Society Museum. (Southeastern Region files)

Southern California Region

The Southern California Region is based in the beach community of El Segundo. You can bet this group takes advantage of the beautiful California weather to enjoy its cars in the greater Los Angeles area. The Valley Chapter is part of the Southern California Region. Joe Pirrone was the region's president for 1998.

Southern Chapter

The Southern Chapter of the Ohio Region covers the Beavercreek area. J.F. Schreel was its president for 1998.

Southern Illinois Chapter

The Carbondale area is home to the Southern Illinois Chapter as well as 1998 president William L. Morse.

Southern Kentucky Region

The Southern Kentucky Region covers the Bowling Green area. Lynn A. Goodman was president for 1998.

Southwestern Two-wheelers Region

The Southwestern Two-wheelers Region is a group specifically interested in motorcycles and bikes and is based in the Southern California town of Imperial Beach. Harry McGill was its president.

Sowega Region

Bainbridge, Georgia, is home to the Sowega Region. Lee West was president for 1998.

Space Coast Region

Floyd Dodd was president of the Space Coast Region in the Titusville, Florida, area during 1997 and was followed by John W. Larson in 1998.

Sparkle City Region

Spartanburg, South Carolina, hosts the Sparkle City Region. C.C. Wheeler was president in 1998.

Staten Island Region

Staten Island, New York, may seem like a pretty confined area to host a full-fledged AACA region, but the Staten Island Region is one of the more active on the East Coast. The group hosted its 21st Annual Car Show and Swap Meet September 14, at the Petrides Educational Complex. Paul Arena was elected president for 1998.

Art Nelson's 1929 Hupmobile rumble seat coupe was one of many cars at the Staten Island Regional Meet in September 1996. (Victor Losquadro photo)

Stones River Region

The Murfreesboro, Tennessee, area is home to the Stones River Region. Lanny McGowan was president in 1997 and Deloris Stephenson followed in that role in 1998. Kjell Gjerde updates a wonderful and colorful website on the internet for the Stones River group. The site lists everything from directions to the club meetings to future events.

Sugar Bush Region

Just south of Route 30, the old Lincoln Highway in Central Pennsylvania, you will find the town and scenic area around Somerset. You will also find the members of the Sugar Bush Region enjoying their antique cars along with 1998 president Donald E. Meese.

Sugarloaf Mountain Region

The Sugarloaf Mountain Region is located in the Sandy Spring area. The 1998 president was Charles H. Zierdt. This group held its 28th Annual Indoor Parts Meet and Rolling Auction at the Frederick Fairgrounds.

Sumner County, Tennessee Region

Hendersonville, Tennessee, and Sumner County are home to the Tennessee Region. Wendell J. Marshall was the president in 1997, and T. Wayne Stutts from Nashville became the region president for 1998.

Sun and Sand Region

Based in Palm Desert, California, you can bet this group enjoys plenty of sun and sand. Lloyd Miller was the group's 1998 president.

Sunshine Region

The Sunshine Region is from the Sarasota, Florida, area, home of the Belm Cars and Music of Yesteryear Museum and the Ringling Renaissance Art Center. The region includes the Rare Birds of Florida Chapter. The 1998 president for this region was Carter Roth.

Susquehanna Valley Region

The Susquehanna Valley Region is just up river from the Pennsylvania state capital of Harrisburg, in the town of Nescopeck where 1998 president Alvin C. Rex resides.

Susquehannock Region

This is another region located just upriver from the Pennsylvania state capital in Williamsport. Ferd D. Page, Jr. was the 1998 president for the region.

Suwannee River Region

The Suwannee River Region is from the area near and around Lake City. Ralph Towner was elected this group's 1998 president.

Swap Fox Region

The Florence area of South Carolina is home to the Swap Fox Region and 1998 president Charles A. Robinson.

Tacoma Region

The Tacoma Region covers the Tacoma/Auburn, Washington, area. Robert H. Brooks was its president for 1997, and Louis L. Berquest took over the position in 1998.

Tallahassee Region

Ken Hart was president for the Tallahassee Region in Florida in 1997 and those duties were performed by Diane McCarthy in 1998.

Tall Corn Region

This group from Boone, Iowa, took its name from that state's most famous crop. The president for this group in 1998 was Dennis Christianson.

Tennessee Valley Region

The Tennessee Valley Region is based in Decatur, Alabama, with Lloyd W. Culp as its president.

Texas Region

The Carrollton-based Texas Region enjoyed having Sandra Lankenau as its president for 1997 and J.M. Farrell as its president in 1998.

Three Rivers Chapter of the North Carolina Region

William Horton served as president of this chapter in 1998.

Tidewater Region

The Tidewater Region, from the Virginia Beach area, elected Neil S. Sugermeyer as its president for 1998.

Tiftarea Region

Tifton, Georgia, is home to the Tiftarea Region of the AACA and 1998 president Frank E. Branch.

Tims Ford Region

Belvidere, Tennessee, and the area around it is home to the members of the Tims Ford Region. Robert Morris became the region's 1998 president.

Tioga Antique Auto Club Region

The Tioga Antique Auto Club Region is from the Newark Valley, New York, area. Jerry Adams was the group's 1998 president.

Tobacco Belt Region

Greenbrier, Tennessee, home to much of this nation's tobacco harvest, is also home to the Tobacco Belt Region of AACA. Rudolph M. Reddick was the region's president for 1998.

Topeka Region

Topeka, Kansas, is home to this Midwestern group of AACA enthusiasts. At the Topeka Region's AACA Central Spring Meet, June 11–13, 1998, the National Club hosted eight AACA Seminars similar to the ones offered annually at the Philadelphia Winter Meeting. These seminars are highly popular when held in locations such as Topeka for those who can't make it to Pennsylvania in the winter. Herbert G. Whitlow was the group's president for 1998.

Transylvania Region

No, we're not talking Eastern Europe and spooky castles—this region is made up of a bunch of antique auto enthusiasts in the Brevard, North Carolina area. The group's 1998 president was Jerry M. Arnold.

Treasure Coast Region

The Palm City group elected Jay Smith as its president in 1998.

Triangle Chapter

Cary is home to the Triangle Chapter of the North Carolina Region. Glenn G. Saunderson was its president in 1997 and was followed by John Agayoff in 1998.

Tri-county Region

The Tri-county Region covers a good bit of AACA territory around the Linville, Virginia, area. Hensel L. Randall was president for 1998.

Tucson Region

The Tucson Region covers the area surrounding the Arizona community by the same name. The region hosted the Annual Grand National and Western Divisional Spring Meets. Peter M. Gariepy was elected president of this group for 1998.

Tulsa Region

The Tulsa Region takes care of AACA members' needs in northeastern Oklahoma. Richard F. Barbee was the 1998 president.

Twin County Region

This Elk Creek group of AACA enthusiasts elected Charles Rudy as its president in 1998.

Twin Lakes Region

The Twin Lakes Region services the Murray, Kentucky, area with Howard Brandon as president for 1998.

Uwharrie Chapter of the North Carolina Region

The Uwharrie Chapter of the North Carolina Region was pleased to have Howard Smith as president of this North Carolina group for 1997, followed in 1998 by Charles A. Ford.

Valle Del Sur Region

The Valle Del Sur Region is based in San Martin, California. David Delmue was president for 1997 and was followed by Philip A. McClain in 1998.

Valley Chapter of the Southern California Region

The Valley Chapter of the Southern California Region is based on the northern edge of the San Fernando Valley in Newhall, California. John Avans was the chapter's 1998 president

Valley Forge Region

The Valley Forge Region covers the Vallcy Forge/King of Prussia area in eastern Pennsylvania. The area is rich in Revolutionary War history and George Washington's bitter winter encampment. Alfred C. Schneider was president for the AACA region in 1998.

Valley of the Flowers Region

The Valley of the Flowers Region enjoys the moderate California climate of the Lompoc-Santa Maria area. Lee Brackin was president during 1998.

Valley Vintage Motor Car Region

Having fun with old cars is certainly not "alien" to this group from Roswell, New Mexico. Phil Corbett was president for 1998.

Vanderbilt Cup Region

Named for one of the most famous early auto races, the Vanderbilt Cup Region is from the North Babylon, New York, area. Salvadore A. Grenci was elected as the group's president in 1998.

Venice Chapter of the Lemon Bay Region

The Venice Chapter of the Lemon Bay Region enjoys warm weather in the Sunshine State of Florida. Betty J. Poetker was the chapter's 1998 president.

Vernon L. Nash AAC of Fairbanks Region

Vernon L. Nash AAC of Fairbanks is an Alaskan-based region. William Chace, from North Pole, Alaska, was the president for 1998.

Viking Chapter

Minnesota's Scandinavian heritage was the inspiration for this chapter's name. This group is from the Winona area in this frigid land and elected Sherman Smith 1998 president.

Vintage Auto Club of Palm Beach Region

AACA members in the Boynton Beach/Palm Beach area can count on the Vintage Auto Club of Palm Beach Region to provide plenty of fun in the sun with their cars. Buddy Pearce was president for 1998.

Vintage Wheels of Manatee County Region

Another group in the Tampa Bay area of Florida is the Bradenton group known as the Vintage Wheels of Manatee County Region. Robert C. Green from Bradenton was president in 1998.

Volusia Region

The Volusia Region is from Edgewater, Florida, and enjoyed Jennie Pausewang as president in 1998.

Walden Ridge Region

The Walden Ridge Region is located in the Kingston area. Fillmore Hendrickson served as president in 1998.

Watchung Mountain Chapter

The Watchung Mountain Chapter of the AACA New Jersey Region is located in the Colonia area. The 1998 president was John Bedner.

Waukegan Chapter

The Northern Chicago suburb of Waukegan, Illinois, hosts this group. The Waukegan Chapter is part of the Illinois Region. George Schurrer was president of this northern Illinois club for 1998.

Wayne Drumlins Antique Auto Region

The AACA group which honored Wayne Drumlin is located in the Waterloo, New York, area. George F. Grube became club president for 1998.

Wayne-Pike Region

The Wayne-Pike Region covers the Hawley/Lake Ariel, Pennsylvania, area. Carol Birdsall was president for the group in 1998.

Waynesboro-Staunton Region

The Waynesboro-Staunton Region elected John M. Stone from Port Republic, Virginia, president for 1998.

West Florida Region

The West Florida Region covers the area near Pensacola. Harold Jackson was elected president for 1998.

West Georgia Region

The West Georgia Region is located in and around the Carrollton area. Bill Crowley was the 1998 president.

West Michigan Region

Delbert D. Carpenter is from Hudsonville, Michigan, and was elected the 1998 president of the West Michigan Region.

West Texas Region

The West Texas Region enjoyed having Ralph Webb as its president in 1997 and 1998.

West Virginia Region

Marvin E. Zinn from Indepenence, West Virgina, was elected as 1998 president for the West Virginia Region.

Westchester New York Region

The AACA's eighth region, the Westchester Region, was recognized on November 26, 1950. It elected Richard E. Marks as its 1998 president.

The Westchester Region held a Silver Jubilee of more than 100 antique and classic cars in Milbrook, New York, in 1960. Cars from the local HCCA and VMCCA regions also participated. IHC highwheelers owned by Ted Sattler and Ralph Curtis are shown. (Antique Automobile)

Westerly-Pawcatuck Region

The Westerly-Pawcatuck Region is listed as representing the state of Rhode Island. Some of the group's members, though, including 1998 president Robert Burdick, live in Connecticut.

Western Pennsylvania Region

The western part of Pennsylvania became the AACA's sixth recognized region in September 1950. The Western Pennsylvania Region is scheduled to host the 1999 Founders Tour in the Greensburg area. Greensburg is home to this group as well as Vincent P. Altieri, the group's 1998 president.

Western Reserve Chapter

The Northern part of Ohio was historically referred to as the "Western Reserve" in colonial days. This Ohio Region Chapter covers pretty much the same northern boundaries including Cleveland. The chapter's 1998 president was Robert J. Marhefka.

Western Reserve Chapter

by Dave Payne

The roots of the Western Reserve Chapter, AACA actually took hold way back in 1969.

In the fall of 1969, Bud Klingler, a member of the Vintage Chevrolet Club of America, called for a meeting of anyone in the area that owned old Chevrolets or had an interest in them. This meeting was held in the basement of the Geneva First Federal Savings and Loan - a location that later our Western Reserve Chapter used for many January events.

Klingler and his wife chaired the meeting and it was their sole desire to form a local chapter of Vintage Chevrolet Club (VCCA) as the closest Chevy Chapter was in the Southwest Cleveland area.

Two of those in attendance were Bob Neubacher and Dave Payne. I had met Bob only one time before, at the Ashtabula Downtown Merchants Fall Festival car show of 1968. In any event, it turned out that Bob and I had gone to that meeting with exactly the same idea in mind. Bob got up and declared that there were just not enough people in the area that were interested only in Chevrolets. He felt, and I agreed, that we should form a club of all antique car makes. Bud Klingler was still in favor of a Chevy Club, but was willing to go along with the idea.

As I remember, he appointed Bob (Neubacher) to seek out other people in his area (Geneva and west), and I said that I would locate people from Ashtabula and east. We ran several articles in the newspapers, and did several photo sessions, with articles featuring Dick Mead, Joe Hassett, Bob Neubacher, and Dave Payne and their cars. This was in the winter of 1969-70.

The initial meetings were held in the meeting room of the Ashtabula Telephone Co., Park Avenue, with Dick Mead as acting chairman (since he worked there).

By the second meeting, we had over 50 people in attendance, some from Painesville and Mentor. We had originally figured on an all - Ashtabula County Club - but quickly added Lake and parts of Geauga County - the areas that our Western Reserve encompasses today.

The fledgling club grew quickly, with one of the primary goals being to select a name for the group.

This club was to be strictly local with no other affiliation. By the second or third meeting at the Telephone Company, a name was chosen. Submitted by Joanne Ray, and overwhelmingly approved, the club became The Yesteryear Auto Club with annual dues set at $5.00. The first year, we hosted a very good invitational car show at the Fairgrounds in Jefferson.

The next two years found even better car shows as they were full judging meets with trophies in several classes.

Dick Mead had judged at the Classic Car meets in Dearborn, so he was chosen to put on the judges school held every year before the car show. During this period, the many talents of Bob Babcox were discovered and it was decreed that he become the Chief Judge for any events held. Many interesting tours were held on a monthly basis, new officers were elected each year, and generally everything went well for about three years. But, like all good things, some people began to lose interest in the club. It was about this time, during early 1972, that we were approached with the idea of joining AACA, the Ohio Region, and forming a new chapter thereof. Up to this time, many of us had never heard of AACA.

There were many people who did not want to join a larger organization and, therefore, dropped out completely.

Some of us decided to pursue the idea of joining AACA. At that time, it took seven members to form a chapter. After the Ohio Region announced to National the intent to form a new chapter, seven people signed up as charter members of The Western Reserve Chapter in the late fall of 1972. One of the stipulations of the Region's forming a new chapter was that Bob Babcox become the first Chapter president, since he had the most affiliation with the Ohio Region at that time.

The other charter members were: Ed Robison, Rod Stemen, Bob Neubacher, Dave Payne, Norm Thorpe, and Paul Herr, from Northern Chapter, who handled all the paperwork for submission to National. On November 5, 1972, we held our first meeting at Unionville Tavern where we were presented our charter by Howard and Gladys Wyles, President and First Lady of the Ohio Region, who were members of the Northern Chapter.

At that time, no one in the infant chapter knew anything about putting on an Ohio Region meet except Bob Babcox, Rod Stemen, and Bob Neubacher. We were all a little horrified to find out that the first meet we were "given" to host was the Winter Assembly in January 1974. However, it came off with only a few hitches and was the first of the Region Meets held at Quail Hollow Motel, Concord Township.

The chapter has come a long way since those days guided by the following presidents: Bob Babcox, Joe Hassett, Bob Neubacher, Dave Payne, Bill Shreves, Charlie Paine, Joe Britcher, Earl Masiello, John Ray, Mike Danzig, Ralph Bowen, Tom Bates, Barbara Paine, Joe Britcher, Don Blaney, Dave Payne, Donna Bowen, Tom Bates, Royal Woodworth, Ralph Bowen, Charlie Paine, and Shirley Payne for 1996.

Wheels In Motion Flager County Region

You can bet the name "Wheels In Motion Flager County Region" is a lot more than just symbolic to this Florida beach community-based group. Patrick N. DelSordo was in charge of keeping those "wheels in motion" as the 1998 president of this group.

White River Valley Region

Franklin, Indiana, is the area serviced by the White River Valley Region. Maurice L. Kyle was president for this group in 1998.

Whiteface Mountain Region

The Whiteface Mountain area of "Upstate" New York is home to the Whiteface Mountain Region. Leading this group in 1998 was president Spencer A. Egglefield.

Wichita Falls Region

Wichita Falls, Texas, is home to this region and 1997 president Tim Donovan. Donovan was followed by Billy Rogers in the position for 1998.

Wildflower Region

The Temple, Texas, Wildflower Region enjoyed John R. Flanagan as its president for 1997. Richard Winn took over the presidency in 1998.

Wisconsin Region

The AACA's eleventh region, located in the Badger state, is the Wisconsin Region, recognized in March 1951. Donald G. Breitbach from Shorewood, Wisconsin, was elected to the presidency of the group for 1997, followed by Walter A. Wilde in 1998.

It is common to see many Wisconsin Region members in attendance with their cars at the huge Iola, Wisconsin, car show every July.

★★★

WISCONSIN REGION

By John Rosenberger

The recent upsurge or interest in antique automobiles in the state of Wisconsin suggests that the national members might be interested in the eighteen year growth of the hobby.

As far back as 1933, Robert LeFeber Feind initiated interest with his 1914 Model "T". A year later, David Uihlein bought the car when Bob acquired the 1910 sport roadster, which he still possesses. These two men became the first Wisconsin directors after our charter was obtained in 1949. They had accumulated a good sized stable of cars in 1942, when David Bartlett gained interest in his acquisition of Fords, Peerless, and Pierce. Immediately following the last war, activity was solidified with the addition of Carl Mueller, Brook Stevens, and the Rosenbergers. Today, there are well over fifty active enthusiasts in this region.

The first car obtained by Feind and Uihlein dated 1914. Over eighteen years, these men and the majority of the collectors have made it a practice to maintain interest in cars that are no newer than 1914. At meets, when Feind appears in his 1914 Rolls, or Uihlein in his 1912 Mercer—both are improvements—we often hear comments such as "Here comes the modern trash."

Among the earlier cars of the region is John LeFeber's 1906 Cadillac roadster. The car still bears its original lacquer and varnish in magnificent fashion. Dave Bartlett is restoring his 1905 Peerless and expects to have it finished in the spring. The 1906 Mercedes of Tom Rosenberger has been completely disassembled and sandblasted; it is now in the process of reassembly. Tom's 1909 Kissel Kar is performing well as usual. Occasionally we see his 1907 Ford about town. The latest addition to his barn is a 1906 Cadillac which may be viewed between Bugatti and American LaFrance fire engine. It seems that Dave Uihlein is blowing the dust off his early (1906) gas Locomobile. This is a big step for a man who restores his own cars and has to choose between Mercer, Speedwell, Alfa-Romeo, National, Kissel, Stutz ad infinitum. Besides his Mercer, we often see his 1910 gas White at meets. Ed Hansen should have his 1909 Cadillac restored but we haven't seen it as of this writing. It is rumored that Jack Rosenberger has the 1910 Brush running, but not one has seen any smoke billow from it this year. Andy Rosenberger's two-cylinder Buick seems to be suffering due to the trout season. Carl Mueller's 1910 Ford has been seen once this year, but we are afraid he has more interest in Pierces and Bentleys.

We have had three meets so far this year and expect several more. Due to our late spring, the first was in May and consisted of a tour through the Holy Hill region of Wisconsin, which may be compared to the Walden Pond in Thoreau. It climaxed with dinner in an early American hostel nestled in the middle of the woods. The second meet, on June 17, was a centennial celebration in the village of Lannon, not far from Milwaukee. Our last gathering was at the lake home of Dave Uihlein's parents. There were no planned events except for swimming and croquet, which was a welcome surprise after the routine of regular meetings.

That's about all the news from Wisconsin. To date no new acquisitions have reported.

The first appearance of the Wisconsin Region is listed as Dave Uihlein, June 1951. Notes and articles were written in the newsletter Sidelights, which is still written in Illinois.

★★★

Reminiscences (A History Of The Wisconsin Region)

by Arthur Seidenschwartz, Jr.

How did the AACA start in Wisconsin? Well, in the beginning there was Bob Find, the first member of the state. He had his first car, a 1914 Buick, before he was old enough to drive it—legally, that is! I can remember it scooting around Wauwatosa when I was still in high school, and you all know how long ago that was. Incidentally, it was about the time the AACA was founded.

The second member in the state was Dave Uihlein. (In the VMCCA Dave was "numero uno" and Bob was number two.) The whole thing was very informal until 1948, when Bob put on a meet for the Wisconsin Centennial; 115 cars showed up, all pre 1915. I was on the curb of Wisconsin Avenue with my camera, and that was the day I decided to get a car. At that time, the entire Midwest was one huge region known as either "Midwest" or "Chicago." D. Cameron Peck, in charge of the whole thing, was from Evanston. Then in 1948, it was broken into smaller pieces, and in January of 1949, Cameron Peck held a meeting at the Lake Shore Club in Chicago, where the Illinois, Iowa, Minnesota, and Wisconsin Regions were formed. My memory is a bit hazy, but Bob Feind and Dave Uihlein were along with several Rosenbergers, John Day, Web and Winnie Woodmansee and your scribe. Web and Winnie rode down with me in what was then just my everyday car—a 1940 LaSalle convertible. I'm sure all of you have admired Winnie's gorgeous white hair, and perhaps this day was responsible for it. The weather was appalling. It was before the days of motorized saltshakers, and U.S. 41 looked like the bobsled run at St. Moritz. Thrilling!

As a result of this meeting, the Wisconsin Region was chartered, and Bob Feind became its first director. Some of the members from the early years were Bob Feind, Dave Uihlein, John Day, Tom and Andy and Jack Rosenberger, Carl Mueller, Brook Stevens, Jim Floria, Fred Stratton, Jim Magin, Web Woodmansee, Art Seidenschwartz, Jr., Ed Hanson, Jack Fults, Herb and Bill Westhoffs, Al Fyffe, Tom Dunham, John Julien, Art Seidenschwartz, Sr., Dave Bartlett, Ivan Baxter, and Bob Kern. One of the early meets that I can recall was a picnic at John Day's house where everyone swapped rides, and Andy Rosenberger's 1910 Buick spent a lot of time going up hills backwards. Another was held a State Fair Park on the mile track, with real, live drag racing! Several delightful picnics were held in Willow Twig Park. A sobering thought is that the entire club treasury circa 1950 would not have been sufficient to pay the rental of the Port-a-Johns at the 1971 picnic.

The big bore meets were held south of the border in Illinois, and the Granddaddy of all was the first Illinois State Fair meet in 1949.

In order to ensure old cars, the Illinois officials sent a transporter to Wisconsin to haul down several of the Region's choice pieces. This was preceded by an Illinois State Patrol car with a patrolman who measured the heights of all the underpasses! With Bob Feind's 1914 Rolls on top of the transporter, lengthy detours were required. After safely delivering the entourage to Springfield, the patrol car departed. Moments later, some fat-headed public servant moved the rig and tore the top off the Rolls on an overhead wire! Fortunately, the budget for the meet approached six figures. The free cocktail party was the most sumptuous I've ever seen, and few of the guests were able to do justice to the free roast beef dinner. Some of the participants even lodged gratis in Springfield's best hotel.

WEBSTER'S 1922 SILVER GHOST

By Verone Kalista

The 1922 Rolls Royce Silver Ghost, owned by Webster Woodman-see, was stored in the downtown Milwaukee Welch Building. The Welch Building was really two buildings with a common elevator. It was a former car dealership, with work done on cars on the floors above. Now it was storage with a sporting good store on the first floor. The building was owned by Sherkow, who stored his Packards and a 1930 Pierce Arrow on the second floor, and on the third floor were Webster's Silver Ghost and a MGTC, parked for the winter.

A fire was started on the first floor in the Sporting Goods store, and the owner—who pretended to be beat-up—ran for the fire fighters down the street. At 10:30 Webster got a call that the building was on fire. The next morning it was determined that the cars were still on the third floor.

At 9 a.m. the crane arrived. The day was sunny and cold with a moderate breeze off the lake. The entire operation appeared to be "a piece of cake." Traffic on 7th Street was not blocked off as we might have thought, but allowed to flow through in single lanes, both north and south.

Part of the wall had to be knocked out in order to remove the cars. The first two cars stored on the second floor, belonging to Bill Sherkow, were removed with a minimum amount of problems. The workers then repeated the removal of part of the wall on the third floor in order to tackle Web's cars.

The MG, being so small, caused no particular problems. But the Rolls Royce was something else! There was less head room on the third floor and a great deal of difficulty was encountered in attempting to raise the Rolls enough to ease it out. As the Rolls perched close to the edge in the first picture on the last row, workmen removed ceiling joists in order to lift the car enough to clear the wheels. Remember, the roof of the building had collapsed on the fourth floor!

No one spoke...no one took a breath...during the time the car was in this dangerous position. Not until the car was safely free of the building and dangling peacefully above the street.

With a sigh of relief we watched her graceful ease to the street below. Web's daughter Jean, now seeing the damage for the first time, was saddened by the sight...This is the car she used when she learned to drive, and as she said, "How many times I have washed and polished her."

Time now is 3 p.m. and the job is over. Art Seidenschwartz was the only other club member present. We talked to the man in charge, "Tiny," whose great size suggested something else, and he told us it was anything but "a piece of cake." He called the job a "real sweat."

The only car we have heard anything about since that day is the Silver Ghost. Web says all new wiring is a must, a new complete paint job, and all new upholstery. In the strong light of day, blistered spots were visible and the odor from the fire would make this upholstery intolerable.

The Great Lady is now in the process of having her wounds healed, and we hope that in the future, we can again show her on the cover after a first class restoration.

Here it is—the famous upper story 1922 Rolls-Royce Silver Ghost on the 1991 Wisconsin Region Fall Tour. (Wisconsin Region photo)

One of the great traditions in the Milwaukee area is the Wally Rank and Sons Buick annual show. The event draws participants from all over the region. Here we see the AACA Region booth inside the dealership. (Wisconsin Region photo)

Wolf Creek Region

The Wolf Creek Region is located in the Grove City, Pennsylvania, area. The group's 1998 president was Michael D. Urbassik.

Wolverine State Region

The Wolverine State Region enjoyed Robert Scheffler as its president in 1998.

Wool Capital Region

The Wool Capital Region is in the San Angelo, Texas, area. Arlen Lohse was president in 1997 and 1998.

Wyoming Valley Region

This New York state-based region covers the area of the Wyoming Valley, in and around Attica. James Fox is the 1998 president.

Ye Olde Auto Club Chapter

The Ye Olde Auto Club Chapter can be found in Brighton, Colorado. Joe L. Baker was president for 1997 and 98.

Zooland Chapter

This Thomasville, North Carolina, chapter enjoyed Jerry Rook as its 1998 president.

Events,
Tours,
and Meets

Club members continued to participate in the antique automobile derbies on the East Coast throughout the 1930s. Some estimate more than 13,000 AACA events have taken place since that time, and we doubt if anyone has ever kept an exact count. Obviously, once again, there is little hope of documenting them all. However, we have included a substantial number of typical events from all over the country for your enjoyment and interest.

Participants at the Lamb Tavern Meet in 1943 included George Hughes and his 1902 Rambler, Louise van Sciver and Ralph Weeks in a 1909 Maxwell, Walter "Sparkie" Matter in his 1910 Ford, and a driverless 1911 International Harvester highwheeler. (Chilton News)

An impressive group of vehicles congregate in front of the historic Lamb Tavern in Springfield, Pennsylvania, in 1943. (Chilton News)

Early Shows and Significant Meetings

The Washington Horseless Cavalcade

In the Volume One, Number One edition of *The Bulletin,* an account of The Washington Horseless Cavalcade was described by Fred Parsons. There were sixteen cars lined up with a sound-car playing old-fashioned music. About 3,000 people were in attendance to see the group off as it paraded through what was described as crowded streets (if they only knew what that really meant today)!

Participants wore period clothing for the vehicles, while the AAA was on hand with tow cars, oil, and gas, declaring all participants honorary members of AAA.

Cars and owners on the November, 24, 1936, Washington Cavalcade included:

William Coleman	1915 Ford Model T
Economy Oil Company	1909 Simplex
John J. Eichorn	1914 Ford Model T
Josiah Ellis	1902 Cadillac
Richard Greenfield	1914 Ford Model T
Haley Body Works, Inc.	1906 Columbia Electric
Parkway Motor Company	1913 Ford Model T
C. Raymond Levis	1902 Cadillac
Mrs. Margaret Ludwig	1910 Studebaker E.M.F.
Paul Marvel	1906 Rambler
Northeast Motor Company	1906 Ford
Fred Parsons	1902 Pierce-Arrow
Robert Patterson	1910 Buick
Thomas K. Smith	1914 Ford Model T
Stitt Motor Company	1902 and 1904 Cadillacs
Morris Stoyrer	1912 Ford Model T
Noah Swartley	1911 Overland
Chas. E. Utermahlon	1910 Hupmobile
William Vehrencamp Jr.	1902 Virginia Buggy
Joseph C. Williams	1902 Oldsmobile
Wisconsin Motors, Inc.	1902 Oldsmobile
Wolf Chevrolet Sales	1914 Chevrolet

Prizes were awarded by the Washington Automotive Trade Association. The Levis' 1902 Cadillac took first place, considering appearance of the occupants (period dress), cleanliness, and "hardihood," reported the *Washington Times* newspaper.

My Personal Experience at the Cavalcade

by Morris O. Stoyrer, Harrisburg, Pennsylvania

My 1912 Model T Ford ran the distance of 250 miles that one day. It took us about five hours going down to Washington and five hours back to Harrisburg. The car, as always, ran smoothly and "kept stepping" along, encouraging us all the way. We rode just as comfortably as though we were seated in a 1937 car.

At the parade, there were sixteen cars in line, and, as for appearance, not one could touch our Ford car with all its brass glistening. It certainly amazed everyone we met in Washington. Personally, I think that was a wonderful performance for a Model T Ford.

At Washington, we met Barney Oldfield, the great automobile racer. He looked all over the car and then gave us 100 percent for appearance. We also met the announcer of the National Broadcasting Company (NBC), who allowed my wife, my son, and myself to talk over the radio and describe our trip.

The Trenton Antique Car Exhibition

On November 14, 1936, the club also participated in the Trenton Antique Car Exhibition. The event was considered highly successful, with nineteen cars entered for the procession through the streets of Trenton, New Jersey. The event ended at the Trenton Armory for the opening of the Trenton Auto Show; $250 worth of prize money was distributed among the nineteen. If we presume the cut was equal, that's $13.16 each—a good day's wage in 1936.

Early event regulations stated no advertising would be placed on cars, and the car could be driven by the owner or the owner's representative (male or female). Cars manufactured prior to 1912 were eligible for prizes. The Pennsylvania Department of Revenue gave a special dispensation. It would permit antique cars in an event of this nature to be towed to and from the parade and then participate in the procession without current license plates. Because trailers were so rare, we presume this was not taken advantage of by many. No car could win more than one prize and had to operate under its own power in the parade.

Prizes included: oldest car, second oldest car, best appearing car, most authentically costumed driver and passenger, and most original or amusing entry.

Martin's Dam—Annual AACA Outing, Annual Spring Meet

The club had its official first annual outing on June 25, 1938, at Martin's Dam near Wayne, Pennsylvania. This event would eventually evolve to become the annual spring meet. There were only five cars at this event. The participants did have a great time. They enjoyed a road run, hill climb, starting contest, and one appearance award. Obviously, car cosmetics where not the top priority in those days for participants. Five members attended:

Frank Abramson	1910 Hupmobile
Hyde Ballard	1905 Packard
Ted Brooks	1912 Buick
Ted Fiala	1906 Waltham-Orient
George Hughes	1915 Ford Model T

In 1939, the second annual Spring Meet was held at the P.D. Folwell Estate in Merion, Pennsylvania. The estate was the home of Hyde Ballard's father-in-law and was substantial in size. Twenty-five members attended with eleven cars. They enjoyed more performance tests, plus new awards for long distance, oldest car, and appearance. The prizes consisted of AACA medallions, coins, cans of oil, and a brass lamp.

The spring event continued to grow during the 1940s, with members thinking nothing of driving more than 100 miles to attend. Since trailers were almost non-existent, there were very few "trailer babies" taken to events. Members really enjoyed driving their old cars and were not afraid to do so. Louise and Joe van Sciver Jr. were frequently in attendance at the early events, traveling at highway speeds in their very dependable Maxwell or 1909 Mercedes.

At the Ballard's invitation, the event was repeated at the Folwell estate for 1940 and 1941. A picnic lunch was part of the event, with the club supplying beverages.

Prizes were awarded for:

Appearance and condition of the vehicle

Costumes

Oldest car

First, second and third

Longest distance: 1 cyl., 2 cyl., 4 cyl., more than 4 cyl.

Most unusual car

Longest distance for any car

In addition, several performance tests and novelty contests were featured.

Hatfield Fair

From Sept. 1–6, 1941, AACA members took part in the Hatfield Fair. The Montgomery County event was held under the leadership of Sam Bailey.

Participants included:

S.E. Bailey: 1918 and 1921 Mercers, 1915 Packard Twin-Six, and 1916 Ford Model T

G.M. Hughes: 1907 Orient and 1915 Ford Model T

G. Gereneck Jr.: 1909 Sears

T.B. Brooks: 1911 White

B. Rubin: 1914 Hupmobile, 1911 Maxwell, and 1909 Brush

AACA members Mr. and Mrs. George Green took antique car use to the extreme. In 1941, they drove their 1904 curved-dash Oldsmobile to California, Canada, and Mexico from their East Coast home.

New cars were rare in 1942, but the AACA was still on the move during these war years. In 1942, the club's spring meet was moved to the historic 200-year-old Lamb Tavern in Springfield, Pennsylvania. Eighteen cars were entered including:

Abramson/Fiala: 1906 Waltham-Orient, Best miles per gallon award

S.E. Bailey: 1914 Mercer, Best car appearance and condition award; 1925 Ford Model T

P. Cadwell: 1910 Maxwell, Best costume award

P. Cressman: 1916 Mercer

John Fetterolf: 1913 Mercer

George Gerenback Jr.: 1915 Packard

W. Hadley: 1910 Mercedes

C.R. Levis: 1911 Oldsmobile, Most interesting car award

Walter Matter: 1910 Ford Model T, Best all-round car

J. Mercer: 1917 Dodge

J. Murchino: 1905 Renault, Oldest car and Long Distance awards

Charles Stich: 1909 Mercedes

When was the last time you saw three early Mercers and two pre-teen Mercedes at one event? Make that driven to an event! Times certainly have changed.

The 1945 annual spring meets had outgrown previous locations and were moved to more spacious facilities around the country.

First Annual Meeting, Annual Meetings

Winter inactivity was cured by having the annual AACA meeting in the chilly off-hobby season. The first annual meeting and banquet were on March 1, 1941, at historic Bookbinder's Restaurant in Philadelphia. Membership ranks had risen to 144 members by 1941. The roster included: Chairman Paul Cadwell, Toastmaster George M. Hughes, speakers Hyde Ballard, Merle K. Duryea, P.D. Folwell, Charles B. King, and Ralph dePalma.

At the 1946 annual meeting, member Sid Strong from Atwater, Minnesota, showed up at the winter affair towing a 1900 Prescott Steamer that he had just purchased in Camden, Maine. He stopped at the Philadelphia meeting on his way back to Minnesota. He thrilled the crowd by showing his 1946 Glidden Tour™ movies as well.

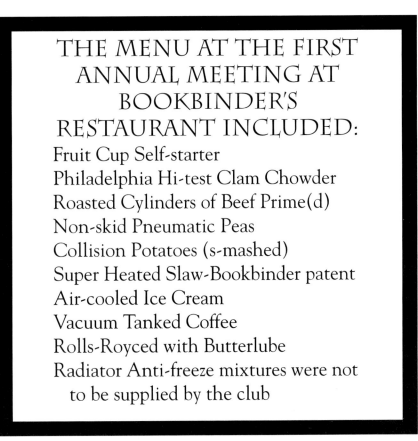

THE MENU AT THE FIRST ANNUAL MEETING AT BOOKBINDER'S RESTAURANT INCLUDED:
Fruit Cup Self-starter
Philadelphia Hi-test Clam Chowder
Roasted Cylinders of Beef Prime(d)
Non-skid Pneumatic Peas
Collision Potatoes (s-mashed)
Super Heated Slaw-Bookbinder patent
Air-cooled Ice Cream
Vacuum Tanked Coffee
Rolls-Royced with Butterlube
Radiator Anti-freeze mixtures were not
    to be supplied by the club

Special Summer Meeting

A special summer meeting was held in Philadelphia at the Robert Morris Hotel on July 23, 1943. There was a brief business meeting and a large display of brass lamps and horns owned by Sam Bailey and other members. Member Cadwell also displayed photos and models of antique automobiles. There were several reels of movies from previous AACA events shown as well.

The Golden Jubilee of the American Auto Industry

The year 1946 was a banner year for the auto industry. It was the Golden Jubilee celebration of the American Automobile Industry. There was a mammoth Golden Jubilee celebration in Detroit and an Antique Automotive Exhibition. On June 1, there was a parade with more than 150 cars driven down a gold-painted Woodward Avenue, past an estimated crowd of one million people. Many of those cars were owned by AACA and VMCCA members.

Devon Horse Show Grounds Meet

In 1946, the Devon Horse Show Grounds became the site of one of the most popular Eastern events. Photos and movies of the Devon event in the late '40s show everything from the typical antique cars you would expect to Duesenbergs and Cords from the mid-1930s. This seems to be a curiosity, as the latter cars were barely 10 years old when they were exhibited.

The Devon show was bursting at the seams by 1953. The event had 200 cars in attendance.

The winners at the 1946 Devon Meet are called to the track for a parade lap. Chief Judge Fred Wicholson is standing in the center. George Hughes is about to crank his Hupmobile and Sam Baily is in his Mercer. (Antique Automobile)

218

The old car line-up at the 1948 Devon Horse Show Grounds event featured a flock of Model Ts. (Chris Hannevig photo)

The ever-present Walter "Sparky" Matter and his Model T at the '48 Devon show. (Chris Hannevig photo)

Clarance Marshall brought his 1912 Stanley fifteen-passenger Mountain Bus to the 1948 Devon Horse Show Grounds meet. (Chris Hannevig photo)

Another 1948 Devon attendee was Ted Brooks with his fabulous Simplex. (Chris Hannevig photo)

Sam Bailey attended the 1948 Devon meet in his 1909 Pierce. (Chris Hannevig photo)

The wonderful Pennsylvania weather in October was a proper atmosphere for Jack Mercer to bring his 1917 Dodge to the Devon Horse Show Grounds. (Chris Hannevig photo)

This 1919 Cadillac Victoria coupe was one of the few closed cars at the 1948 Devon Horse Show Grounds meet. (Chris Hannevig photo)

George Corson brought his American Underslung to Devon for the meet in 1948. (Chris Hannevig photo)

A Rolls-Royce and a Packard were among the larger cars to arrive at the 1949 Devon Horse Show Grounds meet. (Chris Hannevig photo)

Sam Bailey brought his 1931 Bentley tourer to the Devon Horse Show Grounds in 1949. (Chris Hannevig photo)

The well-traveled '24 Studebaker touring not only had been to Skyline and Luray Caverns as the bumper placards would indicate, but it was one of many cars in attendance at Devon in 1949. (Chris Hannevig photo)

This 1914 Stutz Bearcat featured a little extra weather protection for the drive to the Devon Horse Show Grounds meet in 1949. (Chris Hannevig photo)

This big Pierce-Arrow touring was another 1949 participant at Devon. (Chris Hannevig photo)

Even a Model T fire engine was part of the meet at Devon in 1949. (Chris Hannevig photo)

Hershey National Fall Meet

In the fall of 1954, the event was moved to the athletic stadium in Hershey, Pennsylvania. This was thanks to an invitation by Hershey Estates, part of the huge Hershey Chocolate Company, and the efforts of William Pollock. The event was to be hosted by the Pottstown Region. Hershey would become the largest collector car event in the world.

At the first event, Pollock was quoted as saying, "how lucky the club was to have Hershey Estates support." He felt this was a sign the club would truly grow to world stature and the event would have all the room it would ever need. His predictions were ironic because the event would actually outgrow the facility's ability to continually expand and club officials would at times have disagreements with the Hershey Company over the event. The club certainly did grow to be a formidable force in the worldwide antique car community.

Most members feel the Hershey event, the largest antique auto event in the world, is truly something to be proud of. The event is a true symbol of the club's size in the car-collecting world. Today, a quarter of a million people flock to the

Les Henry, then AACA President, in his 1911 Chalmers touring at the first Hershey Fall Meet in 1954. (Les Henry Archives photo)

Atlantic Refining sponsored free gas to the participants of the first Hershey show in 1954. A long line of cars pull into the Atlantic Station in downtown Hershey. Note not only the incredible antique cars but the new Fords at the dealer in the rear. (Atlantic Refining photo; Les Henry Archives)

picturesque property. Just outside Hershey Park, more than 10,000 swap meet vendor spaces, 3,500 show cars and trucks and vehicles for sale create the world's greatest antique auto event.

Die-hard Hershey attendees know that the weather is unpredictable and hotel rooms non-existent without long-term reservation. Participants' friends expect them to bring home several chocolate bars (just like the ones they can buy at home).

Rain, mud, heat, dust, clogged roads, traffic, surly traffic cops, and hundreds of golf carts cannot dissuade a Hershey veteran from making the annual pilgrimage. That illusive special part, car, or collectable may be available. There are many old friends with whom to visit. One can see rare cars and soak up the essence of what the AACA is all about in one concentrated weekend.

From that first meet in 1954 when the show was contained in the Hershey Stadium, the event has continued to grow and grow. The first swap meet in the shadows of Hershey Stadium featured seven vendors and no sign of the Pennsylvania tax department. Lillian Pamphilon, spouse of the club's secretary, also set up a booth with club items and jewelry for sale. The booth benefiting the club grew with each meet. Today, the AACA has a fine line of collectibles and merchandise to help members show their pride of belonging to the greatest old car club in the world.

More cars getting sponsored fuel at the Hershey Atlantic station in 1954. (Atlantic Refining photo; Les Henry Archives)

Atlantic went all out in its sponsorship of the first Hershey Fall Meet in 1954. In addition to providing gasoline, it decorated its station in downtown Hershey with antique car cutouts. (Atlantic Refining photo; Les Henry Archives)

A sampling of the early vendors included National Costume Chairwoman, Mrs. William Browne, selling period clothing, Frank T. Snyder had anything you could name for a Model T Ford, and Paul Marvel had an amazing display of early brass lamps. This small band of hobbyists represented the birth of an industry. This was the first year Hershey Region hosted the Fall Meet.

There was no formal booth space charge for vendors in the flea market area under the stadium. Paul Marvel would visit each booth near the end of the show and ask, "What do you think you made and how much of that can you contribute to the club?"

The AACA Fall Meet in Hershey was held under the direction of the National Activities Committee from 1954 to 1958.

In 1955, two of the hottest sellers were the Chevrolet Bel Air and Ford Crown Victoria. For that year's fall meet, the Hershey Region organized a breakfast run from Hershey to Elizabethtown and back, and then staged a number of events at the stadium.

By 1957, the flea market moved from under the stadium's shadows. Area hobbyists were encouraged to bring surplus parts to sell in an effort to help others with their restorations. Some participants, not seeing the value of the vendors' "Parts Row," thought it was an insult to the quality of the car show. Some considered it a blight to the scenic beauty of the event.

By 1959, "Parts Row" had expanded to cover both sides of Stadium Road and the adjacent field. L. Scott Bailey, then editor of *Antique Automobile*, stated in his own account of the event in the Fall-Winter 1976 *Quatrefoil*, that he was reminded of the storied market in Paris, referred to as a flea market. Paul Marvel and Paul Stern, chairmen of the part's area, liked the term that has stuck since that time.

The Atlantic Refining Company also brought its 1920 White oil tanker to the 1954 Hershey Fall Meet. Here it is being driven onto the show field "in" the stadium. (Atlantic Refining photo; Les Henry Archives)

227

The show field "in" the stadium at the 1954 AACA Fall Meet in Hershey. Note that cars such as the Cord, Packard, and Auburn in the back row were only 17 to 18 years old! (Atlantic Refining photo; Les Henry Archives)

Crowds gather to watch the cars being driving onto the show field at the first Hershey in 1954. (Atlantic Refining photo; Les Henry Archives)

There were many committees and the event was quickly becoming well organized. The host, the Hershey Region, brought the famous "Chuck Wagon," a Model T Depot Hack loaded with free cider to refresh the weary shoppers.

Occasional complaints over the "flea market" came from area merchants to the board of directors. Some members were afraid the commercial section might outgrow the club's control. Concerns over local ordinances were discussed. Concerns of this nature consumed many meetings then and since, but the club always managed to seem to do whatever it took to keep the Eastern Fall Meet moving along. The fear that the event could destroy the fall meet was certainly unfounded.

1960 Silver Jubilee Meet

The Silver Jubilee Meet was held in Hershey in 1960 with 891 cars gathering. Len Rhinehart and his crew were in charge of directing what was the largest old car gathering to date. Judging was supervised by George French, with final tallies supervised by Karl Israel. The weather was beautiful and there was a small swap meet under the eaves of Hershey Stadium. The AACA was selling jewelry, souvenirs, and emblems. The Hershey Region had its cider wagon dispensing cider all day. Oakley Sumpter brought and demonstrated his World War I Model T tank to the amazement of the crowds.

Dr. James H. Gray's 1910 Franklin at the 1960 Silver Jubilee Meet in Hershey, Pennsylvania. (Antique Automobile)

Robert Harrison was in attendance at the Hershey Silver Jubilee Meet in 1960 with his 1912 National Roadster. (Antique Automobile)

The Flea Market (swap meet) during the 1960 Silver Jubilee at Hershey was a busy, if not much more informal place than today. (Antique Automobile)

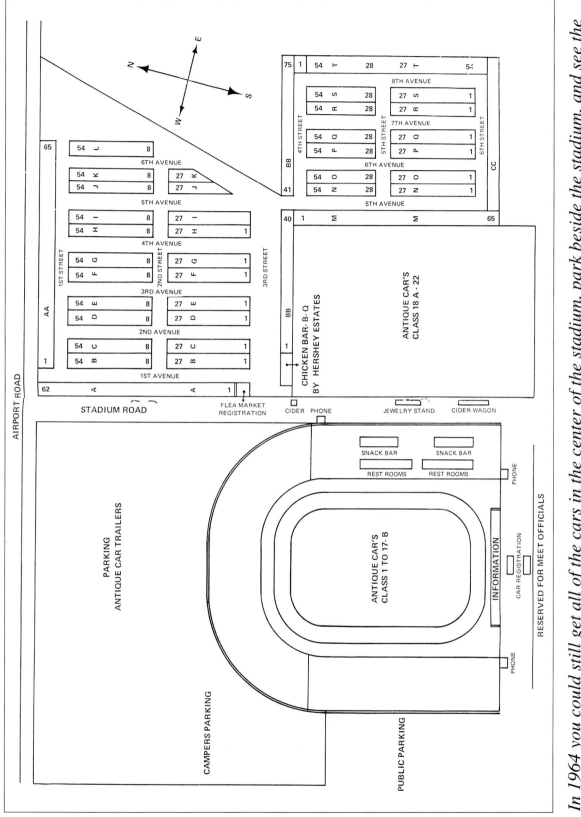

In 1964 you could still get all of the cars in the center of the stadium, park beside the stadium, and see the swap meet in a few hours.

Prices for items at the 1960 event are downright depressing to see today. The Hershey Region reported in a later account of a fully restored 1913 LaGonda Tourer selling for $1,560.

In 1963, car show registration jumped to 913. Only a year later, the number increased to 1,045 cars. The same year, 205 vendors would request 3,330 frontage feet of exhibit space in 10-foot increments. The budget for the event that year was a whopping $9,152.87 with more than $11,000 received.

In 1970, 912 registered cars were in the fall show and the vendor stalls increased to 1,083. More than 800 attended the banquet, where Jim Ladd received a Senior Trophy for his 1929 Pierce-Arrow.

Tours to the new AACA National Headquarters were added to the activities list for the 1971 fall meet. Hershey Estates announced it would begin to charge the club for the use of the flea market field area and set-up day for vendors moved to Wednesday at noon. At the awards banquet, Charles E. Duryea's daughter, Grace, was the honored guest. George Waterman exhibited his 1896 Duryea in the display hall for the occasion.

This 1939 Plymouth convertible coupe was one of the cars still being shown on the grass just outside the stadium in 1969. It is to note that the car is also one of the newest eligible to compete at Hershey in those days. (Ken Buttolph photo)

The car show field at Hershey 1969 shot from the top of the stadium looking down. (Bob Lichty photo)

Some 1,299 vendors arrived from forty-two states for the fall meet in 1972. At the awards banquet, three Fords were displayed: a 1903, 1933, and a new 1973. The cars were on hand to celebrate Ford's 70th Anniversary. By the following year, discussion was set into place to consider making the Hershey fall meet a permanent international event. This seemed ironic since the event had reached that worldwide status anyway.

Nineteen seventy-four was yet another banner year for the event. This was the same year the Hershey Region was incorporated. However, the rental contract with Hershey Estates was initially rejected by the region at the March 9 meeting. The 1974 event was almost not sponsored by the region. Hershey Estates executives Charles M. Wolgemuth, Ned Book, Bruce McKinney, and Roger Conner aided in the negotiations as the contract was signed on May 6. That year saw chairpersons Warren and Beverly Steele add street signs in the flea market. The banquet was moved to the Hershey Convention Center from the Milton Hershey School.

The Hershey event has grown to actually exceed AACA membership numbers and a constant question has been how to get Hershey participants to join the club. Many visitors simply take advantage of the free admission and reasonable parking to do their annual car shopping and viewing.

It was even attempted, in the early 1970s, to ask for proof of membership to enter the car show area. Huge lines formed, tempers flared, and a few punches were even thrown. Directors tried to look up membership names on-the-spot in the club directory but that proved time consuming during the event. The idea was abandoned as a fiasco. There have been very few checks to ensure that spectators are club members since that time. Vendors and car corral participants must be AACA members to participate. In fact, the right to vend at Hershey and other national meets has proved to be a good tool in building membership ranks of AACA.

HERSHEY/PA.

The cover of Ron Nelson's 1971 Hershey book was indicative of the beautiful photography the publication contained. (Ron Nelson photo)

The Chrysler parade phaeton was on display in the early morning fog at Hershey '71. (Ken Buttolph photo)

The parking lots proved to be interesting at Hershey in the early days. A beautiful '56 Cadillac limousine was caught by the camera in 1972, still unable to compete in the show due to its young age. (Ken Buttolph photo)

The parking lot was always just as interesting as the show at Hershey back in 1969. Here, a late '40s Chrysler Town and Country is parked, looking for a new owner. (Ken Buttolph photo)

Sales eligibility of cars and parts have always been a controversy in AACA, ranging from set dates to the current 25 year cut-off date. During the 1970s, strict enforcement of parts sold by date and type resulted in vendors being evicted by show officials. The same carried over to the car show. Easier to enforce and without fanfare, cars prior to a certain year were simply not allowed to enter. Today the rule does not seem as controversial as it once was. When popular cars such as early Corvettes, 1957 Chevrolets, and 1965 Mustangs could not be entered, tempers also flared. The need for postwar cars to be recognized was so great other "for profit" events were created in the region to fill to void. It was feared the AACA would dwindle if something was not done and the 25-year rule was resurrected from the earliest days of the club. Membership has grown since that time. That early strict enforcement of rules and the Derry Township Police Department's strict interpretation of traffic codes and direction began to give Hershey a reputation of being run by the Gestapo. Fortunately, most of that feeling is long gone today. You will always have some friction between participants when you put a couple hundred thousand people on little more than 100 acres for one weekend.

It was predicted in the mid-1970s that the event had peaked and the hobby would begin to deteriorate. Quite the contrary took place with an upsurge in the hobby during the late '70s and onward and upward to this day. By the 1980s, reserved flea market spaces became possible with computerization of the 10,000 spaces. A car corral was added just for the sale of vehicles. If we were to chronicle the progression of shifting spaces and fields due to the ever expansion of Hershey Park, we could make a book out of that with maps and diagrams. Every time Hershey Park would build a new roller-coaster, a piece of the original "Blue field" would chip away. However, the ever creative planners always seem to find new ways to accommodate the vendors' needs.

Many hobby industry companies would launch new products annually. Companies such as The Eastwood Company, Coker Tire, and the major hobby periodicals are just a few such commercial efforts which looked to Hershey for product introductions and direction. *Old Cars Weekly* was born at Hershey in 1971. The Iola, Wisconsin, firm, Krause Publications, brought tens of thousands of pilot issues to Hershey. It was the launch of the hobby's first and only newspaper. Just a few years later, the firm would pioneer giving shopping bags to the participants. The shopping bags became a Hershey marketing coup for the firm until the size of the show ran the cost too high. Companies like Redi-Strip would give hands-on demonstrations, almost mini-seminars, on how to perform a specific restoration process, such as paint removal.

It was said that Bill Harrah was the only man who could attend Hershey without getting dirty. No matter how much mud there was he always looked as clean as he did here, viewing brass lamps for sale with an employee at Hershey '74. (OCW photo)

HERSHEY MUD

Report To The Board Of Directors Of The Conglomerate Corporation Of America Subject - The Collection, Packaging And Marketing Of Hershey Mud

As requested your Research and Development Department has investigated the marketing potential of Hershey Mud and makes the following recommendations.

1. Timing. Hershey mud is at its best immediately following the National Pall Meet, Eastern Division Antique Automobile Club of America held early in October of each year. Harvesting of the product must be completed within three days after the event as the following weeks are completely devoid of rain and the product becomes rigid and difficult to handle.

2. It is recommended that the product be packaged in one pint metal cans with a friction lid and that an appropriate label be prepared illustrating the contents in its pristine form in full color.

3. It is recommended that each can be accompanied by a recipe book covering the following applications, all of which have been thoroughly tested by R and D and we are convinced that Hershey mud is ideal for its various intended purposes and cannot be duplicated anywhere else in the world. Suggested copy for the recipe book follows.

Use Of Hershey Mud As An Abrasive And Polishing Compound

Hershey mud in its raw state contains three sizes of grit carefully homogenized and intermingled. To separate and fully utilize these various grit sizes it is necessary to first thoroughly dry the contents of this package. Now sift the contents through an ordinary kitchen strainer, putting to one side what goes through and spreading what remains in the sieve on some large flat surface such as your paved driveway.

The next step is to take several sheets of medium weight cardboard and spread on a thick layer of glue. Place the glue side face down on the dried grit, let the glue set and you have a product called 'Sand-Paper', an excellent material for leveling lumpy bondo patches. (Bondo can also be made from Hershey mud and this is covered in another chapter.)

By successive straining of the remaining product you can come up with ever decreasing grit sizes that will carry you right down to the final substance, an ideal polishing paste. Used in its liquid state you can Hersheyize your car resulting in a brilliant shine with a slightly brownish cast. If not satisfied with the result, remember our motto - *CAVEAT EMPTOR*.

Hershey Mud For Noisy Rear Ends

Do your transmission or differential gears howl and grind? Has this unwanted noise prevented you from selling your desirable antique or special interest car? Sweat no more - just replace the grease in transmission or differential with the contents of this can. Far superior to sawdust or oatmeal, the contents of this can will silence the most stubborn clanking, grinding, growling gear-teeth noises, make your pride and joy sound like a pacified pussycat.

To prepare the product for gear silencing, carefully remove stones, bits and pieces of metal and other foreign objects (indigenous to genuine Hershey mud) from the enclosed mixture and spoon it little by little into whatever gearbox is causing all the trouble. If this doesn't completely and forever silence your gears, return the contents of this can for full refund. (Be sure to send $5.00 to cover handling, postage and the consternation caused the perpetrators of this concoction.)

Hershey Mud Paint

The delicate brown shade of Hershey mud has made it a favorite among the devotees of the color commonly known as Baby Brown. It has taken years of rain storms early in October, plus the trampling of thousands of feet, to obtain this highly desirable, exclusive brown color. Strands of green grass intermingle with the chocolate brown sub-soil and bits and pieces of hot dogs, spilled mustard and cigarette butts have produced a pigment consistency and color unmatched by DuPont or PPG.

238

Hershey Mud Paint (cont.)

Simply strain the contents of this can through cheese cloth (or nylon pantyhose), mix with your favorite thinner or reducer and you will have the most enviable Baby Brown car in your neighborhood.

The Medical Uses Of Hershey Mud

Hershey mud makes an ideal dentifrice while at the same time perfuming the breath, eradicating the bile and alleviating heartburn.

Taken internally refined Hershey mud *is* an instant cure for diarrhea, and at the same time causes your hair to grow long and curly and your fingernails obtain a diamond brilliancy. Take only under complete and explicit orders from your doctor, chiropractor, optometrist or orthodontist. If in doubt over the efficacy of this medication, have your practitioner write the Hershey Mud Medical Foundation, Chocolatetown, USA (Enclose a contribution of $10.00 and a self addressed stamped envelope).

Hershey mud is ideal as a poultice, designed to drain the most stubborn boils, eradicate warts and leave you with a beautiful Hershey tan (ask your beautician about the youth giving powers of Hershey mud packs).

Puree Of Hershey Mud

The nutritive value of Hershey mud has yet to be completely explored but the following recipe will serve as a good start. Carefully split a handful of dried peas and drop the results one by one in rapidly boiling water. After ten minutes of vigorous boiling, search through your can of mud for bits and pieces of hot dog or substitute any bits and pieces of meat you may have left over in the refrigerator. Continue to simmer while you strain the contents of this can, using a 350 mesh copper screen as nothing but pure mud must enter the puree. Discard bits and pieces of grass, stones, cigarette butts, etc. However, if a coin shows up in the residue it may be returned to the Conglomerate Corporation of America for a refund on the following basis.

One penny, a free can of Hershey mud

Five cents, you may keep - no communication is necessary

Ten cents, return the dime and the can for full refund of purchase price

Back to the stove, stir constantly for several hours or until thick or muscle cramps set in - whichever occurs first.

The resulting mixture is a low calorie, highly nutritive, palate pleasing satisfying soup or can be used as the basic ingredient of Hershey mud pancakes. If not satisfied, send the contents to the Hershey Chocolate people as they are always looking for something new.

Hershey mud c. 1995.

Hershey Mud Building Blocks

As everyone knows, the Egyptians had considerable success with a mixture of mud and straw in the manufacture of bricks that have survived to this day. Fortunately the ingredients of Hershey mud as it comes directly from the can duplicates the heretofore uninvestigated and unknown proportion of mud to straw and other secret ingredients that act as dryers and preservatives.

Hershey Mud Building Blocks (cont.)

One can *of* Hershey mud will make one brick. Simply construct a small wooden box, 8 inches by 2 inches by 4 inches (these materials can be purchased from your friendly lumber yard for pennies), pour in the contents of this can and let cure in the hot sun for six to eight weeks. You will now be the proud owner of your first brick and with luck, and a thousand or so cans or Hershey mud, you can build your dream house, marry an Egyptian girl, remove her veil, and what happens after that is up to you.

Final Note To The Board Of Directors

In anticipation of Food and Drug Administration labeling requirements, we suggest the following be included on the can's label. Unadulterated and undiluted Hershey mud as it comes directly from the Blue or Red Fields is a pungent mixture of a number of unique ingredients found nowhere else in the world. It is the result of a torrential rain the second day of the AACA Car Show and Swap Meet plus the continuous homogenizing of approximately 2,850 booted and bare feet and various and sundry discards from the own-ers thereof. A typical sample contains the following ingredients: Central Pennsylvania mucus-mudicus (brown) - 63%. Cultured and manicured grass (green) - 8%. Hershey chocolate (resulting from the 1917 factory explosion and overflow - 5.5%. Used gum and candy wrappers - 4.7%. Tar and nicotine in the form of cigarette butts (including used filters) - 4.2%.

Hershey Mud

Iron oxide drainings *from* the vendors of old iron - 3.8%

Water in the form of H_2O - 3.5%

Traces of unidentified bolts, nuts, stones and discarded advertising literature - 2.7%

Note - as we go to press the R and D computer has not yet come up with a total of the above ingredients but if by any chance it should exceed 100%, that's our good luck. If not, we feel the consumer is privileged to sue the corporation without any advance warning or hope of a satisfactory settlement.

"Hershey or bust" was the motto of this Hershey '74 vendor. (OCW photo)

The shopping didn't stop at night in the '70s. At Hershey '74, customers searched through vendors' booths well after dark. (OCW photo)

This Autocar truck was one of many winners in the car show at Hershey '74. (OCW photo)

An outstanding car show entry at the Eastern Fall Meet in Hershey 1974 was this Miller-Ford race car. (OCW photo)

Mary Abrams made the coverage of Hershey '74 by Old Cars Weekly *when she gave Lil' Gatsby a lift in one of the shopping bags given out by the publication that year. (OCW photo)*

Harrah's Auto Collection was always in attendance at Hershey in the '70s and 1974 was no exception, bringing several cars including this Chrysler Thunderbolt. (OCW photo)

In 1975, the 62 acres of flea market turned to a quagmire of mud. Bill Pollock's 1906 Cadillac was the featured car on commemorative items and plaques this year. It was not much better for rain in 1976, which began on a Thursday and increasing in intensity through the car show parade of incoming vehicles on Saturday. HERCO, as it was called by now, built a new maintenance building displacing some of the blue field. The new building was a welcome refuge for weary and wet flea market shoppers.

By 1977, a system of co-chairpersons was in place at Hershey and a red and blue field was instituted. Old car films were shown in the maintenance building for participants. Chairman Roland Dunkelberger brought in the director of the U.S. Weather Service, as a guest speaker at the banquet, but the rains came late in the event anyway.

The Silver Anniversary Hershey Meet was in 1978 and included the years the Pottstown Region aided in the procedures prior to the official founding of the Hershey Region. There were many impromptu jam sessions popping up in the flea market during the evening. As a result, a Friday night talent show was begun.

The map of Hershey '75 continued to show the car show contained in the stadium and a swap meet in what was to become known as the "blue field."

FIFTY CENTS

THE AUTOMOBILE QUARTERLY
QUATREFOIL

A Connoisseur's Serendipity of Select Readings and Sundries for the Automotive Enthusiast
Produced by the World's Largest Publishers of Automotive History

VOLUME TWO, NUMBER TWO   **FALL-WINTER 1976**

Hershey Flea Market
BOOM OR BUST

A Brief Critical History

1

In 1954 the National Fall Meet of the Antique Automobile Club of America moved into Hershey Football Stadium. For eight years previous, the meet to judge national prize winners had been held in Devon, Pennsylvania—it had grown during that time to become the biggest single annual attraction for members of the AACA, and it was too big now for the Devon Horse Show grounds. The club, founded in 1935, was growing too, but it remained predominantly a Pennsylvania-oriented organization. Bill Pollock had arranged for the Pottstown Region to host the affair in its new home, with the blessiing and assistance of Hershey Estates—a part of the vast organization responsible for an empire encompassing not only the chocolate factory, the electric and water companies, farms, dairies, seemingly unlimited acreage, two Hershey hotels (the Cocoa Inn and the Hotel Hershey), but the Hershey School for Boys as well, all left in legacy by Milton S. Hershey, father of the chocolate bar.

In looking over the stadium, the parking area and the neatly cut grass fields lying at the base of a hill topped with the beautiful rose gardens of the Hotel Hershey and school, Pollock remarked, "How lucky AACA is to have the support of Hershey Estates. We have everything, all the room we will ever need. With this as a base, AACA can become a truly national club from coast to coast. We are just beginning to really grow. Wait and see. Hershey will draw cars from all over the country."

And so the pilgrimage to Chocolate Town began. Cars did come, they came from the Far West, from the South, from Canada and Texas. The AACA Fall Meet would attract vehicles from the Veteran Motor Car Club of America's stronghold in New England and would compete handily with the Horseless Carriage Club's domain in California. Hershey, Pennsylvania, through the efforts of Bill Pollock, Bill Boden and Jim Ladd, would become the National Headquarters of the AACA. And the AACA, already the oldest organization of its kind in America, would become the largest automotive historical society in the world.

The move to Hershey was indeed propitious. There was a fever abroad in the land of postwar America. Collecting antique cars, making them run, was mushrooming into one of the most prestigious and exciting of leisure-time hobbies—and Hershey Stadium was on its way to becoming the mecca of the old car cult. No longer would it be sufficient merely to restore a car to pristine authenticity; the results of one's efforts had to be brought to

By L. Scott Bailey

Hershey, to endure scrutiny, to be fine-tooth-combed, to be measured against uncompromising national standards by the most knowledgeable and demanding of judges. An AACA National First Prize was a Holy Grail. The quest was ardently pursued. No greater reward was imaginable, nothing else would increase one's reputation more among his peers in the hobby, nowhere else could a car be certified more positively for authenticity and none but a Hershey prize could determine without question its monetary value.

Following the cars to Hershey from Devon—and almost unnoticed—came a handful of members who set up card tables with automotive literature, catalogues, advertisements, books and a few small parts, all for sale. The first year they assembled inside the stadium on the narrow strip of grass near the entrance—subsequently they were relegated to a less-conspicuous grassy mound almost hidden by trees and shrubs at the rear of the stadium. A little closer to the field, Lillian Pamphilon, wife of the club's secretary, and a few national directors' wives sold jewelry on a table that seemed to grow longer each year.

In 1957—probably at the instigation of Paul Marvel, one of the original founders of the AACA, who each year had walked from table to table in a hat-in-hand approach asking, "Well, what do you think you made and how much do you think you can contribute to the club?"—the card tables were

In the Fall-Winter issue of Automobile Quarterly's Quatrefoil, *L. Scott Bailey devoted a large portion of the issue to what he termed "A Brief Critical History." In it he gave an account of the history of the Hershey Flea Market and his editorialized ideas as to its direction. (Automobile Quarterly)*

In 1978 a memorable Hershey event occurred. The rains were so torrential that mud would have been welcome. Water flooded through the swap meet slowing, but not stopping, the activities. (OCW photo)

A young Corky Coker sets out tires for display between rain showers at Hershey '78. (OCW photo)

A Jeep was a pretty handy vehicle to have during the 1978 Hershey Fall Meet. (OCW photo)

Even the local law enforcement officers can't escape getting hooked by hundreds of acres of great antique items, including a toy Texaco tanker. (OCW photo)

Water, water, everywhere.... That's what the swap meet at Hershey '78 looked like. Undaunted, vendors displayed their wares and buyers put on their hip waders, and it was business as usual, just soggy. (OCW photo)

An aerial photo of the 1979 AACA National Fall meet in Hershey.

Another aerial photo of the AACA National Fall Meet. That's the Hershey Chocolate factory in the foreground. No one goes home without Hershey's chocolate.

Twin Chrysler Town and Countrys where displayed as the theme cars for the 1979 event. By 1980, the car show attracted 1,067 cars requiring 405 AACA judges. A total of 5,500 flea market spaces were rented and 12,000 event directories were sold, as it had become impossible to find your way around the event without a program. Weather was an ironic mix with dry conditions causing HERCO to spread calcium on Thursday to control dust, only to have a wet Friday and Saturday.

Many vendors have gone to multiple locations in the event based on the theory that a spectator cannot cover the entire event. Of course, only the most ardent shopper and fast walker can cover the many miles of aisles in just a few days.

The 1980s saw a period of amazing growth in the old car hobby reaching its zenith around 1989, with car prices skyrocketing. Demand for restoration parts and materials flourished in this golden age of the old car hobby. Business boomed for everyone. You could hardly go wrong on an old car purchase and restoration economics made sense even for that loyal hobbyist who did not care anyway. The Hershey and surrounding flea markets drew the attention of the Pennsylvania tax department and the concern of vendors. Before long, even the most innocent of hobby dealing took on the appearance of a business to the tax people. Tempers and nerves were kept on edge, but the cooperative efforts of a flea market promoters for both non- and for-profit, got the issue under control. Vendors simply had to comply by reporting sales and taking sales tax. Once the vendor reported his activities or exemption, he was pretty well left to do business as usual. Nexus tax concerns and state income taxes would cause more alarm for vendors. In 1996, a large Ford parts company that had annually brought a huge tent of parts to Hershey, announced it would no longer return to Pennsylvania due to tax laws. Later, this problem was resolved.

The early '90s saw several years of torrential rain deluge the flea market and show. Hershey followers, being the dedicated hobbyists they are, came anyway. Tractors, tow trucks and sometimes military vehicles had to pull vendors into and out of spaces. Vehicles sitting still would slide down roadways; rare old cars that had never been wet in their lives were axle deep in gooey Hershey chocolate-like mud.

Additional commercial gain to the area is obvious. Area motels raise rates dramatically and often require a specific number of days to stay. Many participants have stayed at the same motel for twenty or thirty years and are close friends with local operators. Restaurants are packed and even the local tourism bureaus have chronicled the economic impact the event has on the region.

Bob Pass of Passport Transport has been coming to Hershey for many years. In 1980 he brought this Morgan to sell in the swap meet. (OCW photo)

If you needed wooden wheels, this was the booth to stop at during Hershey '81. (OCW photo)

Old Cars Weekly *celebrated its 10th anniversary at Hershey in 1981. (Bob Lichty collection)*

"Friendly" Bob Adams from Wisconsin was always just that. He always had a handshake and a smile for everyone who would stop by his car sales space in the swap meet at Hershey. (OCW photo)

This is the place! The headquarters building for the Hershey Region of the AACA located in nearby Palmyra, Pennsylvania. It is from this location that the Region takes care of the business of running the Hershey event, committee meetings and the housing of the famed "Chuck Wagon."

1953 Oldsmobile Fiesta convertible at Hershey '84 is a rare sight anywhere. (OCW photo)

Antique toys have been increasing in popularity at Hershey—this photo is from a 1984 swap meet. (OCW photo)

This sample row of vintage cars is a typical example of what was offered at Hershey in 1985. (OCW photo)

Renault Dauphines were not known for longevity, but this one certainly was in great shape as seen at Hershey in 1985. (OCW photo)

In contrast to the adjoining diminutive Dauphine is the magnificent Cord L-29 convertible sedan also seen at Hershey '85. (OCW photo)

This old '40s era Greyhound "Silversides" bus came to Hershey in 1985. (OCW photo)

A nice old Buick for sale in the swap meet at Hershey '85. (OCW photo)

Clubs, chapters, and commercial businesses frequently use Hershey as a meeting place or venue to offer mini-seminars or lectures (1985). (OCW photo)

Only at Hershey can you expect to find the unusual such as this Citroen ID/DS model as seen in 1985. (OCW photo)

Gregarious Henry Austin Clark (right), one of the club's earliest members and the founder of the Long Island Auto Museum, was popular everywhere he went, including Hershey '85. He is seen talking with Richie Clyne of the Imperial Palace. (OCW photo)

You can always see a few steam cars like this beautiful brass era Stanley at Hershey, and 1986 was no exception.

By 1986 pickup trucks like this early postwar Chevy where becoming commonplace at Hershey. (OCW photo)

This Chrysler Airflow's advanced styling was still turning heads fifty years later at Hershey '86. (OCW photo)

When was the last time you saw a late pre-war Willys or pickup such as this one that was "not" a street rod or old drag car? You could have seen this one at Hershey '86 in the car show. (OCW photo)

Another pickup at Hershey '86—a great looking '47 Hudson in the car show. (OCW photo)

A '55 Chevy panel version from Hershey '86. (OCW photo)

A rare sight even when new, this early Volvo station wagon could have been found in the car show at Hershey '86. (OCW photo)

Hershey '86 was loaded with rare cars including this 1938 Oldsmobile convertible coupe. (OCW photo)

This 1954 Chrysler station wagon could have been bought in the swap meet at Hershey '86. (OCW photo)

If you like brass era cars, Hershey always offers plenty and a rare opportunity to see them drive onto the show field. (OCW photo)

This Jeep FC-170 fire engine was available Hershey '86. (OCW photo)

Motorcycles like this one have become more popular every year (Hershey '87). (OCW photo)

Edsels seem more popular now then when they were new. This 1958 Citation hardtop was at Hershey '87. (OCW photo)

This bird's-eye view of Hershey '87 looks more like "Woodstock" than a gathering of automotive historians. (OCW photo)

The race car division at Hershey is always popular. This example was seen at Hershey '87. (OCW photo)

This great-looking Hudson convertible was on display at Hershey '88. (OCW photo)

Dodge's last roadster, a '51 Wayfarer, was in the car show at Hershey '88. (OCW photo)

No, this beautiful old ambulance was not on an emergency call at Hershey '88—it was part of the show. (OCW photo)

The big Classics come to Hershey, too! This Lincoln "K" convertible sedan was on display at Hershey '89. (OCW photo)

Old Cars Weekly *has been going to Hershey since the publication was launched with its pilot issue in 1971. This was the OCW booth at Hershey '89. (OCW photo)*

Even a casual observer could spot this Pierce-Arrow's trademark fender-mounted headlamps at Hershey '89. (OCW photo)

Most major museums make a point to have a display booth at Hershey. The Owls Head Museum of Transportation was on hand at Hershey '89. (OCW photo)

A pair of rare trucks in the 1989 Hershey swap meet: a Diamond T rescue van and an International KB panel truck. (Bob Lichty photo)

This touring car was drawing lots of interest in the paved Chocolate Field Annex at Hershey '89. (Bob Lichty photo)

This well-accessorized 1953 Ford Victoria was part of Hershey '90. (OCW photo)

A wet, but none the less beautiful, 1941 Oldsmobile coupe braved the weather to participate in Hershey '90. (OCW photo)

The wet weather at Hershey can give anyone the willies...and this Willys Aero gave the crowd at Hershey '90 a thrill. (OCW photo)

Hershey is known for mud, rain, and unpredictable weather—and yet hundreds of thousands of devotees attend annually. Soggy feet is a small price to pay for a weekend at the world's largest swap meet and car show. (Hershey '90) (OCW photo)

The heavy equipment was brought out for pulling vendors into and out of spaces, aisles, and each other. (OCW photo).

The race car trial runs in Hershey Stadium are always popular. To see an Indy car from the past run at such close range is a thrill many will never forget. (OCW photo)

An early race car is prepared for its run in Hershey stadium for 1990. (OCW photo)

This Ford race car is indicative of the type that ran in the famed Elgin Road Races in the '30s, except this was 1990 and in Hershey, Pennsylvania. (OCW photo)

A rare sight this side of the Atlantic was this 1950 Simca roadster observed at Hershey '90. (OCW photo)

The Antique Automobile Club of America's National Headquarters at 501 Governor Road in Hershey, Pennsylvania. (W.E. Bomgardner photo)

David Strong's early regional membership cards illustrate what was awarded members of Regions in the early 1950s. (Dave Strong collection)

HARTFORD'S GOLDEN AUTOMOBILE JUBILEE
1897-1947

25¢

THIS BRIGHT RED PIERCE-ARROW ROADSTER was but one of many participants in the 1963 Glidden Tour™. (C. L. "Doc" Pressler photo)

HARTFORD'S AUTO SHOW IN 1947 celebrated the city's Golden Automobile Jubilee a year after the American automobile's 50th Anniversary. The event was typical of many that AACA cars participated in in that era. (AACA Library & Research Center)

Glidden Tour™ participants are not afraid to drive their cars. Dirt roads can be just part of the fun as this Packard proved in 1976.
(C. L. "Doc" Pressler photo)

A TRAFFIC COP stops oncoming modern cars to permit the vintage cars access to the New York Auto Show. Note: "Old 16" is second in line. (AACA Library & Research Center)

ANTIQUE AUTO SHOW

71st REGIMENT ARMORY — NEW YORK — MARCH 8-14-1948

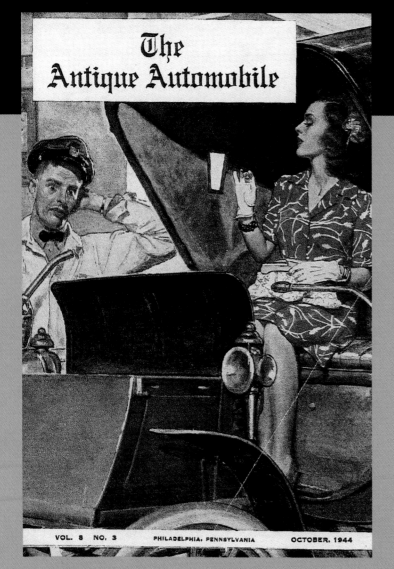

AACA TOURS take members to many beautiful places such as the Biltmore estate in Asheville, North Carolina, in 1985. (C. L. "Doc" Pressler photo)

COVER OF *The Antique Automobile* Vol. 8, No. 3, October 1944 shows a befuddled service station attendant looking to supply fuel for this lady's antique car.
(AACA Library & Research Center)

GLIDDEN TOUR™ cars enjoy a visit to see the latest in military aircraft in 1960. (C. L. "Doc" Pressler photo)

D. CAMERON PECK OF CHICAGO is shown in his rare 1920 Cunningham Speedster on the cover of The Antique Automobile Vol. 8, No. 1, April 1944. (AACA Library & Research Center)

THIS 1937 PACKARD LIMOUSINE from the Canton Classic Car Museum ready to head out on a local AACA chapter tour in 1998.
(Bob Lichty photo)

THE 1975 HERSHEY Fall meet program continued to carry the Hershey Region's famous Model T Ford "chuck wagon" on the cover.

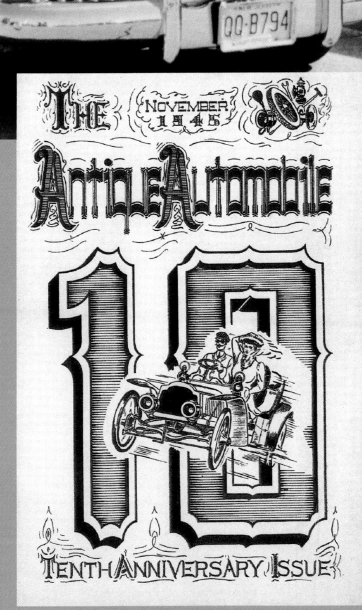

Open wide for the judges. A 1949
Buick convertible awaits the judges
in the 1996 Hershey show area.
(Victor Losquadro photo)

The November 1945 issue of *The
Antique Automobile* commemorated
the 10th Anniversary of the AACA
in yellow and navy blue.
(AACA Library & Research Center)

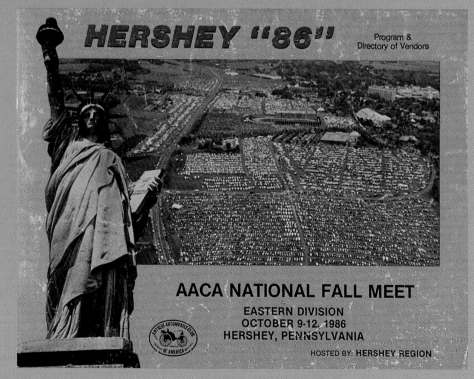

HERSHEY "86"

Program & Directory of Vendors

AACA NATIONAL FALL MEET

EASTERN DIVISION
OCTOBER 9-12, 1986
HERSHEY, PENNSYLVANIA

HOSTED BY: HERSHEY REGION

IT IS HARD TO KEEP IN MIND today that contemporary photos such as this one taken at Hershey in 1969 include highly collectible cars such as the 1964 Chevy Impala and 1955 Chevy Nomad that were only five and fourteen years old, respectively. (Ken Buttolph photo)

HERSHEY 1986 took on a patriotic theme with the Statue of Liberty and an aerial photo of the event on the cover.

JOE'S TAXI, A 1938 PONTIAC, was one of the first cars to be shown in taxi finish. It was a hit with the crowd. (Ken Buttolph photo)

THE THEME CAR FOR HERSHEY 1991 was a 1957 Chevrolet Bel Air, owned by meet chairperson Peggy Derr, which was illustrated on the cover of the event program.

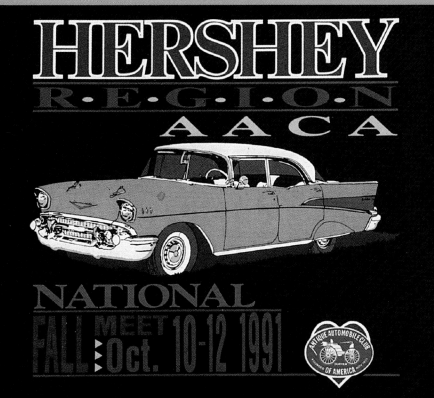

HERSHEY

R·E·G·I·O·N

AACA

NATIONAL

FALL MEET Oct. 10-12 1991

WORLD FAMOUS automotive artist Ken Eberts created a series of four posters to commemorate the American Automotive Industry Centennial in 1996. The series was commissioned for the AACA by Oldsmobile. In this scene, several cars drive by a 1937 Oldsmobile dealership on opening night. (Ken Eberts painting)

IN THE SAME SERIES, Eberts shows a flashy Oldsmobile 98 convertible pulling into a Texaco dealership behind a Kaiser. (Ken Eberts painting)

FIRST IN THE SERIES was this famous scene depicting the Trans-continental curved dash Oldsmobiles. (Ken Eberts painting)

THE FINAL PAINTING in the series was this typical scene on the show field at the AACA's Annual Fall Meet in Hershey, Pennsylvania. Eberts shows a curved dash Olds, two Fords and a new Aurora. (Ken Eberts painting)

IN THIS PAINTING by automotive artist Ken Eberts the popular Fallbrook, California meet is depicted. Typical of many AACA events we find a car show, swap meet and fun for all. That's Ken's wife Liz offering you a poster. (Ken Eberts painting)

IT WAS ALMOST IRONIC for an automobile club to feature whisky ads on the back of its club publication, but Four Roses Distillers featured its "Antique" brand on *The Antique Automobile* for several issues in the 1950s.

Still *The Bulletin of the Antique Automobile Club of America*, the organization's publication continued to become more professional including a second color each issue. (Frank Abramson collection)

The BULLETIN
of the Antique Automobile Club of America

Vol. 5, No. 5   Published Bi-Monthly   December, 1941

Chicago Exhibit Will Be One of Nation's Finest

by J. Russell Heitman

One of America's most interesting and best planned exhibits of antique automobiles will open in Chicago early in 1942.

Pioneer models of automobiles will tell their part in the development of this country in a transportation exhibit now being prepared at the Museum of Science and Industry, at 57th Street and Lake Michigan, in the mid-west metropolis. Incidentally, this fine display of early cars will be within a short distance of the start of the first road race in America —in Jackson Park on Thanksgiving day in 1895, won by a Charles Duryea entry.

This announcement was made several weeks ago by Major Lenox R. Lohr, president of the museum who was operating head of A Century of Progress exposition in Chicago in 1933-34, who has recently become an enthusiastic antique auto collector.

D. Cameron Peck, a member of the Antique Automobile Club of American, an official of the Bowman Dairy Company of Chicago, and an authority on motor transport history in America, has been appointed as associate curator, Transportation Section, of t h e museum, to have complete charge of the museum's growing collection of models.

Mr. Peck has a private collection of upwards of 30 antique models. Major Lohr recently has acquired about ten old-timers, and with the cars owned by the museum itself, and including others in the vicinity of Chicago, more than 80 early vehicles will be available for the museum's exhibit.

From twelve to fifteen cars only will be shown at a time. The old vehicles will be displayed in their "natural setting." They will be shown "parked" along a street of the early 1900's, complete with cobblestones, l a m p posts, gas lights, old-fashioned store fronts, etc. There will be a complete bicycle shop with models of early bikes, and an early motorcycle shop also is planned.

The museum, Major Lohr and Mr. Peck recently acquired the entire collection of Dissman and Sours of Havana, Illinois. This included 20 old cars in running condition, severals others that can be made to run, and three old bikes. This group, which is counted in the eighty mentioned in this

1. International, built in 1905. This two-cylinder model is being cranked by D. Cameron Peck, newly appointed Associate Curator, Transportation Section, Museum of Science and Industry, Chicago. With its air-cooled motor and chain drive, this car had a maximum speed of 20 miles per hour. 2. The 1914 Brewster was considered the most luxurious car of its day—with its four cylinders and leather fenders, this town car was the last word in motoring elegance. 3. Mr. Peck seated behind the tiller bar of a 1914 Stanley Steamer. 4. Haynes—built in 1900. Single tube tires, water-cooled motor. 5. Mildred Anderson, of the Museum Staff, about to step into a 1904 Mercedes seven-passenger touring car. (Another picture on page 3.)

story, include a Sears Roebuck, two M a x w e l l s, a Mier, four Buicks, an Auto Car, a 1900 Locomobile steamer and a 1901 Locomobile steamer, a Gleason, a Rambler, three C a d i l l a c s, a Brush, a Schacht, a Reo, a Metz, a Hupmobile, a McEntyre, a Franklin, a Woods Mobelette, a Corbin electric, and another electric model.

"Because of the important part played by t h i s section of the country in creating a sound automobile at a reasonable price, the featured exhibit will be a significant part of t h e museum's story of industry," Major Lohr says. "We are fortunate in securing a man of Mr. Peck's qualifications and interest to head the new section."

Mr. Peck, who will serve the m u s e u m without remuneration,

has been studying historic cars for many years, and his collection is considered one of the most outstanding in this region.

C o n t r a r y to the traditional practice of museums, the historic automobiles will be displayed in proper setting, so that the public may view these vehicle landmarks against an authentic background. Mr. Peck and a group of histori-

(Continued on page 3)

OFFICIAL PUBLICATION OF THE ANTIQUE AUTOMOBILE CLUB OF AMERICA

VOL. 11 NOS. 3 and 4   PHILADELPHIA, PA.   LAST HALF, 1947

1913 AUSTRO-DAIMLER
Owned By
D. CAMERON PECK

HARRAH'S DISPLAYS at Hershey were always impressive: from the cars shown, the parts offered for sale, the stories of Bill Harrah making purchases in the swap meet, to the beautiful customized trucks in which the road show was brought to Hershey.
(Ken Buttolph photo)

D. CAMERON PECK made the cover of *The Antique Automobile* late in 1947 with his 1913 Astro-Daimler. The cover was printed in only two colors, red and green for Christmas.
(AACA Library & Research Center)

A DODGE TOURING CAR leads a line of
cars for the 1959 Glidden Tour™.
Note the almost new cars in the
background.
(C. L. "Doc" Pressler photo)

THE COVER of the 1949 Philadelphia
Auto Show program illustrated the
link between automotive history
and the latest offerings from around
the world. The show made a point
of featuring both old and new cars.
(AACA Library & Research Center)

1992 CALENDAR

(Left): This 1992 calendar is typical of the many ancillary products developed and sold annually by The Antique Automobile Club of America. (AACA)

25th ANNIVERSARY

HERSHEY REGION

ANTIQUE AUTOMOBILE CLUB OF AMERICA

1955 - 1980

(Right): The cover of this publication commemorated the Silver Jubilee of the AACA Hershey Region.
(AACA Hershey Region)

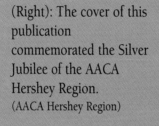

The cover of the 1990 Hershey program illustrated one of the meet's two featured cars — the A.J. Foyt 1962 Indianapolis 500 winning race car.

HERSHEY REGION AACA NATIONAL FALL MEET

Oct. 11, 12, 13, 1990

Cars from the '60s were becoming well accepted at Hershey by 1990. This 1962 "turbocharged" Olds Jetfire was certainly a collectible oddity offered that year. (OCW photo)

The AACA is all about restoring great cars and the people willing to take on the responsibility of that challenge. This fine old Packard certainly lived up to the concept of being a restoration challenge at Hershey '90. (OCW photo)

Sports cars have come to play an increasing role in the car show as they reach collectible status. This Jaguar XKE coupe was at Hershey '91. (OCW photo)

This 1954 Hudson coupe was one of many nice '50s cars shown at Hershey '91. (OCW photo)

Thunderbirds are always in abundance at Hershey. This beautiful '55 was shown at Hershey '91. (OCW photo)

Wood is good and Hershey produces some rare specimens of woodie wagons like this Pontiac that attended in 1991. (OCW photo)

Rain. Mud. Nothing stops Hershey from going on. Hundreds of thousands of participants slog through and enjoy every minute of it just as they did in 1991.

Another wooden car at Hershey '91 was this exceptionally rare Ford Sportsman. (OCW photo)

Number 24, a Ford race car, was part of the show display at Hershey 1991. (OCW photo)

The commercial class at Hershey '92 saw this 1959 Volkswagen Ambulance displayed with all the interior paraphernalia. (OCW photo)

This 1953 Ford wrecker owned by George Kaiser was ready for action at Hershey 1992. (OCW photo)

Bill Smith brought his 1917 Model T Ford roadster pickup to show at Hershey '92. (OCW photo)

The commercial category at Hershey '92 was filled with rare and interesting vehicles like Lester Sheely's 1934 International. (OCW photo)

Hershey 1992 was host to this outstanding 1949 Fraser. (OCW photo)

A truck you don't often see in this condition was Ray Wilson's 1960 Ford F-150 at Hershey '92. (OCW photo)

As always, the racers, like this 1924 Dodge, where back at Hershey '92. (OCW photo)

Frank Malatesta brought his 1929 chain-drive Mack to Hershey in 1992. (OCW photo)

Cars don't have to be big to be eligible at Hershey as Donald Mizner's 1941 Crosley Covered Wagon proved in 1992. (OCW photo)

Noel Thompson brought his beautiful 1920 Ruxton to Hershey in 1992 as a treat for devotees of this rare brand. (OCW photo)

One of the more outstanding early cars in the show at Hershey 1992 was Ernest Bonati's 1915 Brewster. (OCW photo)

J. Scott Isquick brought his diminutive English 1914 Stellite roadster to Hershey 1992. (OCW photo)

When was the last time you saw a Stanley Steamer delivery van? Hershey 1993 was blessed with one. (OCW photo)

Over in the swap meet at Hershey '93 you could have bought this rare Studebaker built 1958 Packard two-door hardtop. (OCW photo)

The mud at Hershey can be tough, and every Hershey veteran comes prepared. This club member did so big time—no amount of mud was going to stop this fellow from his rounds in the swap meet! (OCW photo)

How about a 1954 Mercury station wagon to haul those Hershey purchases home? (1993) (OCW photo)

This beautiful formal Cadillac was headed for the show field at Hershey '93. (OCW photo)

Hershey '93 saw its share of great race cars doing their obligatory lap around the inside of the stadium. (OCW photo)

All race cars at Hershey don't have to come from circle tracks. A Model A roadster-bodied drag car made an appearance in 1993. (OCW photo)

An early Ford stock car gets some exercise in the Hershey stadium during the 1993 Fall Meet. (OCW photo)

This speedster made quite an impression at Hershey '94. (OCW photo)

There were several nice Graham Hollywoods at the Fall Meet in Hershey in 1994. (OCW photo)

Rare parts are one of the biggest reasons people from around the world flock to Hershey, and 1994 was no exception. One could have purchased this unusual accessory steering wheel. (OCW photo)

A rare accessory offered for sale at Hershey '94—a beautiful rare pair of Woodlites. (OCW photo).

"Taxi! Taxi! Take me to Hershey, Pennsylvania...it's time for the 1994 Fall Meet." Actually this Checker was in the Car Corral for sale, not for hire. (OCW photo)

It doesn't seem possible that Mustangs became eligible to enter the car show at Hershey in 1990 as the twenty-five year rule kicked in for the popular Ford. This 2+2 fastback was caught by the camera in 1994. (OCW photo)

This tiny Crosley Farm-O-Road was spotted in the truck section of the car show in 1994. (OCW photo)

The Corvair has become a popular, if not a highly valuable car in collector circles. This "first year" 1960 coupe was at Hershey in 1994.

You could have bought an early Packard truck to restore at the 1994 Hershey Fall Meet. (OCW photo)

Erv Silverstien's Phantom, a White moving van, was the perfect Hershey vendor truck to sell his extensive line of antique automotive toys in 1994. (OCW photo)

A Willys station wagon was one of the many offerings at the swap meet in 1994. (OCW photo)

Motorhomes are an ever-present sight at Hershey. In 1994, you might have noticed this highly unusual English Bedford with a pop-up top. (OCW photo)

This Oldsmobile Doctors Coupe was a crowd pleaser at Hershey '95. (OCW photo)

From the front this coupe really emphasized the car's narrowness and height, giving the look of a rolling phone booth. (OCW photo)

This 1936 Graham at the 1995 Hershey Fall Meet car show featured unique headlamps that blended into the car's hood. (OCW photo)

Many collectors are not aware that Mack made a few smaller trucks in its history. This great '40s era Mack was in attendance at Hershey in 1995. (OCW photo)

Up close and personal with a Stanley Steamer at the 1995 Hershey Fall Meet car show. (OCW photo)

J. Scott Isquick dazzled the crowd with the bodywork of his Dale Adams-restored Mercedes LaBrodette Skiff. (OCW photo)

Three wheels and two seats came in the form of this basic transportation vehicle at Hershey '95. (OCW photo)

If you were ambitious—and had the cash—you could have bought this restoration project at the swap meet at Hershey '95. (OCW photo)

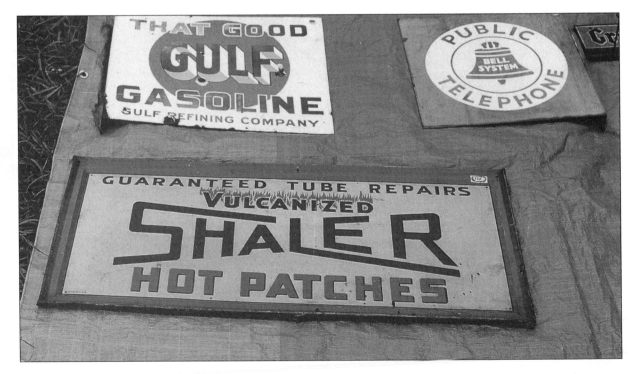

Sign collecting has been a big part of the hobby for many years. These petroliana signs could have been bought during the swap meet at Hershey '95. (OCW photo)

This clean Chevelle was priced at $21,000 at the 1995 Hershey Fall Meet Car Corral. (Victor Losquadro photo)

Not all of the cars at Hershey are for sale. You could have owned this 1965 Mustang being raffled by the AACA Library and Research Center. (Victor Losquadro photo)

A load of Model As and a Jeepster prepare to unload for the Car Corral sale area at Fall Hershey '95. (Victor Losquadro photo)

A 1913 Ford Model T with gleaming white tires and polished brass awaits scrutiny at the 1996 Hershey show. (Victor Losquadro photo)

A LaSalle in the early morning haze prepares for a day on the judging field at the 1996 Fall Meet in Hershey. (Victor Losqaudro photo)

More Hershey National Fall Meet

Hershey's Chocolate World visitor center claims the highest annual attendance and sales figures during the AACA event. Chocolate World features a free ride illustrating the history of the famous chocolate maker, ending in the firm's gift shop, which is barely escapable without a confectionery purchase.

No trip to Hershey was complete without a visit to Gene Zimmerman's Automobilorama, located just a few miles from the car show fields at the Pennsylvania Turnpike exit 17. Mr. and Mrs. Zimmerman are shown in front of the museum in a 1909 Zimmerman. (Zimmerman photo)

Independent promoters have held literature and memorabilia auctions around Hershey weekend. Other events such as the Dutch Wonderland Auction in nearby Strasburg and the dominantly postwar car oriented Carlisle Collector Car Flea Market all take place surrounding Hershey's fall meet in Pennsylvania. In 1993, an exposition of high dollar cars was introduced to the Hershey Lodge & Convention Center by World Classic Auction and Exposition Company from Danville, California. Other auction companies had tried to integrate car auctions at the Eastern Fall Meet only to run into strict opposition by AACA.

Today, Hershey is the place for AACA members from the world over to convene, buy, sell, trade parts, vie for top club awards, and share camaraderie. A tribute to the AACA's flexibility, judging classes expand and the membership comes up with enough judges each year to do an admirable job of reviewing the thousands of cars. The flea market continues to change. Taxation, competition, and even age have taken their toll on some old-time vendors. Ever changing interests push the event to cater to younger and younger members with parts for Mustangs instead of Model Ts. Older members retain flea market spaces to sell a few token items. So, it may be said by some that the event does not have the excitement to the true antique hobbyist it once did. But the reality is, "If you can't find it at Hershey, you can't find it."

On the inside of the Zimmerman Automobilorama cars ranged from the 1909 Hudson on the left to the 1957 Cadillac Eldorado Brougham on the right. Many Hershey participants stayed in the adjoining hotel. (Zimmerman photo)

Hershey is always covered by a host of publications, and never so ably than this special edition of Mobilia *in 1996.*

Northern Hospitality and Southern Humor

The 1983 Annual Meeting was held at the Sheraton in downtown Philadelphia. Shortly after the first AACA members arrived at the hotel, it started to snow. The snowstorm blossomed into a blizzard with 23 inches of the white stuff falling in 24 hours. At one of the meetings the following morning, Bert Harrington from Atlanta, Georgia, announced. "I've heard of Northern Hospitality, but this is ridiculous. I woke up this morning, looked out the window and the whole world was covered with grits!"

Annual Meeting Gets A New Home The Hard Way

1986 was really exciting for Seth Pancoast, Jr., chair of the Annual Meeting Committee and his fellow committee members. The 1985 meeting, held at the Bellevue Stratford Hotel in Philadelphia, Pennsylvania, had been the inaugural event for the club's Golden Jubilee year. Plans for the final event of this special year had gone well. Reservations had been made at the same hotel. Banquets were planned, menus selected, and seminars finalized. It was going to be a grand Golden Jubilee Annual Meeting on the weekend of February 7-8, 1986.

Pancoast, Jr. had everything under control; as he sat down to watch television news on the evening of February 1, 1986, he was shocked and, by his own admission, angered to hear that the Bellevue Stratford management had announced on that day that the hotel had closed its doors for business. There had been no warning of this action, in spite of the fact that the AACA Annual Meeting was scheduled for that same week.

Pancoast, Jr. went into action the next morning. He went to the staff of the Wyndham-Franklin Plaza and found out that they would be able to handle the AACA's needs. He went to the staff of the Bellevue Stratford to determine what could be done to salvage the potential disaster. Fortunately, they were sympathetic to the problems caused by the closure and worked closely with the other hotel. Individual reservations were transferred. Adjustments were made to the banquets and seminar plans. The staffs of both hotels did a remarkable job.

There remained one major problem -- notifying AACA Headquarters and all of the members who were already registered and expected to be staying at the Bellevue Stratford. Pancoast, Jr. had not immediately called Bill Bomgardner, AACA executive director, when the news broke since he felt he needed to handle the immediate problem with the hotels without supervision. When he called Bomgardner things looked pretty good in Philadelphia. An informal phone "network" was implemented at the headquarters to warn the members about the change. This worked remarkably well and only a few people had to get the news when they showed up at the Bellevue Stratford.

The 1986 Golden Jubilee Annual Meeting was, indeed, a grand event. Thanks to Seth Pancoast and his committee, the schedule was flawless and the attending AACA members were hardly aware that there had been a problem. The Wyndham-Franklin Plaza has been the "home" of the AACA Annual Meeting since that date.

More Meets, Swaps And Shows

Winter National Meet of 1989

The 1989 Winter National Meet was in Clearwater, Florida. It was the first time the Florida West Coast Region had hosted a national event. Normally, in the past, AACA regions did not do a lot of promoting of national meets. However, this region advertised in *Hemmings Motor News, Olds Cars Weekly* and other commercial hobby periodicals. The one thing that truly brought in a lot of visitors was a huge billboard the group made and placed near a heavily traveled highway by the local airport.

The result was a packed event with nearly 400 flea market spaces and well more than 400 cars in the show. The event was packed with people wanting to see the beautiful vehicles. There was gridlock from the traffic created. The event truly got the attention of local people, TV, and newspapers.

National Spring Meet of 1992

The 1992 National Spring Meet in Montgomery, Alabama, featured a new National Meet Seminar Program developed by VP National Activities, Janet Ricketts. It was modeled after the seminars held at the AACA annual meeting in Philadelphia. It was approved by the national board to have these seminars alternating between Southeastern, Central, and Western divisions. The first seminars included information on restoration, national events, newsletters, regions and more. More than 600 members attended the talks.

National Meets of 1997

The 1997 National Meets included: Venice, Florida; Greenville, South Carolina; Morgan Hill, California; Winnipeg, Canada (the organization's second International Meet); Gaithersburg, Maryland; Louisville, Kentucky; Cedar Falls, Iowa; and finally the National Fall Meet that is traditionally in Hershey, Pennsylvania.

The 1997 Annual Grand National Meet

A devastating flood struck Grand Forks, North Dakota, in 1997 and, reluctantly, this forced the region to cancel its planned Grand National Meet. The small but determined Cedar Valley Region graciously offered to incorporate the AGMN with its planned fall meet. Both events were rescheduled to the same weekend and were enjoyed by more than 300 entries.

"Fast Blast" was just one of many commercial exhibitors in the AACA Trade Show at the club's Annual Meeting in Philadelphia. (AACA photo)

Touring on the Road with AACA

The Brooks-Cadwell Tour

On November, 17, 1940, the club celebrated its fifth birthday with "The Brooks-Cadwell Tour." This event consisted of a tour, starting from the Bryn Mawr War Memorial, traveling 50 miles and returning back to the starting point. Eight cars entered the event. A dinner at the Dutch Cupboard near Downingtown followed, with 43 members in attendance.

The Revival Glidden Tours™ sparked a new interest in nationally sponsored touring for the members of the AACA and VMCCA. Years passed and the AACA started adding new classes for later model cars as approved for participation in meets. In 1960, it was dictated that the cut-off year for AACA-sponsored Glidden Tours™ be 1936 (and preceding years), which was apparently an arbitrary date that interestingly coincided with the AACA founding date.

It was clearly recognized that designing a tour route which was interesting and challenging for the tourists was becoming more difficult. The ages of the participating vehicles ranged from the early brass era cars to the cars of the 1930s.

With the 25-year cut-off date of AACA, general acceptance and the 1935 AACA cutoff for Glidden Tours™, many members were denied access to the national touring experience. In addition, there was a growing awareness that younger members, meaning younger cars, were not able to participate in the existing tours. This proved to be a critical link in building the organization and the club's future growth.

In the mid-1980s, a committee was appointed to review the touring program. A recommendation from the committee was to add a tour for vehicles that were not otherwise "qualified" for the Glidden and Reliability Tours. As initially defined, the tour would be designated for any type of vintage vehicles determined by the host club. These would be cars not normally expected to run in the Glidden Tour™. It could be a tour limited to motorcycles or powered bicycles. It could be steam cars or electric cars. Most importantly, however, the events would be for post-1935 vehicles excluded from the Glidden Tour™.

Essentially, the AACA Board, in approving the tour, was reaching out to all members to offer touring opportunities at the national level. It intended to make touring available to all members with some specific aim to introduce younger members to touring. All that was left was to name this new tour.

Glidden Tour™ was trademarked and the eligibility requirements were well established between the AACA and VMCCA, even though they use different cut-off dates. The Reliability tour was established in 1970 for pre-1916 cars. The broad range of cars that might be accepted dictated that the name for the new tour be pretty generic. The Touring Committee recommended the title of "Founders Tour" to honor the club's founding members. The Founders Tour was approved and established in 1986.

The North Alabama Region wanted to do something different at a national level after hosting the Southeastern Division Golden Jubilee National Meet in 1985. On hearing about a new type of tour to be called the Founders Tour, the group immediately requested authorization to host a tour in 1988 for all cars after 1935, up to a cut-off date of 1963. That was the first Founders Tour approved by the AACA Board. It became known as the Premiere Founders Tour.

Several members of the region who had been on other tours before were aware of some of the basic requirements that had to be accomplished. Specific guidelines for this new tour were limited with the intention of making it a truly unique activity for AACA members. The original guidelines were so limited that the Tour Committee had fairly broad latitude to try some things differently. Tour Director Ron Barnett and Tour Chair Bob Thurstone used this to their advantage when setting up the basic organization and plans.

For example, hitting the road with cars with good headlamps, brakes (and, hopefully, reliability) a night tour, though short, was planned. Seventy to 100 miles is considered about the maximum for one day of touring in early cars. The Founders Tour opened the door to traversing greater distances in one day. The Alabama group had a wonderful opportunity to show off more of its state and central Tennessee.

This twist also created a new problem—stretching the capability of the relatively small North Alabama Region beyond reason for the group's size. The solution turned out to be somewhat less than a stroke of genius, but still quite clever. Why not include several other regions in the fun? Other regions in the anticipated tour area were contacted and offered one of the tour dates. They would plan the tour and provide the required support for the day. Wanting to give recognition to the groups' efforts, something was in order. Because there is usually only one tour plaque, the solution was to have a different tour plaque for each day of the tour for the host region, then give one master cloisonné plaque for the whole event—sort of a tour host club *de jour* concept. This was to be, after all, the Premiere Founders Tour, and it was felt that something special was indeed warranted.

As it turned out, most of the ideas were, in fact, sound, and the other regions readily agreed to help; some of the tour routes turned out to be too long—in some cases, more than 200 miles. Subsequent tour committees were apprised of the situation and the Founders Tour remains relatively unstructured with more flexibility for planning.

There was no guidance relative to a daily touring newsletter similar to the *Glidden Gazette*. It was not intended that the Founders Tour replicate the other tours. Most of the committee had enough experience to know that daily reminders and good computers, printers, and a committee with a fair amount of newsletter experience dictated that a daily newsletter would be appropriate. The *Founders Flyer* was born and has become a part of Founders Tour tradition.

The night tour also turned out to be a great idea. Huntsville, Alabama, may not have the "skyline" of New York, but there is one magnificent night view from the top of Monte Sano. Two things the committee forgot to consider were that some of the cars still had light bulbs instead of sealed-beam headlamps and a lot of seasoned tourists are day-people. The tour up Monte Sano was enjoyable but not without significant complaints and the idea of night tours was dropped on subsequent events.

One navigator turned out to have an even bigger problem with the "night tour." It was scheduled for Tuesday and as the car departed the hotel parking lot, he turned to the Wednesday section of directions. Several miles out, and into the night, the driver looked at the tour book. Discovering the problem, he returned to the hotel. The navigator was awarded the Most Lost Navigator Award for the tour.

Awards were another overlooked guideline for that Premiere Founders Tour. The touring committee took advantage of its oversight and decided to make them simple, inexpensive, and people-oriented rather than focused on the car. There were awards created for: Family Participation, Longest Distance Driven, Most Lost Navigator, and other awards dictated by the spirit of the event and the informal fun.

The worst disaster for a Founders Tour came during the now infamous "Ice Cream Social." On a hot Alabama summer day nothing would have been better than to have enjoyed a round of ice cream for the tourists. Unfortunately, there was a communication problem. The plan was to have ice cream and plenty of it. When the order was placed with the caterer, it was for a "desert social," which meant there would be an ice cream social. Unfortunately, the caterer was a "Yankee" transplant from an area of the country where "desert social" means cakes, cookies, and other delicious goodies, but no ice cream. The shock of no ice cream at the Ice

Cream Social turned out to be a rallying cry for Founders Tours ever since, and no touring committee has let it happen since. No self-respecting AACA tour is complete without ice cream at some point en route.

Pete and Jeanette Dobbs drove on this tour in their 1937 Packard limousine. Jeanette had been in frail health and could only walk short distances. She tried to convince Pete that the trip would be a disaster. "No one to talk to her, the Packard would break down, etc., etc." Pete pressed the issue and they not only went on the first Founders Tour (the first either had attended), but the People's Choice Award went to the Packard at the award dinner. Jeanette proclaimed she had a wonderful time, the Packard ran fine, and all the tourists were so friendly and she only hoped there would be ice cream the next time. The couple continued to attend Founders Tours in years to come.

One of the fundamental goals of the Founders Tour was to attract younger members whose primary interests (and financial resources) are geared toward newer vehicles. Not many of the younger members can afford the brass era cars or even most of the Glidden Tour™ automobiles. This was a concept that somewhat backfired on AACA planners.

Older tourists like the creature comforts of not having to crank the cars and having air conditioning for summer trips in their vehicles. However, they still wanted to participate in AACA touring. The average age of the Founders Tourist is actually older than the Glidden Tour™ or Reliability Tour. This may tell us that all the right things were done for the wrong reasons.

The Founders Tours have become one of the most popular activities in AACA. The tours have become a mainstay of the club and the hobby.

Glidden Tours™

The original Glidden Tour™ was started by wealthy industrialist Charles J. Glidden. He wanted to prove his automobile to be dependable. He organized the Glidden Tour™ in 1905 to prove his point, traveling 870 miles from New York to Mt. Washington and back. The tours were stopped after 1913 due to becoming overly commercial in nature.

The revivals of the famous Glidden Tours™ were started in 1946 with the help of James Melton as a prime influence. The first two years were run by the Veteran Motor Car Club of America. The efforts of the Firestone Tire and Rubber Company made it possible for cars to participate in the Revival Glidden Tour™ and the Golden Jubilee, thanks to the retooling for the rare and discontinued size tires that antique car enthusiasts could not buy since before World War II. VMCCA issued invitation to participate in the first Glidden Tours™ to both the AACA and HCCA.

Early AACA member Sid Strong remembered participating in the first Glidden Tour™ with his family including his son Dave Strong (a current well-known AACA enthusiast) in their 1909 Model T Ford. They drove the car from Albany, New York, to Columbine, Ohio, August 18-24, 1946.

According to Strong, the first event was hosted by Henry Ford, General Motors, and Firestone Tire and Rubber Company. He came home so enthusiastic about the cars he had encountered on the tour he bought ten more for his collection upon returning home. Sid gave a showing of his 1946 Glidden Tour™ movies at the 1947 AACA annual meeting in Philadelphia.

Strong also participated in the 1947 Glidden Tour™ with the same Model T. The tour, held in September, left Hartford, Connecticut, and ended a week later in Newport, Rhode Island. The Strongs drove the Model T from Minnesota to the tour and back, obviously earning the "Long Distance" award.

The AACA was asked to take over the tour in 1948 and 1949 because the event was a major effort to produce. From 1950 on, the two clubs have done a marvelous job of sharing the task, alternating years in producing the event. The rules vary a bit between years based on the club in charge. Glidden Tours™ are very special events in which to participate.

As legal counsel to the AACA, former president Hyde Ballard decided the AACA should take legal action with the VMCCA to secure the rights on the name "Glidden Tour." He took his case to the board of directors who promptly dismissed the idea. Ballard proceeded with the action, causing embarrassment among board

Participants from the 1957 Glidden Tour™ assemble for a photo opportunity at "Transportation, Yesterday, Today and Tomorrow" display. (Les Henry archives photo)

Col. Augustus Post, founder of the AAA and honorary AACA member, is shown inspecting the Glidden Trophy. Post ran in every one of the original Glidden Tours™ and all revival tours until his death in 1952. (Les Henry archives photo)

members and President Franklin Tucker. Henry Austin Clark stepped in and helped smooth ruffled feathers at the VMCCA, and the two clubs have gone on to a congenial sharing of the event ever since. The two groups still alternate years running the event. It was not too long after that Mr. Ballard was replaced as legal counsel.

It was determined the AACA would sponsor the Glidden Tours™ on odd-numbered years with a vehicle cut-off date of pre-1936. VMCCA tours on even-numbered years permitted cars to 1942 to participate. Today, the Glidden Tour™ is respected in both clubs as "the" paramount tour of the year for cars of these vintages. Follow our extensive photo collection and see how this tour has changed very little in its duration.

AACA honorary member and world-famous artist Peter Helck and his son in his "Old 16" Locomobile during the 1957 Glidden Tour™. (Les Henry archives photo)

The Gilberts slow for a photo opportunity in Lake Placid, New York, in their curved dash Oldsmobile. Note the car's interesting curved wicker basket. (Helen Mattson photo by E. Treloar; Art Bragg Collection)

A 1946 Glidden Tour™ participant is flanked on a city street by then contemporary greats, a '41 Cadillac Sixty Special and a '46 Chrysler Town & Country. (Helen Mattson photo by Oscar G. Owen; Art Bragg Collection)

Cars head out over city streets, dodging street cars in the '46 Glidden Tour™. (Helen Mattson photo by Oscar G. Owen; Art Bragg Collection)

A touring car stops for a quick bit of shopping at the "Stage Coach Stop" Antique Store on the 1946 Glidden Tour™. (Helen Mattson photo by Oscar G. Owen; Art Bragg Collection)

A touring car stops for a quick bit of shopping at the "Stage Coach Stop" Antique Store on the 1946 Glidden Tour™. (Helen Mattson photo by Oscar G. Owen; Art Bragg Collection)

Jerry Duryea, AACA President, starts back down from Mt. Washington on the 1948 Glidden Tour™ in his Pierce-Arrow. (Helen Mattson photo; Art Bragg collection)

Sidney Strong, from Atwater, Minnesota, prepares to head out on the 1948 Glidden Tour™ in his 1909 Model T Ford. (Helen Mattson photo; Art Bragg collection)

Museum founder and AACA past-president W.F. Swigart from Huntington, Pennsylvania, in a 1909 Model T Ford at the 1948 Glidden Tour™. (Helen Mattson photo; Art Bragg collection)

A part of the 600 cars assembled in Hershey stadium for the 1957 Glidden Tour™. (Don McCray photo)

1948 Glidden Tour™ cars stop for a rest at the Bedford Springs Hotel. The "new" Buick would make a great tour car today! (Les Henry archives photo)

Early collector Barney J. Pollard was a participant in the 1948 Glidden Tour™ with his 1909 Austin. (Helen Mattson photo; Art Bragg collection)

A young-looking Henry Austin Clark, then of Flushing, New York, hits the road in his 1907 Locomobile for the '48 Glidden Tour™. (Helen Mattson photo; Art Bragg collection)

World-famous automotive artist Peter Helck from Boston Corners, New York, is shown at the wheel of his equally famous "Old 16" 1906 Locomobile racer at the 1948 Glidden Tour™.

Bill Spear rounds the corner in downtown Bedford Springs during the 1948 Glidden Tour™. (Les Henry archives photo)

Two cars staged for a photo during the 1948 Glidden Tour™. Coming... a 1909 Pierce-Arrow "Toy Tonneau" with owner/driver Mrs. Samuel E. Baily of Bala-Cynwyd, Pennsylvania. And going...a 1910 Cadillac "Miniature Tonneau" with owner/ driver Dr. Jay Rice Moody of Newport, Rhode Island. (Les Henry archives photo)

Louis and Joseph B. Van Sciver Jr. in their 1909 Winton in front of the Bedford Springs Hotel during the 1948 Glidden Tour™. (Les Henry archives photo)

Earl Eckel, an AACA founding member, in his 1914 Stanley Steamer during the 1948 Glidden Tour™. (Les Henry archives photo)

AACA Honorary Member Mr. Cadwalder Kelsey, owner/driver and builder of his 1910 Kelsey Motorette, in the 1948 Glidden Tour™. Kelsey continued to build roto-tillers in his Troy, New York, factory through 1957. On Sept. 7, 1957, he donated the car to the Henry Ford Museum. (Les Henry archives photo)

Sam and Maybelle Bailey arrive at the Bedford Inn during the 1948 Glidden Tour™ in their 1909 Pierce-Arrow. Sam is given credit for coining the phrase "Ground-Up Restoration" in early AACA judging. (Les Henry archive photo)

A Hudson touring, owned by the Lavasseurs, on Highway 2 near Cardinal, Ontario, during the 1950 Glidden Tour™. (Helen Mattson photo by E. Treloar; Art Bragg collection)

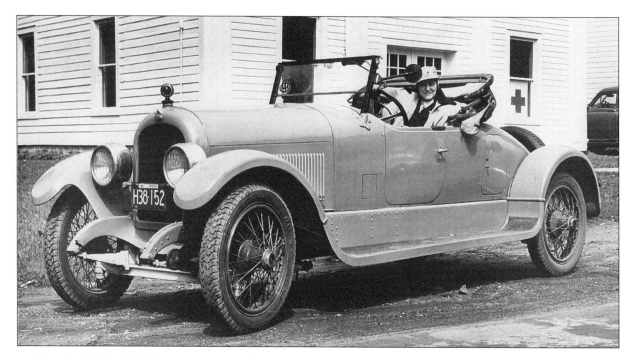

Helen Mattson in her sporty Marmon roadster on the 1950 Glidden Tour™ in front of the Red Creek Fire Department. (Helen Mattson photo by E. Treloar; Art Bragg collection)

The Miller's White on Highway 2 near Iroquois, Ontario, during the 1950 Glidden Tour™. (Helen Mattson photo by E. Treloar; Art Bragg Collection)

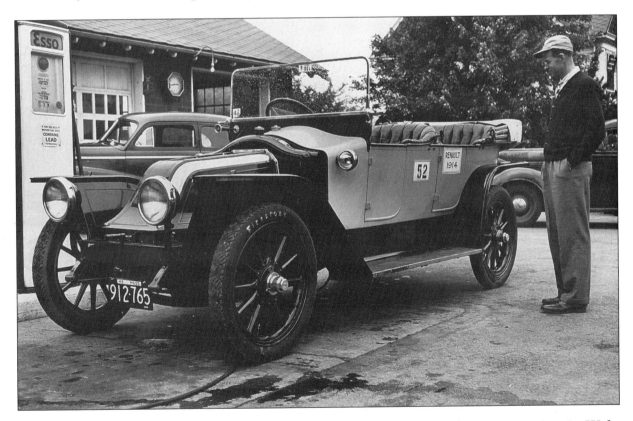

A 1914 Renault fuels up during the 1950 Glidden Tour™ at the Esso station in Webster, New York. (Helen Mattson photo by E. Treloar; Art Bragg Collection)

335

The head table at the 1951 Glidden Tour™ (from left to right): Jerry Duryea, Les Henry (co-chairman), George Hughes (co-chairman), Bob Laurens, Bill Swigart, and Bud Catlette. Paul Cadwell is in the foreground. (Don McCray photo; Les Henry archives)

Another AACA founding member, Walter Matter, driving his 1910 Ford Torpedo Roadster in the 1948 Glidden Tour™. (Les Henry archives photo)

1906 Sears on 1953 Glidden Tour™ sponsored by AACA.

The 1959 Glidden Tour™ in Indianapolis, Indiana, gave tourists a chance to get their cars out on the famous Indianapolis Motor Speedway. (C.L. "Doc" Pressler photo)

The Glidden Tour™ cars as they wind their way through the city of Indianapolis in 1959. (C.L. "Doc" Pressler photo)

For the 1959 Glidden Tour™, General Motors rolled out one of the turbine-powered Firebird experimental cars for participants to see in operation. (C.L. "Doc" Pressler photo)

At the 1959 Glidden Tour™, this open Stanley Steamer allowed its occupants to enjoy a warm, sunny day. (C.L. "Doc" Pressler photo)

A little rain can't dampen the spirit of these 1959 Glidden Tourists from having fun while filling up their Model T roadster. (C.L. "Doc" Pressler photo)

The lineup of participants in the 1960 Glidden Tour™ made for a pretty impressive lot of cars. (C.L. "Doc" Pressler photo)

A touring car makes a rural road-side stop during the 1960 Glidden Tour™. (C.L. "Doc" Pressler photo)

A happy couple poses with their touring car, ready to continue on the 1960 Glidden Tour™. (C.L. "Doc" Pressler photo)

Glidden Tour™ cars pull in for a night at the Holiday Inn Motel during their 1960 expedition. (C.L. "Doc" Pressler photo)

A group of cars about to head out on the 1962 Glidden Tour™. (C.L. "Doc" Pressler photo)

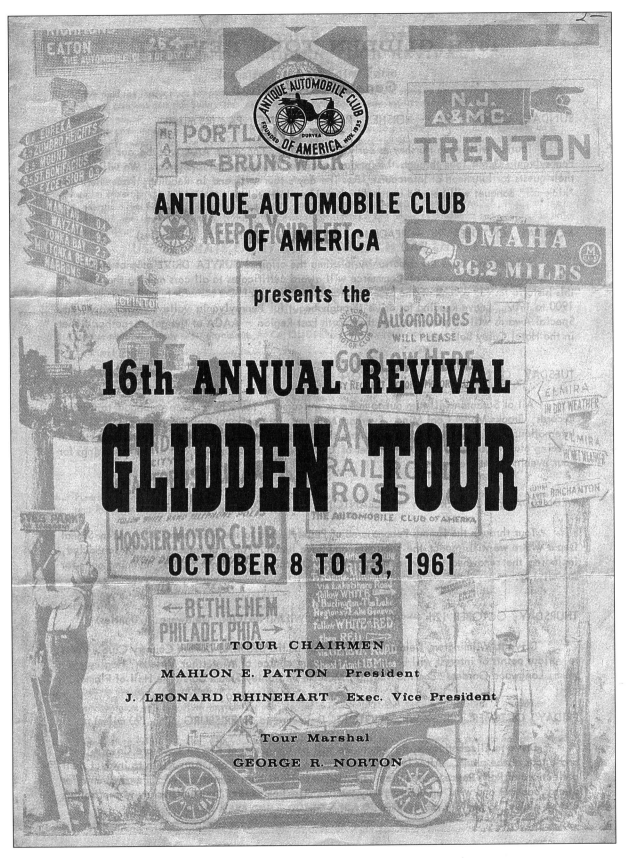

Cover of 1961 Glidden Tour™ program.

An "almost" new '61 Ford station wagon unloads near the staging area for the 1962 Glidden Tour™. (C.L. "Doc" Pressler photo)

Another group of happy Glidden Tourists from 1962 pose in front of their cars during their travels. (C.L. "Doc" Pressler photo)

There is always time for a little fun on a Glidden Tour™ (1962). (C.L. "Doc" Pressler photo)

Lined up and ready to roll during the 1962 Glidden Tour™. (C.L. "Doc" Pressler photo)

Part of the Glidden Tour™ line-up for 1963 was just as impressive as ever. (C.L. "Doc" Pressler photo)

Early morning at the motel during the 1963 Glidden Tour™—getting the cars uncovered and ready to roll. (C.L. "Doc" Pressler photo)

A few cars from the 1963 Glidden Tour™. (C.L. "Doc" Pressler photo)

1963 saw the Glidden Tour™ head for Niagara Falls, a popular tourist attraction. (C.L. "Doc" Pressler photo)

The selection of cars on the 1963 Glidden Tour™ included many interesting marques. (C.L. "Doc" Pressler photo)

Heading for the open road during the 1968 Glidden Tour™. (C.L. "Doc" Pressler photo)

A high-altitude assemblage of Glidden Tour™ cars in 1968. (C.L. "Doc" Pressler photo)

Cars assemble after the trip to the top of the mountain on the 1968 Glidden Tour™. (C.L. "Doc" Pressler photo)

A view of the climb from inside a tour car on the 1976 Glidden Tour™. Tour roads are rarely freeways. (C.L. "Doc" Pressler photo)

A Cadillac convertible leads the way from mountain tops to desert. (C.L. "Doc" Pressler photo)

Some of the 1976 Glidden Tour™ group hang out near the fence made famous by Tom Sawyer. (C.L. "Doc" Pressler photo).

There is always good spirited camaradarie on the Glidden Tour™, and 1976's version was no exception. (C.L. "Doc" Pressler photo)

Tours take hobbyists to many exotic and interesting places. The 1978 Glidden Tour™ featured this remote wooden bridge in the Poconos. (C.L. "Doc" Pressler photo)

Canton, Ohio's "Doc" Pressler prepares to head out for a day of touring on the 1978 Glidden Tour™. (C.L. "Doc" Pressler photo)

Breakdowns occur on any tour and with any old car. On the 1978 Glidden Tour™ plenty of AACA friends came to the aid of this disabled Packard. (C.L. "Doc" Pressler photo)

A line of cars pauses near Calloway Gardens on the 1977 Glidden Tour™. (C.L. "Doc" Pressler photo)

The panoramic view from the top of Mt. Washington was breathtaking for 1980 Glidden Tour™ participants. (C.L. "Doc" Pressler photo)

Participants on every tour come home with many interesting historical facts. Here, participants learned of "the highest wind ever observed by man was recorded here (Mt. Washington)...231 m.p.h." (C.L. "Doc" Pressler photo)

Cars line up as they reach the peak of Mt. Washington in 1980. (C.L. "Doc" Pressler photo)

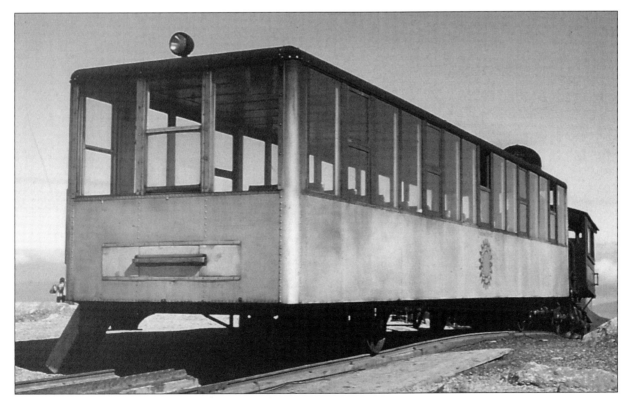

The rail car was but one of the many sights enjoyed by Glidden Tourists in 1980. (C.L. "Doc" Pressler photo)

This trolley display was one of the more interesting things enjoyed on the 1980 Glidden Tour™. (C.L. "Doc" Pressler photo)

A Rolls-Royce and a number of other cars line up for a day on the 1983 Glidden Tour™. (C.L. "Doc" Pressler photo)

The parking lot for the 1986 Glidden Tour™ as many tourists get ready for another day of excursions. (C.L. "Doc" Pressler photo)

Not every car on a Glidden Tour™ has to be fully restored cosmetically. This example from the 1983 tour is proof that a car only needs to be dependable. (C.L. "Doc" Pressler photo)

A beautiful Chrysler Imperial phaeton was but one of many nice cars on the 1983 Glidden Tour™. (C.L. "Doc" Pressler photo)

This beautiful lawn and estate was a wonderful parking area for this red Hudson and other cars from the 1983 Glidden Tour™. (C.L. "Doc" Pressler photo)

Barlow Motor Sales' bright orange Packard tow truck wasn't on call, it was on the tour in 1985. (C.L. "Doc" Pressler photo)

A Terraplane, a Packard, and a Chevrolet were part of the 1987 Glidden Tour™. (C.L. "Doc" Pressler photo)

A tour does not run on gasoline alone. This beautiful snack table is proof that tourists do not go without "fuel" too. (C.L. "Doc" Pressler photo)

This beautiful covered bridge greeted participants on the 1987 Glidden Tour™. (C.L. "Doc" Pressler photo)

Heading into Dixon on the 1989 Glidden Tour™. (C.L. "Doc" Pressler photo)

Antique cars and the cooling towers of the nearby nuclear power plant add stark contrast on the 1989 Glidden Tour™. (C.L. "Doc" Pressler photo)

These trolley cars were an added attraction on the 1989 Glidden Tour™ in western Pennsylvania. (C.L. "Doc" Pressler photo)

The Duquane Incline is one of Pittsburgh's most historic tourist attractions. The 1991 Glidden Tourists got a firsthand look at the famous tram. (C.L. "Doc" Pressler photo)

Tour cars and the owners traversed plenty of beautiful Pennsylvania scenery on the 1991 Glidden Tour™. (C.L. "Doc" Pressler photo)

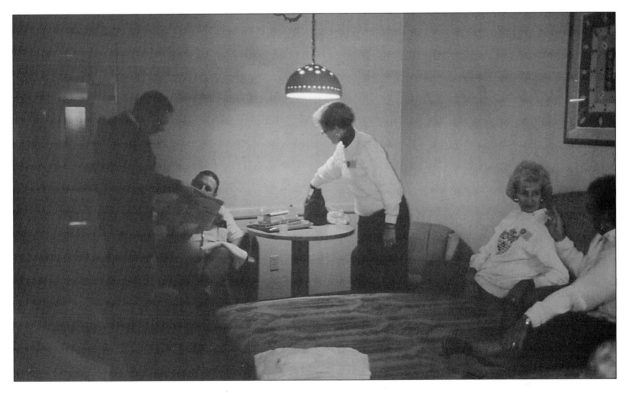

Not all of the fun on a tour is on the road. Camaraderie continues back at the hotel as friends plan the next day's run. Life-long friends can be made on an AACA tour. (C.L. "Doc" Pressler photo)

A lavish floral clock greeted Glidden Tourists on the 1992 tour. (C.L. "Doc" Pressler photo)

Glidden Tourists got a first-hand look at Kentucky horse farms in 1992. (C.L. "Doc" Pressler photo)

March of Dimes Tour

In 1956, Henry Austin Clark chaired a cross-country tour to promote the March of Dimes fight against polio. The tour was jointly sponsored by the Antique Automobile Club of America, Classic Car Club of America, Horseless Carriage Club of America, Veteran Motor Car Club of America and local clubs. Approximately sixty participant cars left Wellesley Hills, Massachusetts, on Friday, January 6, 1956, with a final destination of Los Angeles, California, in February. Unfortunately, this must have been an overly ambitious project and the tour was disbanded in Florida. Each participant received a lovely nickel-silver medallion with the image of the 1895 Duryea. Robert R. Dornsife, of Sunbury, Pennsylvania, made it to Houston in a 1924 Marmon touring with "Austie" Clark in his 1929 Lincoln phaeton.

Wisconsin Centennial Tour

In 1948, the Michigan Region Sponsored the Wisconsin Centennial Tour, August 9–13. The event ran from South Bend, Indiana, to Milwaukee, Wisconsin. Member Sid Strong drove his 1915 Pierce-Arrow in the tour.

1957 Tour to Dunnaway Gardens

In 1957, the Southeastern Region sponsored a tour to Dunnaway Gardens. The event was an excellent example of a regional activity in these early days of our hobby. Cars on the tour ranged from early touring cars to a Lincoln Continental cabriolet barely 10 years old.

The 1957 Tour to Dunnaway Gardens was a great success. The first four cars include (from left to right): Austin Abbot in a 1930 Cord L-29, Bert Harrington in a 1930 Rolls-Royce convertible sedan, Tommy Protsman in a 1930 Rolls-Royce, and Leonard Guttridge in a 1929 Buick sedan. Other early S.E. Region members in the rear include Gene Cofer and Verney Bentley. (Lu Harrington photo)

A lineup of Rolls-Royce are displayed at the Southeastern Fair in 1955. For many years this was an annual event. Some of the cars had an exhibition race on the track. (Lu Harrington photo)

Bert Harrington with his 1930 Rolls-Royce convertible sedan at the Southeastern Fair in 1955. (Lu Harrington photo)

A lineup of Rolls-Royce are displayed at the Southeastern Fair in 1955. For many years this was an annual event. Some of the cars had an exhibition race on the track. (Lu Harrington photo)

1960 AACA Silver Jubilee Tour of Europe

The Silver Jubilee was celebrated with many great events. One of the best was the "Silver Jubilee Tour of Europe." Two-hundred forty-three club members and families visited six countries, nine automobile clubs, and participated in the RAC's London to Brighton Run during their visit. The group left New York's Idlewilde Airport on October 20, 1960, and landed in Brussels, Belgium, with members of the Veteran Car Club de Belgique meeting them at the airport. The trip through France included Paris, Dijon, and the beautiful countryside. Switzerland included Geneva and Lucerne. The group had a fine dinner with the Schweiser Motor Veteranen Club in Alpnachdorf and then it was on to West Germany. Members remarked about the speed of the local traffic during a trip across the Autobahn and then into Holland. Members of the Pionier Automobielen Club hosted the Americans at a banquet in Amsterdam. After crossing the English Channel, the group landed in Hardwick, England. It was on to London for lots of sight-seeing.

The highlight of the trip was seeing the 250 car entries of the London-to-Brighton run. There were two club members, Ray Henry in his 1903 Oldsmobile and Sam Scher in his 1904 Cadillac, the alternate vehicle. Two other American entries were Stewart in a 1902 Rambler runabout and Col. E. Hinman Jr. in a two-seater 1904 Panhard-Levassor.

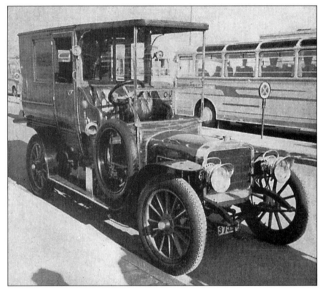

Just one of many beautiful cars from the Veteran Car Club de Belgique that greeted the AACA European tourists in 1960. (The Antique Automobile)

The participants of the 1960 Silver Jubilee European Tour on the lawn of the old League of Nations in Geneva, Switzerland. (The Antique Automobile)

367

Reliability Tour

The Reliability Tour was established in 1970 for owners of pre-1916 cars. This would give them the opportunity to tour at a pace more in tune with the capabilities of brass and earlier cars. It was a welcome addition to the stable of AACA tours and remains popular to this day.

A bevy of brass cars circle for a commemorative photo at the 1974 Reliability Tour.

"Down on the Farm" Tour

The 1994 Down on the Farm Tour was a wonderful collaborative effort between three national clubs: The Antique Automobile Club of America, the Veteran Motor Car Club of America, and the Horseless Carriage Club of America. The event covered a great expanse of Iowa beginning in Iowa Falls on August 10, 1994, to Hampton, Eldora, Ackley, Steamboat Rock, Williams, and wrapping it up back in Iowa Falls on August 13.

The Hardin County, Iowa, event was limited to cars built before 1914. It turned out the newest car was a 1910 model. The group was treated to ice cream socials, craft fairs, a Victorian courthouse, outlet malls, more ice cream, Prairie Bridges Park, a beach party, a historic drug store, a farmers market, a historic theater, and of course, more ice cream.

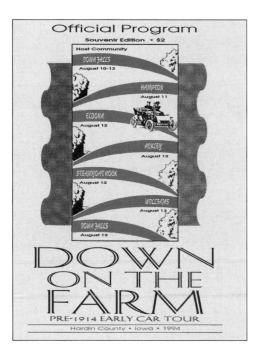

The cover of the 1994 Down on the Farm Tour "official" program traces the events route through Iowa. (Down on the Farm tour files)

Day one of the 1994 Down on the Farm Tour. Brass era cars line up to start. (The Antique Automobile *photo*)

Symbolizing the cooperation of the 1994 Down on the Farm Tour, the three club presidents pose for the camera (from left to right): Richard Neller, VMCCA; Roger May, HCCA; and Roy Graden, AACA. (tour photo)

Clock City Hill Climb, Rome, Georgia

The 1977 Rome, Georgia, meet showed great diversity in the selection of cars displayed on the grassy field. (Warren Steele photo)

AACA'S CELEBRATION OF THE AUTOMOTIVE CENTENNIAL

1996 was a big year as AACA celebrated the 100th Anniversary of the American Automobile Industry. The AACA Centennial Committee kicked off the celebration at the Region Presidents Dinner at the club's Annual Meeting in Philadelphia, Pennsylvania. Beautiful decorations of red, white, blue and gold filled the room. The Duryea family was on hand with their wonderfully restored 1903 Duryea. After Tom Howard, vice-president-regions, opened the meeting, Janet M. Rickets, chair of the Centennial Kick-off Banquet introduced J. Frank Duryea II as the guest speaker.

Sterling Walsh was chair of the Centennial Committee and recognized his committee that had worked hard for almost two years in preparing for the big event. The club celebrated the centennial with special activities, parades, car displays, and commemorative merchandise.

1996 CENTENNIAL MEET

The 1996 Centennial Meet was hosted by the Wolverine State Chapter in Dearborn, Michigan. What better place than the Detroit area where many festivities were already planned for the industry's Centennial. Headquarters Hotel was the Hyatt Regency in Detroit, yet a lot of the activities took place at Greenfield Village in Dearborn from June 17-22, 1996. On the weekend opening the event, two other annual notable events took place: The Greenfield Village Motor Muster and the Eyes on the Classics meet at the Edsel Ford Estate. Bus tours ferried hobbyists to all the great Detroit area automotive attractions and even into Windsor, Ontario, Canada. The next day, bus tours took the group to Richard Kughn's famous Carail Museum filled with great cars and Lionel trains. This was followed by an excursion to the soon-to-close Chrysler museum for the afternoon. Don Johnson, tour chair, and his committee took the group to other tour stops including; the Edsel Ford Estate, Henry Ford's Estate Fairlane, Langiness Antique Auto Sales, Pete's Garage for dinner, Frankenmuth, the GM tech Center, Cadillac Museum, Yankee Air Force Museum, Ford Rouge Plant and on and on. No one went home saying there isn't a lot for car buffs to see in the Detroit area.

Ed Baines received the keys to the city of Dearborn from Mayor Michael A. Guido on Wednesday at The Dearborn Inn evening dinner. At Thursday's sell-out dinner in the Executive Dining Room at Ford World Headquarters, the group listened to famed Ford historian Dr. David L. Lewis speak and deliver a wonderful slide show.

As Friday rolled in the week long rains moved out for the 101 car Centennial Display planned by Tom Howard. The parade included one car from every year including 1896. Every era and type of car from the earliest to a 1995 Buick were on parade. After the parade, the cars were lined up on the Greenfield Village green followed that evening by award ceremonies and a barbecue in a Dearborn public park.

Saturday morning featured a breakfast and vintage fashion show for the ladies while the judges prepared for a 525 car show. 355 judges masterfully did the honors of scrutinizing the cars. 450 attended the evening banquet with James F. Duryea II as guest speaker. Neighboring regions of Saginaw Valley and West Michigan were given credit that evening for aiding in helping to make this Centennial celebration one all would remember.

SPECIAL FALL NATIONAL MEET, 1996

The second special event of the year to celebrate the American Automotive Industry Centennial was the Special Fall National Meet, held September 5-7, 1996. The event was held in Chesapeake, Virginia, and was hosted by the Tidewater Region. Area hurricanes and rain did not dampen this event and, in fact, the weather cooperated with only light rain on Friday.

Thursday evening after registration and shopping, the group went for a ride on a paddle wheel steamboat. Friday morning, Neil Sugermeyer and his crew got swap meet vendors settled in for the weekend and tours began to depart the hotel. A tour of the Norfolk Truck Assembly plant was featured along with a seminar on collectible dolls and vintage fashions. An AACA judging school took place including preparing an Apprentice Team for Saturday's car show. Friday evening hosted a 1950s party complete with ice cream cones and an Elvis impersonator.

Tours of 1997

These tours included: The Founders Tour in Tallahassee; the inaugural Vintage Tour in Johnstown, Pennsylvania; and the Glidden Tour™ in Thomasville, Georgia. Three shorter divisional tours of two to four days were held in Shelter Island, Long Island, New York; Carthage, Missouri; and Cheyenne, Wyoming.

Tours of 1998

The 1998 tours included: Southeastern Division Tour, Arab, Alabama; Eastern Division Tour, Lexington Park, Maryland; Founders Tour, San Francisco, California; Reliability Tour, Dayton, Ohio; and the Central Division Tour, Northeastern, Oklahoma.

TENNESSEE REGION
AACA
HOSTING THE
1998
SOUTHEASTERN DIVISION
NATIONAL FALL MEET
SEPTEMBER 10, 11, 12, 1998
OAK RIDGE, TENNESSEE

Host Hotel   Garden Plaza hotel
215 S. Illinois Ave
Oak Ridge, Tennessee 37830
423-481-2468

DISCOVER
AMERICA'S SECRET CITY . . .
OAK RIDGE, TN

Comfort Inn
433 S. Rutgers Avenue
Oak Ridge, Tennessee 37830
423-481-8200
(One Block from Host)

HERSHEY
AACA Eastern Division National Fall Meet
GREAT IN "98"

HERSHEY REGION AACA
hey, PA • October 7-11, 1998

A - 300 West Cherry Street, Palmyra
im Koons - 1998 Fall Meet Chairman

SNAPPER'S
EST. RIPLEY OHIO 4283
BRASS AND GAS TOURING REGION
Tour Chairman: Fred Collett
● Middletown, Ohio
August 2-7, 1998

Registrar:
Marge Salvatora
4169 Glasgow Road
Valencia, PA 16059
(724) 443-4782

Join Gus and the other Snappers
at the 1998 Reliability Tour in Middletown, OH.

AACA
Eastern Division Tour
May 26 - 29, 1999
Sponsored By
Pennsylvania Dutch Region

Kumme Sehne Deitch Land

Visit the Dutch Country of Lebanon and [...]
Counties in Central Pennsylvania.. Enjoy
[c]rafts of the Pennsylvania Dutch.

53rd Rev.
of the
Glidden Tour®
Bretton Woods,
New Hampshire
September 27 -
October 2
1998
Limited to 300 Cars,
1942 & Earlier

1998 Glidden Tour
White Mountains, New Hampshire
AUTUMN IN NEW ENGLAND

Headquartered at Mt. Washington Hotel and Resort

Glidden Tour® Information
Return to: Sharon Zaniboni, Registrar, P.O. Box 121, Southborough, MA 01772
Phone-Fax: (508) 485-6887

Please send me information about the 1998 "Autumn n New England" Glidden To[ur]
soon as it becomes available

I am a member of   VMCCA____   AACA____

Name (please print)____   State____   ZIP____

YOU'RE INVITED TO
PARIS
TEXAS
IN THE SPRINGTIME
AACA CENTRAL DIVISION
[...]L SPRING MEET
21-22, 1999

[SP]ONSORED BY THE
[...] VALLEY HONKERS REGION

Paris

- WELCOME PARTY
- RV HOOKUPS ON-SITE
- HOST HOTEL HOSPITALITY ROOM
- LADIES LUNCHEON
- TRAIN RIDE AND MUSEUM TOUR
- HISTORIC SAM BELL MAXEY HOUSE
- HAYDEN MUSEUM - AMERICAN CHAIR COLLECTION

1935   1999

BUFFALO'S GREAT IN '98
The Lake Erie Region A.A.C.A. is proud to host the
1998 Special Fall Meet
August 21-22, 1998
at the University Of Buffalo Amherst Campus

Meet Headquarters
& Host Hotel
Buffalo Marriott
1340 Millersport Hwy.
Amherst, New York 14228
(716)   689-6900
1-800-228-9290

"Don't Be Late, Participate"
Early Bird Tour to Niagara Casino
Thursday, August 20

[...]man
[...] Ferber
[...]e Breeze [...]   Chief Judge

TUCSON'S
POWER-PACKED EVENT
APRIL 8 - 11, 1999
HOSTED BY THE TUCSON REGION, A.A.C.A.

[t]he scenic Southwestern Sonoran Desert will be your setting for the combined
[W]estern Spring National and Annual Grand National meets being held on the same
[w]eekend!! Plans Include a fun filled Friday evening of western hospitality,
[e]ntertainment and an old fashioned hay ride. Tours are being planned for the GM
[pro]ving grounds, Pima Air Museum, Franklin Foundation Museum, and other local

1999 FOUNDERS TOUR
July 18-23, 1999

[Founde]rs Tour will be headquartered
[...] Hotel in Greensburg, PA.

[...] be limited to the first 220
[...]om 1936-1974

● Indiana
★ Latrobe

Welcome
to
Latrobe
1999
JULY 18-23
Hosted by
Western Pennsylvania Region
Latrobe, PA

[G]reensburg
● Bedford

[b]y the Western Pennsylvania Region

REGISTRATION CHAIRMAN   AACA TOUR DIRECTOR

AACA WESTERN DIVISION HUB TOUR   APRIL 13-15, 1999
WESTERN RED ROCK CELEBRATION

SCC

SEDONA REGION · SEDONA, ARIZONA

[T]OURING MAGNIFICENT RED CLIFF SCENERY EQUAL
[...]AL PARK; INDIAN RUINS, OLD WESTERN MINING
[...] SPECIAL CELEBRATION ON ROUTE 66.
[...] OPTIONS: APRIL, 12 AND/OR 16....BALLOON AND
[...]E SHOPPING, ART GALLERIES, HORSEBACK RIDING,
[...]LE DRIVE OR NARRATED EXCURSION BUS TOUR
[...] CANYON [ON APRIL 16 ONLY].
[SHO]WS THE TUSCON REGION AACA SPRING DIVISION
[AN]D NATIONAL MEET.
[P]ROMISE YOU FUN PACKED TRAIL RIDES!!!

Annual Meeting Trophies

The AACA Cup

Awarded at the AACA Annual Meeting for an outstanding restoration of the year of a pre-1921 automobile entered in each Division. Award established in 1945 by a member who desired to remain anonymous.

The President's Cup

Awarded at the AACA annual meeting for an outstanding restoration of the year of a 1921 through 1942 automobile entered in each Division. Award established in 1960 by AACA.

The Bomgardner Award

Awarded at the AACA Annual meeting for an outstanding restoration of the year of a post-1942 automobile entered in each Fall Meet. Award established in 1987 by AACA in honor of William and Jean Bomgardner for their years of dedication as executive director and office manager of AACA from 1959 through 1986. The trophy itself was donated by Mr. Edward H. Marion.

The AACA Past President's Racing Cup

Awarded at the AACA Annual Meeting for an outstanding race car entered in each Division. Award established in 1971 by Mr. and Mrs. Seth Pancoast, Sr. and is a cup won by Erwin Bergdoll on June 18, 1910, driving a Benz at the Point Breeze Race Track in Philadelphia, Pennsylvania. P.D. Folwell, Mrs. Hyde Ballard's father, was chairman of the contest board of the Quaker city Motor Club and presented the cup to the winner in 1910.

The Joseph Parkin Award

Awarded at the AACA Annual meeting for an outstanding Packard entered in each Division. Award established in 1973 by Joseph W. Parkin, Jr., former race driver of the Fairmount Park races and the Point Breeze races. Joseph W. Parkin, Jr. won this trophy in 1910 with a Packard "30".

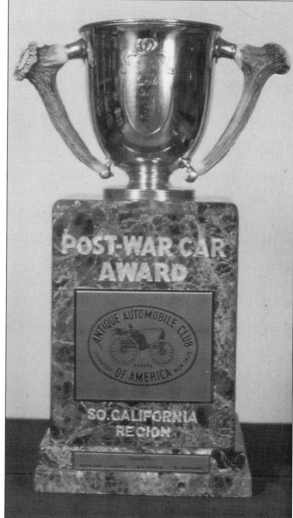

The Post War Car Award

Awarded at the AACA Annual meeting for an outstanding Junior Post-War automobile entered in each Spring meet. Award established in 1982 by the Southern California Region and R.J. LaPorte, Bill Honda and Al Gheradi.

The James Melton Memorial Cup

Awarded at the AACA Annual Meeting for an outstanding Senior Car entered in the Spring Meet in each Division. Award established in 1963 by Dr. Samuel L. Scher in memory of James Melton (1903-1961), former AACA president and internationally known singer. The cup itself is the racing trophy won by the famous Winton Bullet in 1905, and was once a prized possession of James Melton.

The Chocolate Town Trophy

Awarded at the AACA Annual meeting for an outstanding senior car entered in the Fall Meet in each Division. Award established in 1972 by the Hershey Estates and Hershey Foods Corporation in commemoration of the first annual Fall Meet held in Hershey in 1954. The Hershey Fall meet, largest of its kind in the world, has been held continuously since that time.

The W. Emmert Swigart Memorial Cup

Awarded at the AACA Annual Meeting for an outstanding restoration of a rare and unusual automobile entered in a National Meet. Award established in 1950 by Mrs. Swigart in memory of W. Emmert Swigart (1883-1949), former AACA director and an early collector of antique automobiles and automobilia.

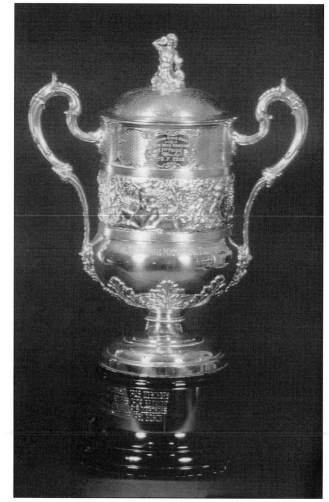

The S.F. Edge Trophy

Awarded at the AACA Annual meeting for an outstanding restoration of the year of a foreign-made automobile entered in a National Meet. Award established in 1956 by Mrs. Edge of England in memory of S.F. Edge (1868-1940), winner of the Gordon-Bennet Race in 1902, and who was known as the "father of the British motor industry." An associate of the Napier organization, he designed the first six-cylinder engine for them.

The Pamphilon Distinguished Car Award

Awarded at the AACA Annual Meeting to a pre-1916 self-propelled land vehicle of outstanding merit entered in a National Meet. Award established in 1965 by Mrs. L. Edward Pamphilon in memory of L. Edward Pamphilon who gave unsparingly of his time and energy to the Antique Automobile Club of America and to the advancement of the hobby.

The Ford Award

Awarded at the AACA Annual Meeting to Fords of the four eras of model years:
Brass Model era & Model "T" era cars —1903-1927
Model "A" Cars —1928-1931
Prewar Ford cars —1932-1945
Postwar Ford cars —1946 to current allowable year
One winner will be selected annually from the nominees from all National Meets. Junior and Senior cars are eligible. Competition and commercial vehicles are excluded. All driven and non-driven cars are eligible, with consideration given to driven cars. The award is made on the basis of authenticity, appearance and reliability.

Bert S. Harrington, Jr. Brighton Era Award

Awarded at the AACA Annual Meeting to a pre-1905 automobile.
Awarded on the basis of restoration, Maintenance or preservation selected from a National Meet or Tour. Donated by Mrs. Lu Harrington in memory of her husband.

The Edgar E. Rohr Memorial Award

Awarded at the AACA Annual Meeting to 1920 or older Buick Junior or Senior automobile the basis that it has participated in AACA events and has been driven at least 500 miles or more since restoration. Donated by Mrs. Walser Rohr in memory of her husband, a great promoter of the hobby, who was a National President (1963-1964). The Rohrs participated in more than 23 Glidden Tours™ in their 1912 Buick.

Ransom E. Olds Memorial Trophy

Presented by Oldsmobile Division, G.M.C. honoring the year's highest scoring restoration at a National Meet by a product of Olds Motor Works or Oldsmobile Division, G.M.C. Trophy donated by Classic Oldsmobile, Merrillville, Indiana.

Louis Chevrolet Memorial Award

Awarded at the AACA Annual meeting to an outstanding Junior Chevrolet shown at an AACA National Meet during the year. This award was made possible by Chevrolet Motor Division, General Motors Corp.

The Motorcycle Award

Awarded at the AACA Annual Meeting for an outstanding restoration of the year of a motorcycle shown at a National Meet. Award established by the Southwestern Two Wheelers Region of AACA.

The Annual Grand National Award

Awarded at the AACA Annual Meeting for an outstanding Senior truck entered in a National Meet. Award established in 1980 by the Hershey Region of AACA.

The Hershey Region
Junior Truck Award

Awarded at the AACA Annual Meeting to an outstanding Junior truck entered in a National Meet. Award established in 1980 by the Hershey Region of AACA.

The Hershey Region
Senior Truck Award

Awarded at the AACA Annual Meeting for an outstanding Senior truck entered in a National Meet. Award established in 1980 by the Hershey Region of AACA.

The Mercer Plaque

Awarded at the AACA Annual Meeting for an outstanding Mercer automobile entered in National Meet and judged on the bases of age, authenticity, appearance, and mechanical condition. Award established in 1956 by the late honorary member, Vincent Galloni, who was a Mercer employee during the existence of that company and who was the greatest Mercer authority until his death in 1958.

The Auburn - Cord - Duesenberg Award

Awarded to an outstanding Auburn, Cord, or Duesenberg automobile present at an AACA National Meet. Selection may be a Junior or Senior vehicle. This award was made possible by the Auburn-Cord-Duesenberg museum, Auburn, Indiana.

HPOF Award

Awarded at the AACA Annual Meeting to the outstanding vehicles in the HPOF (Historical Preservation Original Features) Class in three categories:

Two- or three-wheel cycle vehicle -- Award established in 1988 by the AACA Northern California Antique Motorcycle Region.

Vehicles through 1929 (excluding two- or three cycle vehicles) -- Award established in 1991 by the AACA Hershey Region.

Vehicles 1930 through current allowable year (45 years old or older) -- Award established in 1992 by the AACA Hershey Region in memory of Shirley M. Mader, longtime member and Secretary of the Hershey Region.

The Thomas McKean Tour Trophy

Awarded at the AACA Annual Meeting for an antique automobile that completed a National Tour on the basis of age, authenticity , appearance, condition and distance traveled to and from the tour. Award Established in 1949 by Thomas McKean, former president of AACA.

The Foo-Dog Trophy

Awarded at the AACA Annual meeting for an outstanding Rolls-Royce automobile entered in a National Meet judged on the bases of age, style and quality of coachwork, authenticity, appearance, and mechanical condition. Award established in 1945 by former AACA president, D. Cameron Peck. The trophy itself is an ancient and valuable Chinese work of art.

AACA Post War Buick Award

To be awarded at the AACA Annual Meeting for an outstanding Post War (World War II) Buick entered in a National Meet. Donated by Eileen and Jeffery Brashares of Worthington, Ohio.

The Augustus Post Memorial Plaque

Awarded at the AACA Annual meeting to the AACA member doing the most to preserve or re-create the spirit of the original Glidden Tours™ during a National AACA Tour. Presented first in 1953 by AAA and since 1959 by AACA in memory of Col. Augustus Post, a founder of the AAA, early motorist and aviator, and instigator and participant of every original Glidden Tour™ (1905-1913). He participated with AACA in every revival Glidden Tour™ from 1946 until his death.

The Winters Racing Award

Awarded at the AACA Annual Meeting to an AACA member in recognition of an outstanding contribution to documented racing vehicles by his or her deeds and display of enthusiasm. This award was established in 1996 by James E. and Clarice B. Winters, racing enthusiasts.

The Charles E. Duryea Cup

Awarded at the AACA Annual Meeting to an AACA member for outstanding effort on behalf of the Club on the basis of the value of the member's contribution to the general welfare of the AACA. Presented by Marion and M.J. Duryea in memory of Charles E. Duryea (1860-1938), inventor of America's first gasoline automobile in 1892 in Springfield, Massachusetts.

The Fiala Old Faithful Award

To be awarded at the AACA Annual Meeting to a member of AACA, not elected or appointed to a National office, who best exemplifies the true spirit of our Founders for service and accomplishment to the Antique Automobile Club of America, by his or her deeds and display of enthusiasm through the years. This award was established in 1995 by the children of Theodore and Suzanne Fiala in their parents' memory.

The AACA Library and Research Center Award

Awarded annually to the person who made an outstanding contribution of any kind (personal service, financial support or other aid) to the AACA Library and Research Center. Presented to AACA in 1984 by Harry and Lorraine Logan. Lorraine was the first secretary of the AACA Library and Research Center.

The I.C. Kirkham Membership Award

Awarded at the AACA Annual Meeting to the Region or Chapter with the greatest membership gain according to a weighted formula that considers the number of new National members acquired and the percentage of increase in membership. This I.C. Kirkham trophy is presented by the Genesee Valley Antique Car members for AACA than any other person.

The Samuel E. Baily Memorial Award

Awarded at the AACA Annual Meeting to an AACA member in recognition of an outstanding contribution to the improvement of performance in the AACA Judging System. Presented to the AACA in 1968 by Mrs. Samuel E. Baily in memory of Samuel E. Baily who was the pioneer in complete restorations and prepared the basis for our present-day judging.

1968 BERT HARRINGTON, JR.
1969 JOHN E. BITTNER, JR.
1970 HENRY KRUSEN
1971 GEORGE J. LIDDELL
1972 ALBERT SHAW
1973 SETH E. PANCOAST, SR.
1974 THOMAS J. WELLS
1975 THE SCRANTON REGION
1976 THE PIONEER CHAPTER
     OF THE MINNESOTA REGION
1977 EARL D. BEAUCHAMP, JR.
1978 LEO C. QUEEN
1979 DAVID J. ABEL
1980 HOWARD V. SCOTLAND, JR.

The Thomas J. Wells Memorial Award

Awarded at the AACA Annual Meeting to an AACA Field Judge whose continued performance has contributed to the success of the judging program. Tom Wells set high standards for judging and this award is made to those who give their time and knowledge to support the AACA Judging System. Selection shall be made by the Judging Committee and the National Awards Committee.

The Founders Award

Awarded at the AACA Annual Meeting to the National Director, selected by his fellow directors who, in their opinion, has contributed outstandingly to the guidance of AACA toward its founding principles: the perpetuation of the pioneer days of automobiling by furthering the interest in and the preserving of antique cars, and the promotion of sportsmanship and of good fellowship among all its members. The trophy itself is the actual steering wheel from the 1907 Thomas Flyer driven by Montague Roberts in the 1907 Briarcliff Road Race, given to Robert and Dorthea Laurens in 1952 by their dear friend Montague Roberts, one of the great pioneer race drivers of the early 20th century, and presented to AACA in 1975 through the efforts of Founding Members Frank Abramson, Ted Brooks, Earle Eckel, Sr., and Ted Fiala, Sr., for use as the "Founders Award-Steering Wheel Trophy," by Mr. and Mrs. Laurens in memory of "Monty Roberts."

The AACA Plaque

The AACA plaque is awarded in recognition of outstanding achievement in the preservation of the automotive history

The Ann S. Eady Memorial Award

Presented to the editor of a region or chapter newsletter for their contribution to the general welfare and spirit of the Antique Automobile Club of America. Presented by the Southeastern Region of AACA, the trophy itself is Ann S. Eady's typewriter, which she used as editor of Peachtree Parade *from 1965 to 1974.*

The Thomas McKean Memorial Cup

Awarded at the AACA Annual Meeting for worthwhile effort during the year in automotive historical research on the basis of accuracy, interest to club members, and the use to which the research is put. Presented by the AACA in 1949 in memory of Thomas McKean (1909-1949), former president and bibliophile.

The M.J. Duryea Memorial Cup

Awarded at the AACA Annual Meeting to an AACA member for outstanding contribution to automotive history through Antique Automobile magazine during the year. Presented in 1958 by the AACA in memory of Merle J. Duryea (1895-1957), a former president and editor who contributed more to the success and growth of the AACA than any other individual in his time.

The Editorial Award

Award at the AACA Annual Meeting to a member of the staff of Antique Automobile *magazine in recognition of outstanding editorial services. This award is sponsored by the Raymond E. Holland Automotive Art & Toy Collection, Allentown, Pennsylvania, and is awarded annually.*

Judging
and
Awards

Judging

The AACA Judging Program is one of the most well known features of the organization. It has been established with specified judging objectives, standardized procedures and vehicle classifications that support fair and honest evaluation of vehicles registered to compete at National Meets, regardless of the location. The fundamental purpose of judging and awards has always been to encourage high standards of achievement in preserving, restoring and maintaining antique vehicles.

The judging system, as we know it today, has evolved over the history of the AACA. It has not always been so structured. Judging was part of the early Derby Days and continued with the beginning of AACA meets and events. The first AACA Chief Judge was Fred C. Nicholson. He had helped organize the Derby Days Meets and had some judging experience. For the first 20 years, the Chief Judge was an appointed position held by club members who were not elected officers or board members. By 1965, judging had become important and there was need for a more structured organization. National Director Samuel E. Bailey was then appointed as the first AACA Vice-President of Class Judging. He has often been called the "Father" of the AACA judging system as we know it today.

Judging was much more informal in the early days. The designated AACA Chief Judge would organize a small group of volunteers and give them some indications of how the judging was to proceed. They would then look at all of the vehicle and select the winners. The show or meets in those days were relatively small, so a single group would be adequate for the task. Since we have no records of gross miscarriages of justice nor indications of major battles, we can only assume that this procedure worked quite satisfactorily.

Initially there were no written instructions, formal training sessions, forms or point systems to guide the judges. There was just their personal expertise and subjective, or collective judgment of the team, to select the winner vehicles.

The first record of a point system was in a May 3, 1936, letter from Chief Judge Fred C. Nicholson. It outlined a procedure to identify winners by the following formula:

1. Multiply the number of years the car is older than the minimum set for entrant...
2. By the number of miles traveled, and...
3. Divide by the number of cylinders.

The example given was:

If a 25 year old limit is set, the youngest car would be a 1911 product. Therefore, count 1911 as year 1, 1910 year 2, 1909 year 3 and so on.

A 1910 car - 2 cyl. - 100 miles: $\dfrac{2 \text{ yrs. old} \times 100 \text{ miles}}{2 \text{ cylinders}}$ 100 points

A 1910 car - 4 cyl. - 100 miles: $\dfrac{2 \text{ yrs. old} \times 100 \text{ miles}}{4 \text{ cylinders}}$ 50 points

A 1910 car - 4 cyl. - 50 miles:	$\dfrac{\text{2 yrs. old x 50 miles}}{\text{4 cylinders}}$	25 points
A 1906 car - 2 cyl. - 100 miles:	$\dfrac{\text{6 yrs. old x 100 miles}}{\text{2 cylinders}}$	300 points
A 1906 car - 1 cyl. - 50 miles:	$\dfrac{\text{6 yrs. old x 50 miles}}{\text{1 cylinder}}$	300 points
A 1902 car - 1 cyl. - 25 miles:	$\dfrac{\text{10 yrs. old x 25 miles}}{\text{1 cylinder}}$	250 points

The highest point vehicle would be declared as the winner. This was certainly a rather arbitrary and crude procedure to select winners and since it did not consider condition, it hopefully had limited, if any use at AACA meets.

The "official" statement of a criteria for judging first appeared in print in 1955. Awards were primarily based on authenticity and the ability of the car to function. Smoothness, silence and the excellence of mechanical condition are given the greatest consideration in scoring points for the well-restored car. All accessories should work. The statement went on to say, "...that all other things being equal the car that is restored to a 'most original' condition should outpoint a competitor having in its finish or equipment that which is better than the original."

The judging committee at that time recommended the following method of scoring:

	Maximum points
1. Smoothness of operation, silence, condition of brakes, general mechanical condition and transportation ability	20
2. Condition of engine	5
3. Cleanliness of underchassis and lubricators	5
4. Evidence of "tight" steering gear, king pins, etc., and lubrication	10
5. Condition of finish, bright work, woodwork, upholstery and mats	10
6. Condition of top or "hood"	5
7. Condition of tires	5

A. All other things being equal preference will be given to the car that has been restored by the member as against one that has been purchased already restored, or restored by a professional.

B. No additional points or consideration shall be given for finishing to a higher degree than was original or for superior performance due to installation of non-original equipment. Inappropriate accessories or equipment may be items to reduce the points of scoring allowed, at the discretion of the judges. This does not mean that there be any penalties for superior work of restoration of for contemporary accessories.

C. During judging, drivers should be available to start engines so that their operation may be appraised. Judges must not start the engines unless authorized to do so by the driver.

D. Unless in the case of a tie, the newness or condition of tires shall for the most part be disregarded in judging. The car should be equipped with suitable tires, preferably of original size. This consideration is made due to the extreme difficulty in obtaining tires of certain sizes, and also the expense involved in securing new tires, especially so when the owner has old tires that are wholly suitable for reliable transportation.

This system with a maximum of 60 points was a step in the right direction; however, there is no evidence that it was ever officially adopted as a standard or that a form was developed. It is interesting to note the preference for owner versus professional restoration and the requirement to check the operation of the car and all accessories. One would presume the accepted contemporary accessories mentioned referred to items such as turn signals, etc., and not hot rod equipment.

Vehicle Classification System

The vehicle awards program continued to develop during this period. Junior and Senior Judging was started at the National Spring Meet held at Pottstown, Pennsylvania, in 1952. A classification system had been developed with difference classes for vehicles with similar characteristics, such as age, number of cylinders, brakes, etc. This was to improve competitiveness within the classes. Vehicles would initially compete and be judged as Juniors until they win First Prize in their class. Then they would compete as Seniors against other National First Prize Winners in their class for the Senior award.

Although some vehicle classification rules had been tried as early as 1947, the new 1952 classification system, having been developed by a joint AACA and VMCCA committee, was the first to have official standardized acceptance. It included 18 classes. The year cut-off was cars 25-years old or older, except Classic Cars, which were defined as later model, high quality cars of unusual merit that would be accepted as over 15 but less than 25 years old. This meant that there could be cars on the judging field through 1927 with Classics through 1936.

As years passed it became apparent that one of the best features of the system was its demonstrated flexibility. Classes could be added, separated, or combined and cut-off years could be changed to accommodate the need to recognize "new" antiques and other types of vehicles. The evolution of the Official AACA Car Classifications includes the following most significant changes:

1954: Cut-off at 1929. No new years accepted.

1957: Reinstated the 25-year rule. Antiques limited prior to 1930 and added production cars after 1930 to 25-year cut-off. Added motorcycle class. Added list of accepted specified makes for Classics.

1960: Cut-off year set at 1935. Cars redefined as highway motor vehicles (including trucks) and year meaning model year, not necessarily year of manufacture. Classics changed to 1930 to 15 years old.

1963: Commercial cars (trucks except hearses) class added. Classic cut-off set at 1948.

1968: Production cars' cut-off advances one year during each even numbered year until 1940 model year cars are accepted and then will stop.

1970: Added class for Fire Vehicles.

1971: Added class for Competition Cars (race cars).

1975: Reinstated the 25-year cut-off rule for applicable classes.

Separate classes have been added to separate Ford V-8 cars, Corvettes, Thunderbirds, 1955-1958 Chevrolets and others. New classes were added for post-classic prestige cars and limited production and prototype vehicles. In 1988, the Historical Preservation of Original Features (HPOF) class was added for essentially unrestored cars, a move that has been popular. The cars entered in the HPOF class are not point judged, but are certified by a special team as meeting the criteria established for that class.

Judging Forms and Point Systems

The first Official Judging Form was introduced at the 1960 AACA Silver Jubilee Meet in Hershey, Pennsylvania. This was the first use of the 100 point form. There were ten sections to this form related to different parts of the vehicle, i.e., Paint & Car Finish, Wheels & Tires, Engine & Radiator, etc.

The judges would evaluate the appearance of the car and assign points on a 10 point scale from poor to excellent, with 10 as maximum. Deductions in each of the sections would be applicable if the items in the area were not authentic. The total appearance points, maximum of 100, would be reduced by the total authenticity minus points for a grand total that would be the basis for awards. A minimum of 75 points was required for any award.

The criteria for judging was to judge a car to match the way it looked and operated at the time of its delivery from the factory or custom body builder. Accessories such as toolboxes, spotlights, spare tire covers, etc., were permissible provided they were authentic as to the year of the car. There was great emphasis on owner authentication of the correct model year of the car.

After judging the Senior cars, Judges were to take a tour of the Junior cars, without judging forms. They would walk around the vehicles in each class and eliminate the "non-contenders" based on a visual assessment of potential competitiveness. They would then use the forms only in judging the ones not already eliminated. The resulting scores would be the basis for the Junior awards. Only one Senior prize winner per class was permitted according to the judging instructions in 1960. Similarly, only one Junior vehicle in each class could receive a First Junior. There were no tie provisions.

The Antique Automobile Club of America

Form B — April '61

Date _____

Entry No. _____ Class _____ Car _____ Year _____

Owner _____ Address _____

APPEARANCE ONLY		AUTHENTICITY COLUMN MINUS POINTS Deduct as specified	
POOR +2 **FAIR** +4 **GOOD** +6 **VERY GOOD** +8 **EXCELLENT** +10			
PAINT & CAR FINISH (except wheels) Consider paint workmanship, badly prepared surface, peeling, fading, rust pits showing through, poor striping. (Disregard normal road dust)	+	Wrong color (or metallic paint) on body —5; Wrong color (or metallic paint) on fenders —5; Non-authentic striping —1 to —3; Other (Judges must specify)	
BODY, FENDERS, & FRAME Consider roughness, signs of straightening or welding, fender beads, fender edges and undersides. (Disregard normal road dirt)	+	Completely non-authentic body or body style —25; Non-authentic fenders (or non-authentic lack of fenders) —15; Partial non-authenticity —5 to —15 (judges must specify such as "non-authentic mother-in-law seat", "doors missing", etc.)	
WHEELS & TIRES Consider paint and striping, condition of spokes, felloes and rims, hubs. (Disregard normal road dirt)	+	Natural wood or non-authentically colored wheels —5 (Owner must prove authenticity); Missing or wrong hub caps —1 to —4; Wrong size tires & wheels —5 (Bear in mind tire availability); Dangerously worn tires —10 to —15; Indications of poor alignment or wobbling wheel —3 to —5; Other: (Judges specify)	
SPRINGS, AXLES, STEERING, UNDERCARRIAGE Consider rust, excess grease & oil, signs of baling wire or other makeshift repairs. (Disregard normal road dirt)	+	No signs of lubrication —2 to —4; Dangerously worn steering —10 to —15; Modern shock absorbers —10; Modern overdrive —15; Modern type grease fittings —3; Other non-authentic chassis modifications: (judges must specify)	
TOP OR ROOF If car has no top, see instructions at bottom of this form*. Otherwise, consider top tightness or looseness, lopsided bows, neatness, rear window, condition of headliner and top on closed cars.	+	Non-authentic top material —5; Non-authentic roof or top style —10; Non-authentic fasteners, buckles, straps, etc. —1 to —3; Other: (Judges must specify)	
UPHOLSTERY AND INTERIOR Consider seats, seat backs, floor coverings, side panels, dash instruments, steering wheel, floor pedals, all other inside handles and lockers.	+	Non-authentic upholstery material —5; Non-authentic floor coverings —2; Upholstery style (pleating, sewing) non-authentic —3; Non-authentic trim tape or tack heads —2; Other: (Judges must specify)	
LAMPS & BRIGHT WORK Consider freshness of plating, plating worn off, manufacturer's name and other markings worn off and replated.	+	Plating MUST BE OF THE ORIGINAL TYPE MATERIAL and plated only where plated originally! All plating done in non-authentic material —10; Partially plated in non-authentic material —3 to —10; Plating on parts factory never plated —3 to —10; Non-authentic lamps 5 to 10; Other: (Judges specify)	
ENGINE & RADIATOR Consider excessive oil leaks, paint on engine and engine compartment, rust, radiator damage. (Disregard normal road dirt, normal oil and grease films)	+	Non-authentic substitute engine —25; Engine obviously modified —5 to —10; Engine painted wrong color —2; Non-authentic radiator core —10; Wrong radiator cap —5; Other: (Judges must specify)	
WIRES, ENGINE ACCESSORIES, FUEL LINES, HOSES, FAN BELT, etc. Consider worn or frayed wires, hose condition, worn or frayed fan belt, poor or loose connections in wires and fuel lines, signs of "baling wire repairs", etc.	+	Modern plastic wires —3; Modern fuel pump —5; Carburetor not original type but antique —2; Modern carburetor —5; Modern magneto —5; Other: (Judges must specify)	
OVERALL AUTHENTICITY Automatic 10 points in appearance column. NOTE: It is up to vehicle owner to prove authenticity of any questionable restoration by documentary evidence (catalog, advertisements, A.L.A.M. Handbook, etc.).	+10	Deliberate pre-dating of vehicle —25; Specify any other authenticity deductions. Note to Judges: If individual non-authentic components have been previously deducted in above listed categories, it is unnecessary to deduct any more here. If in doubt of authenticity, request owner to show proof.	

Total Appearance Points _____

Total Minus Points _____

Less Total Minus Points _____

Judges' Names _____

GRAND TOTAL _____

_____

_____

Vehicles must score 75 points or more to be awarded a first prize.

*If factory supplied top as standard equipment, but top is now missing, score 0 in appearance column and —15 in authenticity column. If car has no top (having been sold that way at time of manufacture), mark ✕ in appearance and ✕ in authenticity. Adjust final Grand Total Score by dividing 90 into total points. Carry to one decimal point. i.e. Total points of 82 equals GRAND TOTAL SCORE 91.1.

The Antique Automobile Club of America

JUDGING FORM

Revised May, 1966

Do not deduct more than the maximum points listed by group

GROUP 1
(100 Points)
BODY, FENDERS, RUNNING BOARDS, SPLASH APRONS, HARDTOP, ALL EXTERIOR PAINT AND FINISH INCLUDING WHEELS, CHASSIS AND ALL COMPONENTS ON THE OUTSIDE OF THE VEHICLE

Dents___ Alignment of components___ Fender beads___ Straightness___ Mouldings___ Underside of fenders___

Edges of fenders___ Paint workmanship___ Runs___ Depth___ Gloss___ Orange peel___ Chipping___ Peeling___

Poor preparation___ Fading___ Scratches or pits___ Striping___ Others_____

MAXIMUM DEDUCTION 100 POINTS FOR GROUP 1.   TOTAL DEDUCTION

STANDARD DEDUCTIONS: Incorrect color — 1 to — 20; Metallic paint on cars produced prior to Nov. 1927 — 15; Metallic paint on cars produced after Nov. 1927 and without evidence to show metallic paint is correct — 15; Incorrect striping — 1 to — 10; Incorrect body or body components — 1 to — 50.

GROUP II
(75 Points)
CHASSIS INCLUDING WHEELS AND TIRES (Excluding paint)

Rust___ Excess grease and oil___ Makeshift repairs___ Tire covers___ Lubrication fittings___ Tires___

Spokes___ Felloes___ Rims___ Hubs___ Others_____

MAXIMUM DEDUCTION 75 POINTS FOR GROUP II.   TOTAL DEDUCTION

STANDARD DEDUCTIONS: Power brakes added — 12; Unsafe steering including kingpins — 5 to — 20; Incorrect type of wheels — 5 to — 20; Incorrect size of tires or wheels (deduct only if correct size available) — 5 to — 20; Badly worn tires including spares — 5 to — 20; Incorrect lubrication fittings or lack of Alemite covers — 1 to — 10. Do not deduct for mis-matching of tires if the front tires match each other and the rear tires match each other and the spare or spares match each other or the front or rear set.

GROUP III
(75 Points)
UPHOLSTERY, SOFT TOP, INTERIOR INCLUDING PAINT

Seats___ Seat backs___ Heel boards___ Floor coverings___ Side panels___ Dash___ Instruments___

Operability of instruments___ Steering wheel___ Pedals___ Inside hardware___ Door mouldings___

Door trim___ Tools___ Manuals___ Others_____

MAXIMUM DEDUCTION 75 POINTS FOR GROUP III.   TOTAL DEDUCTION

STANDARD DEDUCTIONS: Incorrect top material — 10 to — 20; Incorrect top style — 10 to — 20; Incorrect fasteners, buckles, straps — 5 to — 10; Top missing (use this deduction only if top was included as original factory equipment. Burden is on owner to establish this fact) — 40; Top down — 20; Incorrect rear window — 5; Side curtains not in evidence or incorrect — 5 to — 20; Incorrect upholstery material — 10 to — 20; Incorrect upholstery style — 5 to — 10; Incorrect upholstery trim — 5 to — 10; Incorrect floor covering — 5 to — 10.

GROUP IV
(25 Points)
LAMPS AND BRIGHT WORK (EXTERIOR ONLY)

Incorrect plating___ (both as to type of plating___ and area___) Absence of paint___

Absence of plating___ (as supplied by factory) Operability of gas, oil, electric lights___

and horn___ Others_____

MAXIMUM DEDUCTION 25 POINTS FOR GROUP IV.   TOTAL DEDUCTION

STANDARD DEDUCTIONS: Incorrect plating and absence of correct paint or plating — 1 to — 20; Incorrect lamps — 5 to — 20.

GROUP V
(100 Points)
POWER PLANT AND ACCESSORIES

Paint___ Operability___ Carburetor___ Magneto___ Coil___ Fuel supply device___ Hose clamps___

Tape___ Incorrect wire___ Fan belt___ Incorrect components added___ Incorrect engine___

Others_____

MAXIMUM DEDUCTION 100 POINTS FOR GROUP V.   TOTAL DEDUCTION

STANDARD DEDUCTIONS: Incorrect engine — 50; Incorrect engine component — 5 to — 20; Incorrect radiator core — 5 to — 20; Incorrect hose clamps — 1 per clamp; Taped wire — 5 to — 10; Incorrect wire and/or connectors — 5 to — 15; Starter added — 12; Power steering added — 12; Incorrect fuel pump device — 15.

GROUP VI
(25 Points)
DISCRETIONARY POINTS

Poor roadworthiness___ Predating___ Features of special demerit___ Others_____

MAXIMUM DEDUCTION 25 POINTS FOR GROUP VI.   TOTAL DEDUCTION

TOTAL MAXIMUM DEDUCTION   4 0 0

POINTS DEDUCTED IN GROUPS 1, II, III, IV, V and VI. ⟶ TOTAL POINTS DEDUCTED   —
(deduct from 400 and enter below)

Circle one: Senior Car   Junior Car   GRAND SCORE

DATE_____ ENTRY NO_____ CLASS_____ CAR_____ YEAR_____

OWNER_____ ADDRESS_____

403

No point preference would be given to "owner restoration" over a professional restoration. Considering the experience of the Judging Committee, they had concluded that both types of restorations were equal. Judges were instructed that in scoring they were to consider only the merits of the vehicle. The car alone was being judged and the particular history and other irrelevant facts of ownership, trials and tribulations from before to after restorations were to have no bearing on the scoring of points.

It was the responsibility of the owner to provide documentary evidence to prove authenticity if requested by the judges. This requirement has remained one of the constants throughout the evolution of the judging system.

The 1960 form was modified several times and in 1970, it was totally revised to introduce the 1000 point system. Each vehicle would enter the judging field with 1000 points. The judges would take deductions according to the items on the form under the following groups:

Group 1 - Exterior and underside finish

Group 2 - Chassis, wheels and tires

Group 3 - Bright work

Group 4 - Interior

Group 5 - Engine compartment

The deductions for each of the groups would be added and the total deductions would be subtracted from 1000. Minimum points for awards were set for Senior (875), 1st Junior (875), 2nd Junior (750) and 3rd Junior (625). For the first time, multiple awards were permitted when vehicles scored within 25 points of the highest score in each category.

A 1972 *Antique Automobile* article by John E. Bittner, National Judges Training Director, indicated that while modifications had been made to the original 1960 form, "...the most fair and most equitable method of judging seems to be the present 1000 point system." The opinion was apparently not widely held in the judging community for changes were already on the horizon.

In 1973, a new form with a 400 point maximum was introduced with a format that has essentially remained constant since that date. Each car entered the show field with 400 points. The form provided for judging in four areas: Interior, Exterior, Chassis and Engine. Specific items within these areas were identified with maximum and in some cases mandatory, deductions. The deductions would be added and that total subtracted from 400. The resulting score would be used to determine the winners in each class.

Minimum points for awards were set for Senior (365), 1st Junior (365), 2nd Junior (330) and 3rd Junior (295). Multiple awards were permitted when vehicles scored within 10 points of the highest score in each category. Visual judging was eliminated, except under certain limited circumstances.

Judging forms were subsequently developed for two-wheeled vehicles, racing vehicles and commercial vehicles. The format and judging procedures were similar, but these forms listed items that were more appropriate to these vehicles.

There was also a criterion change. Under the new system the objective of judging was to evaluate an antique vehicle which has been restored to the exact same state as when the dealer delivered the vehicle from the factory. Any feature, options, or accessory shown in an original dealer or factory catalog, were accepted for judging. Aftermarket accessories, even if added by the dealer, would not be accepted.

The trophy for the Senior award was a miniature AACA logo Duryea car mounted on a wood base. Each time a vehicle won the Senior award it received another trophy. In 1979, this rule was changed and a competitor could only win one Senior award. When the first award was won a Senior Tab would be presented with the trophy. This tab would be placed behind the National First Prize plaque to identify the vehicle as a Senior Award winner. The vehicle could continue participation and compete for a Preservation Award.

In 1979, the Preservation Award was implemented for all National Meets. To encourage owners to continue showing their vehicles, they would be eligible to receive a Preservation Award by scoring a minimum of 350 points at each meet entered. The first award consisted of a wooden board with a large polished metal Preservations Award Medallion (embossed with the AACA logo, a nameplate with the owner's name and year and make of vehicle and a Wheel Tab to be placed on the board. Another Wheel Tab would be awarded each time the vehicle won a Preservation).

Participation cards were included with each Wheel Tab. When a vehicle wins five Preservation Awards the owner can send the five cards to the Vice-President - Senior Car Awards and receive a Participation Award. Initially there was a choice between a metal mug or an oval metal tray. Currently only the metal tray is available.

This has been an effective way to encourage Senior Award winners to continue participation and many owners take great pride in their Preservation Awards. Ironically, the first three vehicles to receive fifty Preservation Awards, all within a few months of each other, represented three important eras of the same make. These were Marshall Van Winkle's 1924 Ford Model T, Herman Hoke's 1929 Ford Model A and Benny Bootle's 1941 Ford V-8.

When the A.G.N.M. was approved in 1980, the scoring criteria was changed for those meets. Minimum points for awards were set for A.G.N.M. 1st (380), A.G.N.M. 2nd (365), A.G.N.M. 3rd (350) and Preservation (350). Initially, ties were not permitted. The wisdom of this decision was questioned quickly when it became apparent that some incredibly well-restored vehicles failed to win at the A.G.N.M. Several changes were tried and it was finally settled that vehicles scoring within five points of the highest score in each category and above the minimum would be tied. In 1992, vehicles that had won the A.G.N.M. 1st were eligible to compete for the A.G.N.M. Senior. Each eligible vehicle scoring a minimum of 390 points would receive the A.G.N.M. Senior.

Judging Manuals

Geographic divisions were created in 1960 to place National Meets in all parts of the country. Initially there would be Spring and Fall Meets in each of three divisions, Eastern, Central and Western. The Southeastern Division was added later, thus there would be a total of eight National Meets. In 1973, a National Winter Meet was added in the Southeastern Division and the AACA Board decided that Special National Meets could be approved if required to support the demand. Then in 1980, they approved the Annual Grand National Meet where only Senior vehicles would compete for an Annual Grand National Prize. One constant that remained was that the Eastern Division National Fall Meet would always be in Hershey, Pennsylvania.

By 1962, the greatly increased number of entries at National Meets indicated a need for a larger judging staff and an organized judging education program. The program would standardize the judging procedures and would provide pertinent information to the judges and restorers. A judging manual would be developed and regional chief judges would be required.

Written explanations for judging procedures were provided in articles that appeared in the *Antique Automobile*. As of the early 1960s, judges were informed that if they did not have a copy of the specific magazine, they could purchase one for $1.25 from AACA headquarters. This was clearly inadequate to ensure the availability of competent, well-trained judges.

In 1966, the National AACA Board of Directors authorized the publication of an Official Judging Manual to set standards for the Judging Program. The manual was 4 x 8 inches and fit nicely in a judge's pocket. There were only eight pages and that included pages for the "Official Car Classifications." In this version, and subsequent revisions, only the essentials of judging instructions were included. This manual was barely adequate, but it was an improvement.

During this period, the evolution of the judging system continued on several fronts, most notably in organizational structure at the meets and recognition that more technical and authentication issues needed to be provided to the judges. This latter problem was particularly critical with the proliferation of new makes and models within the "Official Vehicle Classifications." It was also due to the fact that more judges were doing more research and finding more errors in the "absolutes" that they had been taught. Additional important information related to judging procedures. Technical data was distributed in mimeographed copies of notes, sometimes handwritten, to judges at the judging schools.

In 1984, the Official Judging Manual went through a major revision. The format was changed to 5-1/2 x 8-1/2 inches and increased to 48 pages. The total organizational structure was explained along with position descriptions. There was a section to provide a detailed explanation of awards and how they were determined and copies of the various documents to include judging forms, vehicle registration forms, and judges' registration forms were included. There was an important section to provide the judges with specific information such as, first years for chrome plating, first uses of power steering, first years for Phillips screws, incorrect uses of electric fuel pumps on early cars and many others. This was clearly a step in the right direction to get the swelling ranks of judges better equipped for their duties.

Since the "Official Vehicle Classifications" changed every year because of the 25-year rule, it was also necessary to annually update the manual. With each change there were improvements to the other sections as well and the manual grew to 64 pages. After six years of publication in this format, it was realized that the judges would receive a new copy, read it and then leave it home or in a suitcase when traveling to a meet. Something had to be done.

A new format was developed. In 1990, the manual was published in a 3-1/2 x 8-1/2-inch size—just the right size to be carried in a judges pocket to the show field. The content was basically the same as before, but the new size made it more useful. These manuals are distributed at the Judging Schools and are also available through National Headquarters.

$3.00

OFFICIAL JUDGING MANUAL

ANTIQUE AUTOMOBILE CLUB OF AMERICA

FOUNDED NOV. 1935

DURYEA

Copyright 1966

Revised 1998

Antique Automobile Club

of America

Hershey, Pennsylvania 17033

Judges Training

The judges training program grew during this same period. It stared in 1967 with a Judging School at the Annual Meeting. Experienced Senior Judges were selected as instructors and a Director of Judges Training was appointed to serve with the Judging Committee. After a while, this title became confused with the title of National Director used by members who were elected to serve the National Board. The title was then changed to Chairman of Judges Training.

By 1973, it was apparent that holding the judging school at the Annual Meeting was not satisfying the need. In 1974, judging schools were held at several National Meets. This has continued, eventually reaching the point where there would be a school at every National Meet and the Annual Grand National Meet. The only exception was Hershey. That meet had grown to such a size that the logistics for holding a school were too great to handle. In fact, few judges want to give up precious flea market time to sit through a school.

There was also a program to hold accredited special schools at other locations if requested be a region or chapter. This greatly expanded the opportunity to train and encourage AACA members to become judges. In 1998, the first accredited bilingual judging school was held in San Jose, Costa Rica. The school was presented at a meet hosted by the AACA region in that country, Club de Autos Antiquos de Costa Rica. Ralph Pinto an officer of that club, served as the Spanish interpreter for the AACA instructor, Ron Barnett.

The Apprentice Program was added in 1986. Prior to that time a new judge would attend a school and serve as an observer for the first time on the field. Unfortunately, the Team Captains were not well trained to make this observation time a real learning experience. Often, the shortage of judges would mean that the new one would have to serve as a judge. With this program a new judge was assigned to the Apprentice Team and a Senior Master Judge specifically selected for instruction skills would train that team on the basics of judging. This was one of the most important advances in the training program since the start of judging schools.

Another important event in 1998 was the first Continuing Judges Education (CJE) school presented at the National Spring Meet in Topeka, Kansas. The purpose of this program is to present advanced and refresher training for Master and Senior Master judges. Judges are required to attend a CJE coarse when they reach 10 credits and each time they reach multiples of 25 credits thereafter. The Judging Committee is confident that this program will be effective in maintaining the high quality of the judging system.

Judges Awards

Judges have always volunteered their time and expertise to perform this important job. There has never been any reimbursement if there were costs nor any pay. By 1965, the Judging Committee had concluded that that some form of recognition was needed to reward judges for their efforts.

Starting with the National Fall Meet of that year, each participating judge received a walnut plaque with the "National AACA Judge" brass tag at the top and brass "year tag" for that particular event. There was no provision for retroactive awards for previous years, and the judge would only receive one plaque per year, regardless of how many times they judged. There was room on the board for five "year tags" and when the board was filled, the individual would qualify for the title of "Senior Judge."

With these rules it would take a minimum of five years to become a Senior Judge. However, many of the judges participated at more than one meet each year and attended judging schools. By 1970, the procedure had been changed to give a brass plaque for each time that the individual judge attended a school (school credits were later limited to one per year) and the plaque would indicate that the credit was for a Spring, Fall, Winter and Annual Grand National Meet or School. When a judge reached 10 credits they become a Master Judge and when they had 25 credits they would be a Senior Master Judge.

Bert Harrington was the first to reach 25 credits and become an AACA Senior Master Judge. In 1983, it was announced that Harrington was the first judge to have 100 credits. There were two judging schools at Annual Meeting that year, one for judges with 0-5 credits and one for judges with more than 5 credits. Harrington solemnly proclaimed that now that he had 100 credits, it was time to start over again, so he attended the school for Junior Judges.

By 1997, seven judges had reached the 200 credit level. These were Howard Scotland, Sam High, Charlie Coulter, Forest Sloan, Al Edmond, Earl Muir and Margie Sloan. During his year as AACA President in 1997, Sam High became the first judge to reach 250 credits. These are remarkable achievements and show the dedication of AACA judges.

The Judges Award Program was well received and the number of AACA members volunteering to be judges grew steadily. Someone had to keep track of the credit records so a new position was created within the Judging Committee. This was the Director of Judges Records, later changed to Chairman of Judges Records. That appointee was charged with the task of filing all of the 3 x 5 cards collected at each meet and maintaining accurate records of the number of credits held by each judge. This was an enormous task to do manually and was eventually logged on a computer.

An indication of the size of this task is that in 1997, there were 10 judging schools with 1,351 judges attending. There were nine National Meets with 4,088 registered vehicles judged by 2,559 judges.

An additional responsibility of the Chairman of Judges Records was to publish the "Judges' Newsletter". This newsletter has served to communicate with all the judges, to keep them aware of any significant changes in the rules, and to provide registration information and forms for each National Meet.

Judging at National Meets has been one of the major AACA programs. The obvious impact to the restoration quality of participating vehicles is one of the top success stories for the organization. The judging system is definitely one of the best, if not the best, in the hobby and numerous other clubs have implemented similar systems. From the perspective of AACA judges, this has become a hobby within a hobby for thousands of dedicated AACA members.

January 10, 1998

The Judge

Number 96

ANTIQUE AUTOMOBILE CLUB OF AMERICA   **JUDGES NEWSLETTER**

A FAMILY AFFAIR
by Ron Rubenstein
Chairman National Judges Training

First of all let me thank the National Judging Committee and all AACA Judges for welcoming me as the new Chairman of Judges Training. I hope to continue the level of excellence that has already been established by many predecessors. I also want to thank David Wuntsch as my Assistant Chairman of Judges Training.

My earliest recollection of AACA and the old car hobby dates back to the mid 1970's when my father and I drove past Rose Tree state park, Havertown,

PA. A local AACA car show was in full swing. I remember as a pre-teen stopping to look at the old cars with my father who got caught up in the excitement and thought it would be exciting to be a member of this great organization. I guess my father always had an interest in old cars and high performance Mopars as I was growing up. Little did he realize that by joining this antique auto club on this particular day that he would be sparking an interest in a hobby that would continue to grow for him and his family to this day.

Over the years I recall going to Monday night Keystone Region meetings where my father served as President. We also became active as a family in the National Judging program. My mother and sister joined us in national car show events and "vacations." My mother, father and I accumulated our initial judging credits

at these events.

I have fond memories of going to Hershey in the early years with my father where some of the activities and events included driving events & skills competition in addition to the judging activities. I am living just outside of Hershey, PA perhaps in part due to the close proximity to our AACA National Headquarters. The heart of this great organization.

My wife Lois and I along with our two children Nathan and Brenna continue to enjoy this family tradition and hobby started by my father over 20 years ago.

P.S. Sandy: Ronnie took his bride on their honeymoon to an antique car show. With a start like this I know the Rubensteins are a dedicated AACA family. They are a fine example of the younger generation we need to carry on this great hobby.

IT'S A NEW YEAR
by Carl R. Boyd
Vice President Class Judging

1998 looks to be a very busy year in the judging system, with 12 shows and many miles. This year we will be introducing the new Continuing Judges Education program (CJE). You will get all information about CJE in Philadelphia or the next Judging School you attend. The CJE should keep all judges informed on new or revised information, and help unify the judging system.

We have had a very good year in

'97 with few complaints, however, one of which stoodout is TIRES. As most of you know tires can make or break a vehicle, the Judging manual is vague as to what size, and material they should be made of. I know myself, I would have trouble with some vehicles, so therefore I ask each field judge, if you are not sure, ask your team captain or deputy, two heads are usually better than one. If the team cannot make a decision, please, Team Captains get help from the administration office. We are working on some new material that should help in the area.

For all you Computer Nuts out there, CRAM will be ready this spring. In Philadelphia we will have a full

demonstration of the program.

I would like to take this opportunity to thank all Judges for a great 1997. You did an outstanding job and I am looking forward to working with each one of you in 1998. I would also like to thank all Chairmen involved in the judging program, you make me proud to be a part of the AACA. I should also thank Dave Berg and Ron Rubenstein for all their assistance they have given to me and my duties. Last but not least the ladies in the administration office, these ladies, work long and hard, long after field judging is over. Thanks again, to all of you.

ON THE DRAWING BOARD FOR 1998
by Sandy F. Neidigh
Chairman, National Judges Records

High quality "golf style" shirts with a pocket and bearing the inscription "AACA Judge," will be sold at cost. Look forward to their availability.

New wreaths for 50, 75, 100, 150 etc... judging credits will be a one piece unit of a pin and wreath. The first ones

will be awarded at our Winter meet in Florida. Replacements for existing 2 piece units will be available by mail order only from AACA headquarters at a cost of $10.00 plus shipping & handling for a total of $12.00.

Publications

The history of the AACA if filled with journalists and historians creating wonderful publications for the members to read, learn from and enjoy. From quality national publications to the grassroots local region and chapter publications, there is a wide variety of magazines, manuals and newsletters, giving AACA a rich journalistic heritage.

Editors of these publications have ranged from highly accredited journalists to amateur hobbyists who simply want to contribute to better communication throughout the club. In every case, each publication has done its share to bring enlightenment and pleasure to AACA members.

Antique Automobile

The AACA grew slowly during its first year, and most of the members resided in the greater Philadelphia area. By 1937, the officers recognized the need for some form of publication to increase the enthusiasm of the members and to get them more involved in club activities. The *Bulletin of the Antique Automobile Club of America* first appeared in 1937 as a mimeographed eight page booklet, 7"x 8-1/2" in size. It was designated as Volume 1, Number 1 and was prepared jointly by officers. It did a remarkable job of creating more interest in the club, which in turn increased membership.

The First issue of the *Bulletin*

The following paragraphs are taken from a message that appeared in the first edition of the *Bulletin* -- written by Frank Abramson, president; Earle S. Eckel, vice-president and Theodore J. Fiala, secretary-treasurer.

"Since the election and installation of officers of the club, plans and schemes have been thought of to bind the members together, and to create an interest in the accumulation of material, your officers have produced a few pages of information and short subjects to form this Bulletin.

"... your contributions are the backbone of the *Bulletin*... Just look around you. Perhaps in your city, town, or county there are antique cars that you know of and men who have driven these cars. There are untold stories and facets wrapped around these old-timers which make fine material. Write the history of your own car; write anything in the line of the antique automobile that interests you. Your interests are also the interests of every member of the club.

"We as officers of this club, not only look forward to and expect that you contribute various interesting items, but our very existence demands your cooperation in this respect. Do your part and favor us with your suggestions and ideas..."

In 1938, there was a small change in the size of the publication to 8-1/2" x 11". The *Bulletin* continued to be the work of the officers since no one had volunteered to be the editor. There were several articles submitted by other members, thus starting a tradition of membership contributions that has continued through the life of this primary club publication.

9-21-88
To Howard Scotland
Tod Fiala Jr.

Vol. 1

No. 1
1937

BULLETIN

OF

ANTIQUE AUTOMOBILE CLUB

OF

AMERICA

COPY

Frank Abramson, President.

Earle S. Eckels, Vice-President

Theodore J. Fiala, Sec'y-Treas.

Board of Governors

Earle S. Eckels, Chairman

Theodore Brooks   Fred Parsons   Joseph Williams

Address all correspondence to:

Theodore J. Fiala
8 Overhill Rd.
Upper Darby, Pa.

1937-Vol. 1 No. 1: "The First Bulletin*"*

Fifth Anniversary Number

The Bulletin

of the

Antique Automobile Club of America

> "The purpose of this organization is to perpetuate the memories of pioneer days of automobiling by furthering interest in and preserving antique cars, and to promote sportsmanship and good fellowship among its members."—from the Club Constitution.

Vol. 4, No. 4 — Published Bi-Monthly — December, 1940

Minutes of the October Meeting

A meeting of the Antique Automobile Club of America was held Friday evening, October 25, at the home of Hyde and Mary Ballard in Merion, Penna. Those present were President Hughes, Paul Cadwell, Dick King, Frank Abramson, Al Hutchings, Mr. Brossman, Mrs. Rogers, Grace Hughes, Kitty Dean, Wes Roever, Erskine and Virginia White, Raymond Levis, Sarah Buehl, Ted Brooks, Paul Lufkin, Jimmy Carpenter, Mr. Weeks, Bob Henderson, Mr. Talone, Mr. Bishop, Mr. Kern, Ted Fiala, and George Gerenbeck.

The treasurer's report showed a favorable balance on hand of $47.21.

The question of improving the set-up of getting The Bulletin printed was taken up and it was suggested that the Club obtain its own mimeograph machine. George Gerenbeck was appointed to look into the situation.

George Hughes announced a parade to be given by the Ardmore Business Men's Association on October 30. They are anxious for old cars to enter and have offered prizes for age, condition, and the most unique car.

Ted Brooks suggested that we have one more Outing to wind up the active season. Mr. Talone mentioned The Dutch Cupboard just above Downingtown as a suitable place for the group to meet and have dinner. Ted Brooks was appointed to head the idea and organize the run.

George Hughes read a tentative prospectus of the Club to be used as a brief history and purpose of our organization when answering inquiries. It was also suggested that the prospectus be put into The Bulletin each month.

The floor was then turned over to Mr. Levis who gave a very interesting description of the Historic Car Exhibit in New York. He gave

(Continued on page 4)

A Message from President George M. Hughes

The Antique Automobile Club of America is now five years old, having celebrated its fifth anniversary in November of this year. To celebrate this birthday, the Club sponsored "The Brooks-Cadwell Tour," which event is described in detail in this issue of The Bulletin. On the fifth anniversary, forty-five members and friends gathered together for dinner, whereas on the founding date back in 1935 a small group of thirteen charter members started our organization with fond hopes that a permanent club could be started which would continue to expand with the years.

At the present writing our Club has grown from thirteen enthusiasts to one hundred and fifteen strong, scattered in fifteen states and two foreign countries. From our small but energetic beginning, we have grown until now we are recognized throughout the United States wherever early automobiles are discussed. It is quite possible that our Club proved to be the inspiration for the formation of two fine groups of "Horseless Carriage" adherents, one in Los Angeles and the other in Boston.

For the future we are looking forward to bigger and better things. On June 16th of this year our Club held its third annual outing in which twenty-one early model cars participated and some thirty members with seventy-five friends attended. On November 17th our Anniversary Tour proved to be a huge success and these events promise to be finer than ever next year. All during this year we have held monthly meetings of the members in the Philadelphia area the better to carry on business and activities. All this we hope to do again next year with improvements, plus the issuance of our Club Bulletin in its new form every other month. This year, due to insufficient time, we have been able to publish only four Bulletins; however, this situation is now remedied with the addition of Wesley Roever to the staff of our paper, who will act as Editor, permitting Ted Fiala to devote more time to the business end of our paper. Thus, this final Bulletin for the year 1940 comes to you with the promise that six such issues will be published next year.

As we enter the Christmas season our wish for all our members is a very Merry Christmas and a Happy and Prosperous New Year and we fervently echo the words of Tiny Tim:

"God bless us everyone!"

THE BROOKS-CADWELL TOUR

On Sunday, November 17, an antique car run of approximately fifty miles round-trip was sponsored by Clubmembers Brooks and Cadwell, with Clubmember Fred Talone acting as advance scout. Fred told us that The Dutch Cupboard, just off the Lincoln Highway about two miles west of Downingtown, was a good place to go for dinner. Sponsors Brooks and Cadwell took his advice, which proved to be excellent, and The Dutch Cupboard was chosen as our destination.

The War Memorial in Bryn Mawr was the designated starting point, making an official run of approximately 25 miles in each direction, although most of the cars traveled considerably more than that. At 10 a.m. Messrs. Ballard, Brooks, Brossman, Hughes, Tacconelli and Talone from the vicinity of Philadelphia, and John A. English from Brooklyn, New York, and his brother from Allentown, assembled in their antique chuggers. Fred Talone had arranged with Superintendent Gearhart of the Lower Merion Township Police for an escort through Bryn

(Continued on page 4)

Changes in the Club Bulletin

Due to the press of his personal business, Theodore Fiala has resigned as Editor of The Bulletin. He has consented to remain as Business Manager which is a "break" for his successor and the rest of the Staff, for we can make good use of the knowledge and experience which he has accumulated during his years as Editor.

Henry W. Roever takes over the editorship and has spared neither trouble nor expense in gathering together a staff worthy to carry on our Club publication. Theodore Fiala, as already stated, remains with us as Business Manager. Please refer your advertisements to him. Hyde W. Ballard will head our Steam Car Department and handle all problems relating to steam buggies, while Paul Cadwell will do the same for the gasoline driven cars. Messrs. Clark, Lewerenz and Hulse continue as Associate Editors, and the Staff is complete with its newest member, J. Russell Heitman, and he is indeed a notable addition.

Mr. Heitman, who is a publisher in Lake Forest, Illinois, recently joined our Club. He became very much interested in our Bulletin and made us the very magnificent offer to put his printing facilities at our disposal and publish The Bulletin without cost to the Club. His offer came at a time when we were figuring on buying a new mimeograph, and was accepted with loud cries of joy and a vote of thanks. We all appreciate Mr. Heitman's generosity and hope, with his help, to turn out bigger and better Bulletins.

It has been decided that, instead of designating our publication simply as The Bulletin, we give it a name more connected with, and descriptive of, the early days of automobiling. Mr. Ballard of the Staff has suggested "THE DUSTER," and we like it, but it is always

(Continued on page 4)

The Fifth Anniversary was observed in the AACA publication still referred to as The Bulletin, *Vol. 4 No. 4 issue dated December 1940. (Frank Abramson collection)*

Theodore Fiala volunteered to be the editor in 1939. He changed the name of the publication to be more grammatically correct by titling it *The Bulletin of the Antique Automobile Club of America*. He also changed its size to 10" x 14", thus increasing the amount of space available for activities. In 1940, the club's first anniversary was featured. Fiala held the editor position until 1940 when he felt compelled to resign for business requirements. Henry W. Roever took over as editor in 1941-42.

In 1943, when J. Russell Heitman volunteered to be the editor, the format was changed to 6" x 9", but there were more pages. The content continued to grow and photographs were added to the front cover. The most significant alteration made at that time was that the *Bulletin* began to be numbered. This volume numbering system of the original *Bulletins* has continued.

The first issue of the magazine was erroneously marked Volume 1 Number 1, but it was actually Volume 7, Number 1. Subsequent issues were marked upward from Volume 7, Number 2, thus maintaining continuity with the previous issues of the *Bulletin*.

George M. Hughes became editor in 1944, and was responsible for publishing a special issue in 1945 to commemorate the 10th anniversary of the AACA. Hughes held the editor position until 1946 when it was turned over to Marshall I. Groff. Groff was responsible for returning the format to 8-1/2" x 11". Evolution of the magazine continued, but it became apparent that the short terms of the editors would need to be changed if an adequate publication for the rapidly growing club was to be sustained. A more professional approach was warranted.

L. Scott Bailey at the drawing board creating another edition of Antique Automobile *c. 1960. (Antique Automobile)*

M.J. Duryea, a son of automotive pioneer Charles E. Duryea, replaced Marshall Groff in 1949. Duryea was to remain the editor until his death in 1957. During that period the magazine was published quarterly. The current logo of *Antique Automobile* was first used in 1949. The content continued to increase and by 1957, the issues were published containing 74 pages. The editorial staff grew dramatically to include several assistant and associate editors as well as specialized editors for racing vehicles, steam cars and club activities.

Foreign correspondents were added, most notably St. John C. Nixon who served as European editor for many years and was later named as an Honorary Member of AACA. Famed automotive artist Peter Helck became art editor and noted photographer Don McCray was the photographic editor. The professionalism of the staff and the number of contributors made the *Antique Automobile* one of the most significant journals for automotive history and the hobby.

L. Scott Bailey became the editor in 1957. Publication of the magazine was increased to six issues each year. Some issues were devoted to specific themes, such as the special truck issue published in 1959. Meanwhile, the club continued to grow nationwide. In 1960, when the AACA celebrated its Silver Jubilee, there was a special *Antique Automobile* issue commemorating the event.

William S. Jackson turned the *Antique Automobile* world on its side, literally, with the January-February 1969 issue. That was the first issue to use the now familiar horizontal format. This format is ideally suited to typical horizontal, three-quarter-view automobile photos. Jackson left the editor position in 1970 when he bought the newspaper in nearby Hummelstown, Pennsylvania.

Several years earlier, William E. Bomgardner had been hired as business manager for the new AACA National Headquarters in Hershey, Pennsylvania. This position was later changed to Executive Director. In 1970, the AACA Board decided the Executive Director had to also take the position of editor of *Antique Automobile*. Mr. Bomgardner continued to attract talented contributors and the magazine grew in stature with each passing issue. During his years, he published many exciting issues, but most notable were the specials, commemorating significant events in the club or automotive history.

A special issue in 1971 marked the 75th Anniversary of the U.S. automobile industry. In 1976, there was a special issue for the nation's Bicentennial celebration. The November-December 1986 issue of *Antique Automobile*, Bomgardner's last issue as editor, commemorated the year-long celebration of the 50th Anniversary of the Antique Automobile Club of America. The Golden Jubilee celebration had included many special events at the Annual Meeting, Golden Jubilee National Meets, and a Golden Jubilee Tour. The special issue was considered one of Bomgardner's crowning achievements as he stepped down from the position with the club.

In 1984, Bill Bomgardner announced his intent to retire. The AACA Search Committee selected William H. Smith to be his successor as Executive Director and *Antique Automobile* Editor. His first issue was the January-February 1986 edition.

Bill Smith has continued, in the tradition of his predecessors as editor of the *Antique Automobile*, to attract contributors with great talent to provide articles for the magazine. Tom Reese had been author of "Restoration Tips" for sixteen years and has continued with his series "Brass Tacks." George E. Orwig II, one of the magazine's most prolific contributors, was noted for his series "George's Truck Stops" and numbers of special marque articles. The artwork of Ken Eberts has graced the front cover of the November-December *Antique Automobile* cover for many years. Eberts also did the cover of this book, and annual posters for AACA. Keith Marvin is well known to the readers for his masterful antique auto-related book reviews. The horizontal formation of *Antique Automobile* has remained unchanged; however, there have been some distinctive efforts to improve the graphics, use of color and layout of the magazine.

Above the logo of the *Antique Automobile* on the title sheet of each issue is the modest inscription, "Dedicated to the History of the Automobile." This magazine has lived up to the challenge, and more -- it has also documented the history of the Antique Automobile Club of America.

HIGHWHEELERS

a survey of the buggy auto era

Spin-off publications were possible with some of the excellent material that has been presented in Antique Automobile. *A history on Highwheelers was written by Cornelius Hauck and reprints in softbound form were made available by editor William S. Jackson.*

BULLETIN OF
ANTIQUE AUTOMOBILE CLUB OF AMERICA

Vol. 2   No. 3

Frank Abramson, President

Earl S. Eckels   Thomas McKean, Jr.
 Vice-President   Chairman Mem.Comm.

Theodore Fiala, Sec'y.-Treas.

MEMBERS IN GOOD STANDING

Frank Abramson	Charles Hulse	Arthur E. Twohy
Hyde Ballard	Joseph M. Kern	
Vincenzo Bevilacqua	Clarence W. Letts	
Theodore Brooks	Alfred S. Lewerenz	
Paul Cadwell	Paul Marvel	
Edward Clark	Walter Matter	
Harry Doan	Thomas McKean, Jr.	
Earl E. Eckels	Frederick McKenrick	
Theodore Fiala	Wellington Everett Miller	
Albert Garganigo	Fred Parsons	
Richard Greenfield	Anton Schuck	
George Green	Morris Stoyer	
Robert Henderson	Charles Strong	
Walter Hoffman	George W. Tuck	
George Hughes	Joseph Williams	

All other members kindly return your application for membership blanks, in order to have your name appear on the above club role.

A LONG CAREER ENDS

"No one can do much but every one shud help a little. Leave the world better because we lived" — signed Charles E. Duryea. Thus, wrote Charles E. Duryea, world famous automobile pioneer and father of the American Automobile, when he accepted the honorary membership offered him by The Antique Automobile Club of America.

We of The Antique Automobile Club salute Charles Duryea who died September 28, 1938.

Charles Duryea was born near Canton, Illinois, December 15, 1861. He built his first bicycle at the age of 17 and soon obtained patents on a number of bicycle improvements. The first Duryea car was manufactured prior to September 16, 1893 in Springfield, Mass. The third Duryea car begun in October of the same year was the first to be equipped with pneumatic tires. With his third car Mr. Duryea won the first American Automobile race, a contest sponsored by the Chicago Times Herald on Thanksgiving Day 1895. It's manufacturer won a prize of $2000. Mr. Duryea manufactured cars intermittently from 1892 to 1914. After 1914 Mr. Duryea became a consulting engineer. In later life Mr. Duryea became an ardent propagandist for a number of beliefs in which he was interested. Among other things he publicly advocated community ownership of natural wealth, currency stabilization by means of a commodity index rather than a gold base, loans at 1% "to make America the world's workshop" and prohibition. He believed that English should be the universal language and invariably practiced simplified spelling. Charles Duryea's place in automotive history is assured.

Vol. 2 No. 3, 1938, AACA salute to Charles E. Duryea.

BULLETIN

THE ANTIQUE AUTOMOBILE CLUB OF AMERICA
April, 1939

| Vol. 3 | Published Bi-Monthly | No. 2 |

George M. Hughes, President
29 Ralston Avenue,
Upper Darby, Penna.

Thomas McKean, Jr., Secretary
Ithan,
Penna.

Hyde W. Ballard, Vice-President
227 Bowman Avenue,
Merion, Penna.

Theodore Brooks, Treasurer
201 S. Aberdeen Avenue,
Wayne, Penna.

Editor of Bulletin

Theodore Fiala
650 Copley Road
Upper Darby, Penna.

Associate Editors

Edward Clark   Alfred S. Lewerenz   Charles Hulse

Chairman Membership Committee

Mary F. Ballard
227 Bowman Avenue,
Merion, Penna.

Chairman Activities Committee

Frank Abramson
422 N. 52nd Street,
Philadelphia, Penna.

The purpose of this organization is to perpetuate the memories of pioneer days of automobiling by furthering interest in and preserving antique cars, and to promote sportsmanship and good fellowship among its members and associate members.

April 1939: the new logo!

419

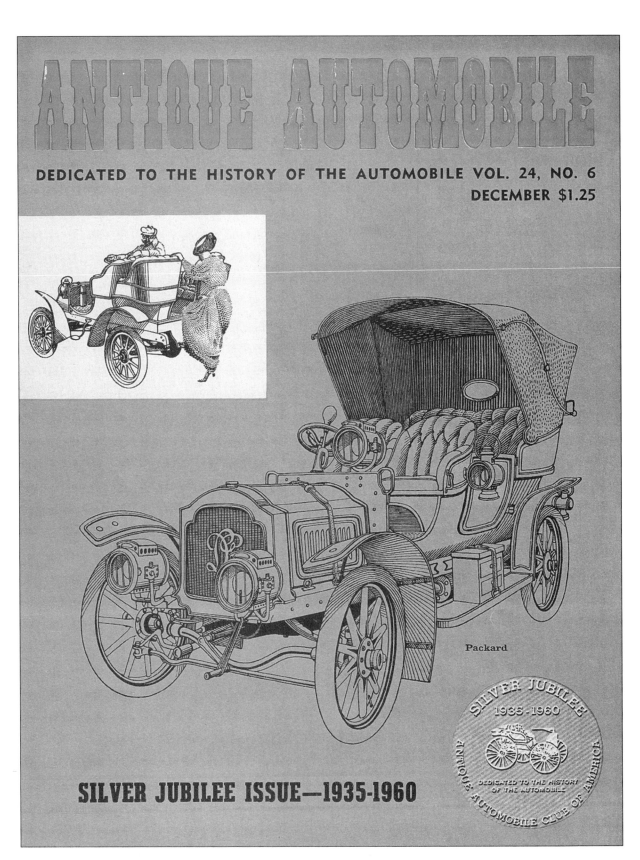

ANTIQUE AUTOMOBILE

DEDICATED TO THE HISTORY OF THE AUTOMOBILE VOL. 24, NO. 6
DECEMBER $1.25

Packard

SILVER JUBILEE ISSUE—1935-1960

SILVER JUBILEE
1935-1960
DEDICATED TO THE HISTORY
OF THE AUTOMOBILE
ANTIQUE AUTOMOBILE CLUB OF AMERICA

The cover of the Silver Jubilee edition of Antique Automobile *featured line art of an early Packard and the emblem honoring the occasion.*

1st Quarter 1946: C. Raymond Lewis and his 1903 Cadillac.

Members' Advertisements

FOR SALE—1905 or 1906 Wayne in fine overhauled condition. Complete except tires. 2 cylinder runabout, beauty. 1901 International, 2 cylinder air cooled. Carriage type. ROY VAIL, Warwick, N. Y.

WANTED—Aid in restoring 1910-11 Metz, instruction book, catalog, and other pertinent literature. Will buy or borrow for photographing with promise of quick return. Also want photos, helpful hints, and spare parts. Need especially head lamps with brackets, carbide generator, side lamps, tail lamp, shift control lever, hood, bulb horn, and four 28x3 tires. BOB ANDERSON, 324 Paris Ave.., Rockford, Ill.

FOR SALE—Circa 1916 Pathfinder V12 sport touring. Disappearing top, concealed spare wheel, excellent 35x5 tires, Houk wire wheels, new Duco paint, overhead valve engine just overhauled. Very fast and powerful. Good side curtains. Instruction book. A very rare and unusual American sport car. WM. G. CAIN, JR., 1918 Washington Ave. Cedar Rapids, Iowa.

FOR SALE—1928 Cadillac sport Phaeton tonneau deck and windshield. Original paint in perfect condition. Top side curtains; trunk cover, all like new. Engine, tires, etc. excellent. Previously kept at summer estate and used only part of year. W. S. KEMP JR., 91 View St., Fitchburg, Mass.

FOR SALE—Buick motor, 4 cylinder about 1909 or 1910. Renault motor. About 1910 or earlier. Complete with mag., carburetor and crank, the smaller 4 cylinder. 5-7.00x18 tubes in fine shape. No patches. Gasoline tank for 1909 Winton. Complete with allcaps. TED BROOKS, Wayne, Penna.

A TIP—A 1909 Chalmers roadster, running condition for sale at Clauser's Service station, 10 Miles West of Harisburg, Pa. on Route No. 15. DON EPHLIN, R. D. No. 2 Mahopac, N. Y.

WANTED—Square acetylene generator for running board. Will buy or swap for round type generator. Five inch centers for mounting holes. Pair of E. and J. flared side lamps for Mercer. Dash bracket for mounting spot light on Mercer raceabout. Wil buy, swap or borrow to have copy made. Instruction book or piping diagram for Locomobile Steamer, last model. Will buy, or swap or pay for photostats. HYDE W. BALLARD, 227 N. Bowman Ave., Merlon, Pa.

WANTED—Top section of 1908-09 Model T Ford Windshield with brass frame. WALTER BITTNER, 1002 W. Washington Bloomington, Illinois.

FOR SALE—Brass carbide generator, Gray and Davis model H, never used, top tank, cracked; two Solarclipse brass headlamps, gas, top handles, 11 inch diameter doors, good condition, make an offer. EDGAR W. FRAZER, 38 Ruimby Place, West Orange, N. J.

FOR SALE—1918 Cadillac model 57 4-door sedan. Mechanicaly perfect. Upholstery like new; interior cleaned and has all original appointments. Six good 35x5 tires J. S. RIGGS, 615 Euclid Ave., Elmira, N. Y.

WANTED—1927-1930 Lincoln five passenger touring or double cowl phaeton. J. S. Riggs, 615 Euclid Ave., Elmira, N. Y.

FOR SALE—Four "Flentje" hydraulic shock absorbers. Need overhauling. Three Firestone 34x4½ rims, ring type. E. W. FRAZER, 38 Ruimby Place, West Orange, N. J.

FOR SALE—Renault sedan 1921. Car driven less than 15.000 miles and is just like new other than paint which is poor. 8 good tires, new battery. Runs perfectly, ready to go anywhere. J. E. VANDERVEER, 26 Emerson St., Kingston, N. Y.

WANTED—Instruction book for 1930 series G DuPont; also sales catalog or other literature, showing 1931 model A Ford cabriolet. BOB GEGEN, 3160 N. W. 2nd St., Miami, Fla.

WANTED—Your want lists, send us your lists and can assure you that from time to time we will supply you with some very much desired items, Literature, Name Plates, hub caps, and all other types of Auto material. All collectors know me or should, The first in the field of supply. The one and only HOUSE OF AUTOMOBILIANA still doing business at the same old stamping grounds. HARRY A. WEISBORD, 5728 Rodman St., Pnila., Pa.

FOR SALE—1915 Ford touring, 1911 Ford Torpedo Roadster, 1909 Model A Madwell 1911 Brush, 1909 Hudson. All cars in running order. DON EPHLIM, R. D. No. 2 Mahopac, Putman County, N. Y.

WANTED—Rear axle and spring for model E Maxwell, High and second gear for 1909 Hudson 20. DON EPHLIM, R. D. No. 2 Mahopac, Putman County, N. Y.

FOR SALE—Magnetoes, Bosch D4 dual, DR6 two spark dual, DU4AB; Dixies; large assortment of used parts mostly Bosch; sell lot or singly; make an offer. E. W. FRAZER, 38 Ruimby Place, West Orange, N. J.

FOR SALE—Have 27 cars and 100 live leads. Lots of parts and accessories. Dissembled 1914 Cadillac, 32 HP Hup, 1915 Grant, 1929 Rolls-Royce. N. C. ENSWORTH, Canaan, N. Y.

FOR SALE—1918 Chevrolet "490" Roadster, needs work. 1914 Buick Tourine, needs work. 1907 Metz in good condition. DON R. BLYTHE, 209 North Ninth, Columbia, Mo.

WANTED—Rear end for 1917 Overland Model 85-4-TLH, differential marked 39 J, transmission is on rear; also instruction book for same and one tire rim for 32x4 straight side tire. ARTHUR R. WERNER, 40 William St., West Orange, N. J.

WANTED—Information - I've been given a share of Pennsylvania Horseless Carriage Manufacturing Company, Ltd., stock. The seal denotes the Company was organized in 1897. Does anyone know what car was manufactured? The capital stock is $500,000.00 at $1.00 a share. JOHN PAUL STACK; Henry Hudson Hotel, New York 19, N. Y.

FOR SALE—Motometers new and perfect, several sizes, including one size marked "Ford". Or will trade. C. F. NORRIS, 801 S. W. Plum Dr., Portland 1, Oregon.

FOR SALE—1913 Ford Touring, completely restored. Car is complete and original throughout. JOHN W. F. ALEXANDER, 222 W. Allen's Lane, Phila. 19, Pa.

WANTED—5 demountable rims size 32x3½ for a 1916 Briscoe. HAYDEN SHEPLEY, Apple St., Essex, Mass.

WANTED—Live axle shaft or complete rear end for 1922 T-6 Reo. Split housing type. Need urgently. J. DOWN, Box 146, East Lansing, Michigan.

FOR SALE—Winton radiator and shell circa 1916, Packard Single Six headlamps and front hubcaps circa 1922, brass and nickle Klaxon electric horns circa 1913, 1929-32 Rolls-Royce body cowling and generator. Brass hand pump (Mercer type), ten 34x4 tires, two34x4 rims (Studebaker). New and used motor meters. Many other items. Or will trade. C. A. GAINES, 2429 W. Fond du Lac Ave., Milwaukee, Wisc.

WANTED—A Colburn or information which might lead to one. RAY E. AMUNDSEN, 4668 Raleigh St., Denver 12, Col.

FOR SALE—Marmon V-16, 1933. Engine in pretty good shape. Body good but needs paint. No top. Good tires. Leather excellent. As is $300. J. DOWN, Box 146 E. Lansing, Michigan.

LEAD—Albert Welles, Old Mystic, Conn. has a collection of old spark plugs for sale.

FOR SALE—Tires - sizes 6.00-6.50—21, 6.00—21 and 7.00—21 SAMUEL E. BAILY, 45 E. Levering Mill Road, Bala-Cynwyd, Pa.

FOR SALE—Have access to Reo blue prints and parts. Prints go back to 1905. 10c-25c according to size. Detailed drawings of assemblies for axles, engines, transmissions etc. for models M,N,R,S,T-6 and others. Also many parts for 1916 6 cyl. Reo for sale. J. DOWN, Box 146 East Lansing,Michigan.

FOR SALE OR TRADE—Intake manifold for 6 cyl Pierce Arrow Model 80 or 81, 1926 to 1928. VICTOR VIROSTEK, 10917 Greenwich Ave., Cleveland 5, Ohio

WANTED—Source of supply for Marmon 16 parts, and literature or repair manual. J. F. KEARNS, 2705 Shorb Ave., N. W., Canton 3, Ohio

WANTED—Intake manifold for 8 cyl Stutz any series except DV-32. Also want other parts and literature on Stutz. VICTOR VIROSTEK, 10917 Greenwich Ave., Cleveland 5, Ohio

WANTED—To buy or trade - Packard and steam literature, especially anything pertaining to the 1902-03 Locomobile Steamer. A list of items needed sent on request. HYDE W. BALLARD, 227 No. Bowman Ave., Merlon, Pa.

FOR SALE—My 1915 Crane Simplex Limousine. Its history was described in last issue of the Bulb Horn. Car in perfect condition both mechanically and with respect to coach work. Have replaced original engine, which had gone 345,000 miles, with new engine with 40,000 miles. Price $1,200.00. JOHN PAUL STACK, Henry Hudson Hotel, New York N. Y.

FOR SALE—1928 Model 81 Pierce Arrow convertible with coachwork by Phillips. Engine rebuilt recently and appearance thoroughly restored. Exceptional condition except for top which is only fair. RICHARD M. PARRY, Shady Grove, Westtown, Pa.

WANTED—26x2 ¼ and 26x3 clincher tires and tubes. Also Amilcar literature and instruction book, preferably in French. F. E. BISSELL JR., 325 Alpine St., Dubuque, Iowa.

WANTED—Contributors to the magazine. EDITOR

WANTED—2 brass Kerosene burning dash lamps to fit 1913 Buick. WILLIAM R. KRAFT, Monarch Buick Company, Inc., Indianapolis, Indiana.

WANTED— Complete top for 1906 Model M Cadillac, also two 28x3 tires and tubes. Also want to purchase cars from 1895 to 1905. especially want an 1903 Ford and 1900 to 1903 Oldsmobile. WALTER BITTNER, 1002 W. Washington St., Bloomington, Ill.

FOR SALE— Motor and chassis parts for 1 cyl. Reo, 1913 Model T Ford. Also two brass carburetors for 38 HP Pierce Arrow about 1905-15.

WANT—catalogs or instruction books on 1 cyl Cadillac, 1906-07; 2 cyl Cartercar, 2 cyl Maxwell, 1916-24 Marmon 34. Also any other early catalogs or magazines. N. W. CROSBY, 66 Brightwood Ave., Pearl River, N. Y.

FOR SALE— Model AB two cyl Maxwell runabout, good running order. Will accept best offer over $150.00 F. E. BISSELL, JR., 325 Alpine St., Dubuque, Iowa.

WANTED—for 1926 Cadillac V-8 sedan: taillight, radiator cap with motor meter or figurehead, split rim for 21 inch tire. Also want good 6.00, 6.50 or 7.00x21 tires; trunk; float and rheostat for gas guage; lens for inside dome light, cigar lighter and control button and trouble lamp. EDWARD C. PROCTOR, 29 Custer Ave. New Holland, Pa.

WANTED—Electric open car, Franklin, White Steamer, Curved dash Olds, Metz, Sears, small Stanley, Locomobile or Mobile Steamer. White Steam engine and blue-print of installation of Naptha launch engine. F. A. WOODZICKA, Lake Tomahawk, Wis.

SERVICES AVAILABLE - THE ANTIQUE AUTO SHOP offers complete facilities for restoration, partial or complete, of any car domestic or foreign. Members RALPH BUCKLEY and HENRY HEINSOHN, Props., Ventnor Hts., N. J.

A sample listing from the "Last half" edition of Antique Automobile *in 1947. Note that there were a lot more "wanted" ads than "for sale" ads, and few were so bold as to put a price tag on the offered vehicle. (*Antique Automobile*)*

THE

ANTIQUE AUTOMOBILE

JUNE 1951 VOL. 15, NO. 2

LOUIS S. CLARKE, FOUNDER OF THE AUTOCAR COMPANY AND AN HONORARY MEMBER OF THE AACA, IN THE 1898 AUTOCAR WHICH HE RECENTLY RESTORED PERSONALLY.

ANTIQUE AUTOMOBILE CLUB OF AMERICA

This June 1951 issue featured Louis S. Clarke, founder of the Autocar Company, in a 1898 Autocar.

423

Ford. Model T with low brass radiator, any condition or body style if reasonably complete and at right price. Want a North-East starter generator unit, an Eiseman magneto type G-4, and an oil pump assembly with gear for early 1914-15 Dodge. Also dash type hand gasoline pressure pump and air pressure gauge for same. M. E. Minton, 26 Tower Hill Ave., Red Bank, N. J.

Float for Ball and Ball carburetor, 2¼" diam. and 1¾" high, brass with hole through same. Also 2 hard rubber covered radiator caps, one 2½" diam. and one 2" diam. Am. Bosch 2R4 magneto if possible. Dr. Paul W. Morgan, 312 Corbet St., Tarentum, Pa.

Instruction manual for 1925 Packard big 8 touring. Also old copies, 1910 or earlier, of Cycle and Auto Trade Journal. Phil Palker, Box 217, Unionville, Conn.

Rolls-Royce. Phaeton as first choice, but a "cream puff" in a limousine, towncar or roadster would interest me. G. J. Palmer, 140 Washington St., Hartford 1, Conn.

Catalogue or picture of (about) 1908 Mitchell touring 4 cyl. Need gas head lights, speedometer, transmission parts. Also need complete set of lights for International Autowagon 1911. Should have IHC stamped on them. Also side mounted carbide generator. William Pollock, 443 Highland Road, Pottstown, Pa.

Radiator, lamps, door handles, cushions for White 1911, 4-cyl. 7-passenger car. W. J. Prentice, 1727 E. 35th St., Baltimore 18, Md.

Tires: 34x3¼ up to 5 tires. I have some tires and tubes on hand: 30x3½ S.S. & Clincher, 31x4.5.5; 32x4. Want a Jordan Blue Boy restored or in a restorable condition. E. G. Reese, E. Third & S. Cedar Sts., Lititz, Pa.

Livingstone radiator, continental rims, lugs, etc., to fit 34x4 SS: tires, 2 head lamps, 2 side oil lamps for 1910 or 1911 Chalmers or Bergdoll cars. George Regn, Jr., 301 Stanwick Road, Moorestown, N. J.

Radiator, mixing valve, set of 8 tire lock rims, brass tail lamp, side lamps, and generator for 1905 Model F Cadillac 1-cyl. Also bulb horn that fastens to steering column. State price and condition of each. Bobby Ruedy, 2650 N. W. 25th St., Oklahoma City 7, Okla.

Buick 1906-7 model G or model F, restored or unrestored but nearly complete. L. W. Sexton, Box 138, Laramie, Wyo.

Unrestored car about 1910, roadster preferred, condition not important, but must be complete and located in states near Ohio. State price and information. Howard E. Shupe, 634 Garfield Ave:, Lancaster, Ohio.

Tube, one 30x3 inner tube. W. P. True, 130 S. Gill St., State College, Pa.

Maxwell, 1911 touring car. Also model K Ford 6 in any condition. Need radiator, pump, crank and year manifold for model N or S Ford; top bows and sockets for 1912 Ford; bows for 1917 D45 Buick; clock, speedometer and manual for 1914 Stutz Bearcat. Gordon E. Smith, RR 3, Orillia, Ontario.

Member Mrs. Gloria (A. H.) Chapin, 180 Long Hill St., Springfield, Mass., is trying to locate and acquire, if possible, the 1929 Rolls-Royce with roadster body by Murphy of Pasedena. Any information concerning this car that Mrs. Chapin owned from 1929 to about 1932, would be greatly appreciated.

Instruction book 1918 Studebaker. Will buy or borrow. Also need wheel lugs and 3" dash clock for above. Dr. A. J. Smith, R 1, Box 36, Salem, Wisc.

Engine: complete for 1934 Packard super eight model No. 1104 and owner's manual for same. W. Roberts Tymeson, Jr., 19 Prospect St., South Orange, N. J.

Instruction book for 1935 Packard super eight. Will buy or rent. H. B. Willis, 527 E. College Road, Lake Forest, Ill.

Touring car, good make, as old as possible with starter and all restored so we can go on 1952 Glidden Tour or any other place. Herbert P. Blake, 135 Westford Ave., Springfield, Mass.

Tires: One set (1 to 4) post war Firestone 36x4½ or excellent soft prewars of other make 36x4½ or 37x5; also tubes same condition and size. John W. Bonnell, 201 N. West St., Falls Church, Va.

Knox, early air-cooled. Curved dash Olds, and Oldsmobile Limited. Walter Bittner, 1002 W. Washington St., Bloomington 3, Ill.

1903 Cadillac, restored or unrestored. Must be complete in every detail. Please send picture with reply. Wm. E. Rowland, 328 E. Lancaster Ave., Downingtown, Pa.

For Sale

Wire wheels. Two 25" Hayes in apparently good condition, picked up by mistake for 24" (including two hubs that are not too hot). A. H. Amick, Jr., Cumberland, Md.

Ford Fire Truck: 1919 and trailer for same, in excellent condition, all repainted, same capacity pumping as when new; rebuilt motor. Harry W. Annear, 24 Warren Ave., Malvern, Pa.

Mercer. 1922, series 5, sporting, partially restored, engine overhauled, good tires, completely equipped. T. C. Barton, Jr., Dorset Road, Devon, Pa.

Miscellaneous Saxon: two 1914 4-cyl. roadsters, unrestored but complete. Will be sold together only at $200 for both cars. Ruxton, 1931, front drive sedan, excellent condition, $800. Cord cabriolet, 1937, excellent condition. 75-year old horse drawn hearse, $100. A nice piece of unusual equipment. 50-year old phaeton type buggy with nice coachwork, $50. Walter Bittner, 1002 W. Washington St., Bloomington 3, Ill.

Miscellaneous Spotlight. Phare-Continental brass acetylene, complete with brass swivel yoke, perfect shape. Generator, Phare-Continental brass square carbide. Tail lamps, several Dietz dainty brass ball. Bulb horn, Model T brass. Side lamps, pair of 1913-14 Ford steel and brass square, and tail lamp. Limited supply of brass side lamp pairs. Wm. Cain, 1918 Washington Ave., Cedar Rapids, Iowa.

Rolls-Royce, 1930 P-I Brewster limousine, new tires, brakes, battery. Body, chrome and interior good, motor little rough. $700 or will trade for classic touring or roadster in good condition. Make offer. A. H. Cameron, 220 7th Ave. North, Texas City, Texas.

International Auto-wagon, 1908. Remarkable state of preservation, sound body, perfect running condition, needs only paint, $400. Peter Reiss, Lake Placid, N. Y.

Rolls-Royce, 1931 Springfield roadster with what I believe to be a Murphy body. Good condition throughout, located just north of Chicago, $900; Lauren L. Suter, Swarthmore College, Swarthmore, Pa.

Dodge, 1917 roadster. Has California top, new paint job, new 12-volt battery, 1951 license, $225. Lloyd H. Swenson, 4044 Fremont Ave. No., Minneapolis 12, Minn.

Packard, 1925 6-cyl. 4-door sedan model 326. Very good condition throughout, 45,000 miles, second owner, original manual, tools and winter storage jacks, interior in excellent condition. Asking $300, but will consider reasonable offer. D. J. Trefney, Som Center Rd., RFD 4, Chagrin Falls, Ohio.

Miscellaneous. Automobile sales catalogs, Packard, Lincoln, Pierce-Arrow, foreign and orphan cars. Motor (N.Y.) Show issues, 1924 and later. Details for stamped, self-addressed envelope. Art Twohy, 400 N. Kenmore Ave., Los Angeles 4, Calif.

Metric wrenches. 8 beautiful, new unused Snap-on type, short handle combination box and open end, 10mm to 18mm. Cost $14.20, will mail postpaid for $10. H. W. Uhle, 65 E. 92nd St., New York 28, N. Y.

Miscellaneous. Pierce-Arrow 1925 roadster model 80, completely and beautifully restored. Cadillac 1909, unrestored, priced very reasonably. Brass side lamps, tail lamps and head lamps (carbide) of all styles. Two all brass carbide generators. 15 bulb horns, all brass and complete. 6 steering post horns, brass, complete. 3 old style Klaxon horns, motors under horn, 6-volts. Bosch magnetos and one Splitdorf 4x6 cyl. Splitdorf and Bosch coils. 3 brass clocks for dash mounting. Large assortment of good tires from 32x4 up, $8.50 up. Rims, split type $4.00. Westinghouse 12 volt generator, $5. Bosch 6 volt generator, $10. Gray & Davis 6 volt generator, very old, $10. J. E. Vanderveer, 26 Emerson St., Kingston, N. Y.

Maxwell, 1908 roadster. Completely restored in perfect running condition. Will consider reasonable offer. Howard E. Wing, 66 Pierce St., Greenfield, Mass.

Miscellaneous. Wayne, 1905, 2-cyl. model C 599 2-seater. A museum piece, restored, runs smoothly, looks almost as good as new, does 30 mph. Specifications and snapshot on request. Maxwell, 1909, 4-cyl 2-seater. Partly restored, not yet in running order, motor needs overhauling. McLaughlin 1917, 4-cyl. touring. In running order, has all original equipment except tires and battery, gone about 20,000 miles, needs minor repairs and a paint job. Chevrolet 1917, "490" touring. Excellent condition, actual mileage less than 7,000 miles, complete in every detail, needs a valve grind and battery. Joseph Wiznuk, Box 386, Stonewall, Manitoba, Canada.

Miscellaneous. Packard, 1935, Dietrich 1205 convertible sedan. Side mounts, runs good. Cadillac, 1932 V12 double cowl phaeton. Runs fine. Pierce-Arrow, 1933, club coupe. Needs paint, but runs very nice. Packard, 1929, roadster. Runs good, needs little body work. Lincoln, 1920, sedan (pre-Ford). Needs engine block welded, otherwise runs very good, news tires, Dodge, 1919, sedan. Not restored, 2000 miles. Chevrolet, 1917, sedan. Runs good, good tires. 18,000 miles. Locomobile, 1899, steamer. Disassembled, but believe it reasonably complete. Must cut down my collection. Richard H. Zacks, P.O. Box 134, Erie, Pa.

A sample page from Antique Automobile *classifieds in December 1951. By now, sellers were comfortable putting asking prices in ads. Note: Lauren Suter offered a 1931 Rolls-Royce Springfield roadster for $900 and Lloyd Swenson offered a 1917 Dodge roadster with California top for $225.*

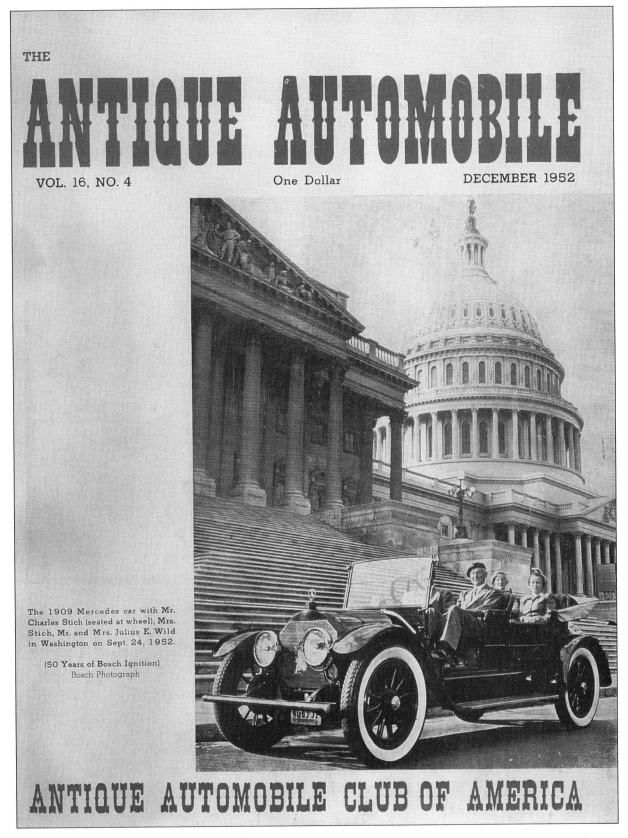

December 1952: Charles Stich's 1909 Mercedes.

*September 1953: R.J. Osher's 1952
photo contest-winning picture.*

*Summer 1955: 1904 Darracq was
featured with actors shown in the
movie "Genevieve."*

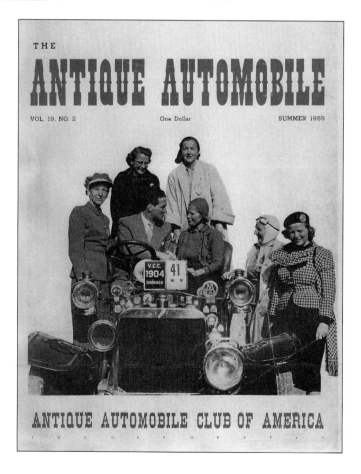

THE

ANTIQUE AUTOMOBILE

VOL. 20, NO. 3   One Dollar   FALL 1956

ANTIQUE AUTOMOBILE CLUB OF AMERICA
I N C O R P O R A T E D

Fall 1956: Illustration showing the Duryea horseless carriage as it appeared in the Barnum & Bailey Circus. It was this card that inspired AACA founders to choose the Duryea as the Club's logo.

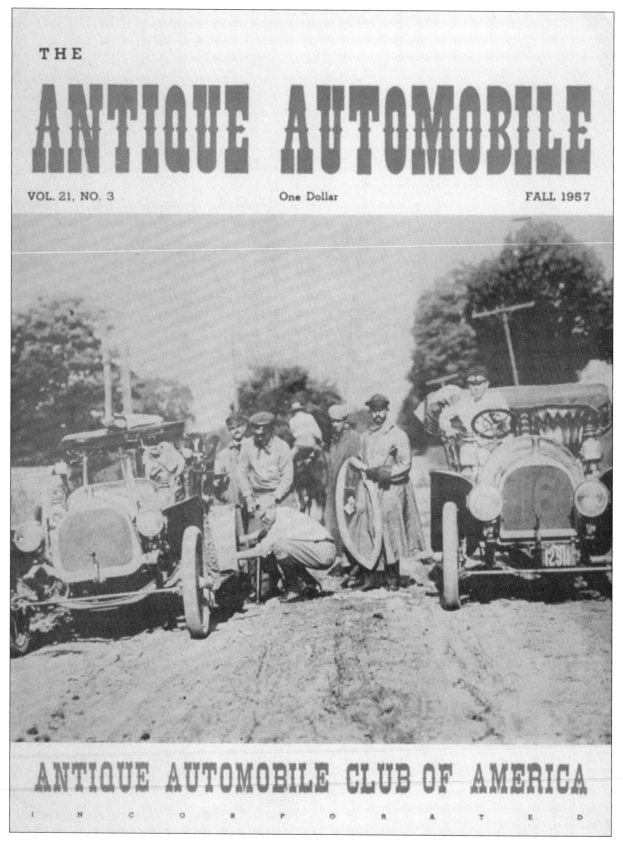

THE

ANTIQUE AUTOMOBILE

VOL. 21, NO. 3   One Dollar   FALL 1957

ANTIQUE AUTOMOBILE CLUB OF AMERICA

I N C O R P O R A T E D

Fall 1957: The 1907 Glidden Tour™.

Spring, Summer and Winter 1957.

October 1958: Special antique car rally art provided to AACA by Cities Service.

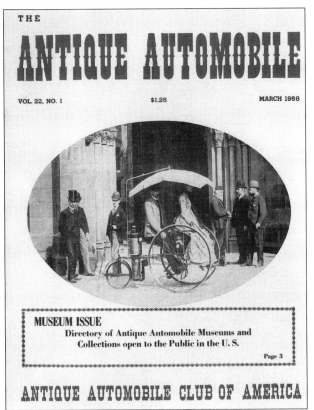

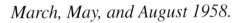

March, May, and August 1958.

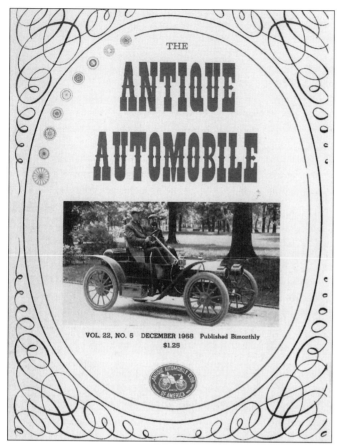

December 1958.

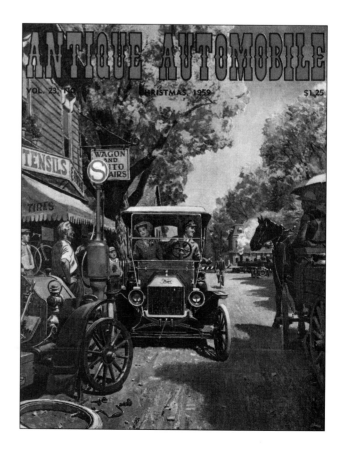

Christmas 1959: 1909 street scene painting by Peter Helck.

February, April, June, and October-November, 1959.

433

April-May, June-July, August-September, and October-November 1960.

January-February, March-April, May-June, and July-August 1961.

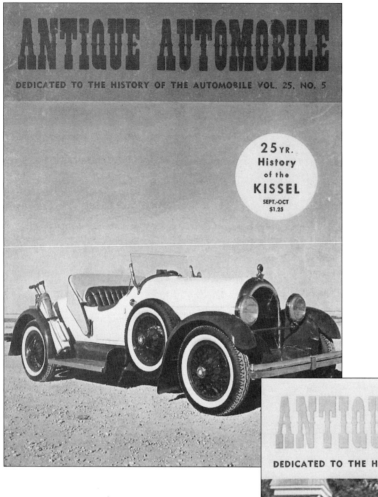

September-October and
November-December 1961.

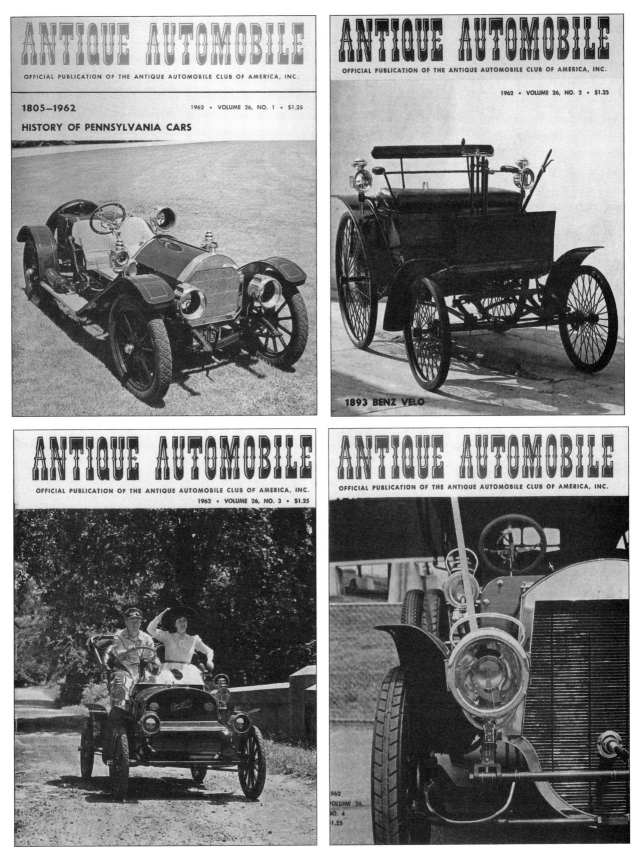

January-February, March-April, May-June, and July-August 1962.

September-October and November-December 1962.

438

July-August 1963: 1931 Chevrolet roadster owned by Jim McKeon.

439

January-February, March-April, May-June, and September-October 1963.

July-August 1964.

January-February, May-June, September-October, and November-December 1964.

ANTIQUE AUTOMOBILE

OFFICIAL PUBLICATION OF THE ANTIQUE AUTOMOBILE CLUB OF AMERICA, INC.

NOVEMBER-DECEMBER, 1965 $1.25   VOL. 29, NO. 6

November-December 1965: Jack Timmis' 1931 Ford Model A Glasier cabriolet.

January-February, March-April, May-June, and July-August 1965.

January-February, March-April, May-June, and November-December 1966.

*July-August and
September-October 1966.*

ANTIQUE AUTOMOBILE

OFFICIAL PUBLICATION OF THE ANTIQUE AUTOMOBILE CLUB OF AMERICA, INC.

MAY-JUNE, 1967 $1.25   VOL. 31, NO. 3

May-June 1967: Carl Ausley's 1904 White Model D.

January-February, March-April, September-October, and November-December 1967.

ANTIQUE AUTOMOBILE

OFFICIAL PUBLICATION OF THE ANTIQUE AUTOMOBILE CLUB OF AMERICA, INC.

MARCH-APRIL, 1968 $1.25   VOL. 32, NO. 2

March-April 1968: Roland Dunkelberger's 1906 Stanley Model F touring.

May-June, September-October, and November-December 1968.

May-June 1969: Warren W. Fitzgerald's 1930 Cord L-29.

*January-February and
March-April 1969.*

First issue with horizontal format.

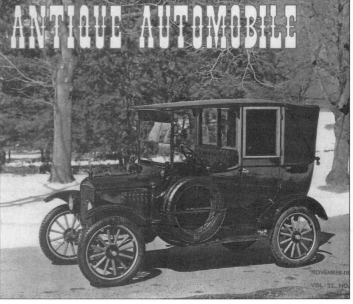

July-August, September-October, and November-December 1969.

September-October 1970: Glen Van Slyke's 1914 National.

January-February and March-April 1970.

March-April 1970.

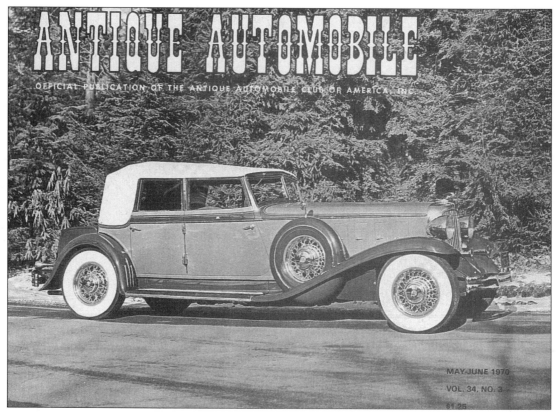

May-June 1970.

July-August 1970.

November-December 1970.

March-April 1971.

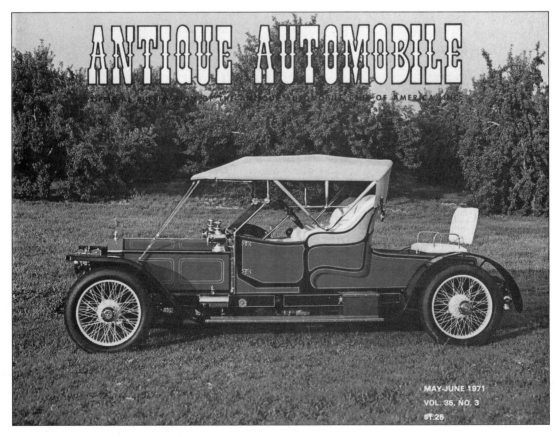

May-June 1971: Millard Newman's 1910 Rolls-Royce Silver Ghost.

*July-August, September-
October, and November-
December 1971.*

January-February 1972.

March-April 1972: Fred Rouse's 1913 Moyer.

May-June 1972.

November-December 1972.

January-February 1973: Harold Coker's 1910 Thomas Flyer.

November-December 1973.

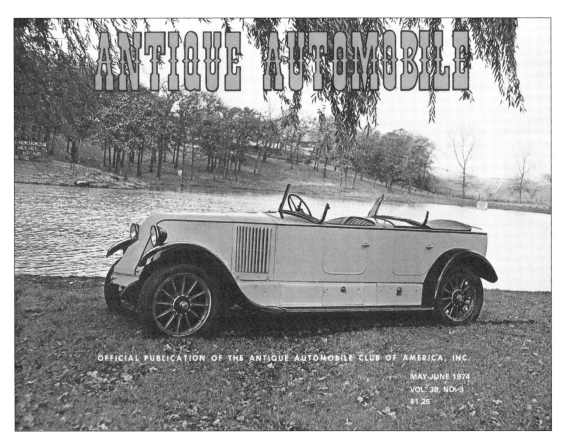

May-June 1974: Gerold A. Rolph's 1927 Renault.

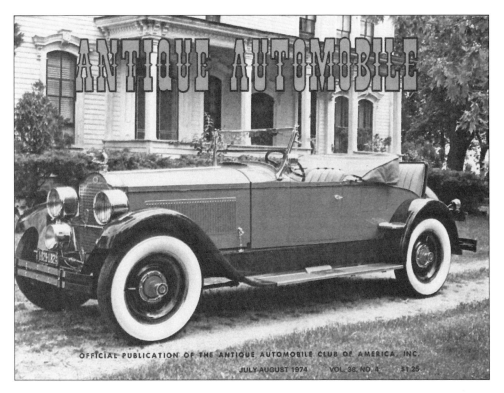

July-August 1974.

September-October 1974.

November-December 1974.

July-August 1975: Carl Starkey's 1934 LaSalle.

*January-February and
March-April 1975.*

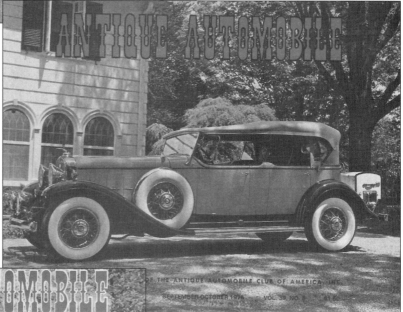

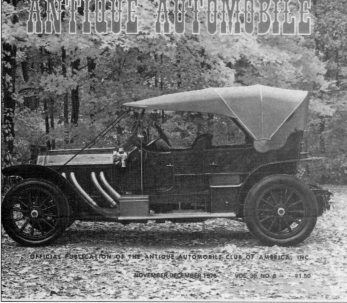

*May-June, September-
October, and November-
December 1975.*

January-February and March-April 1976.

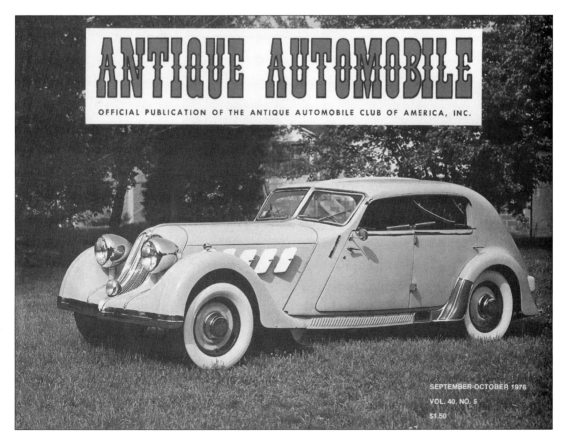

September-October 1976: Edgar H. Rohr's 1933 Rohr.

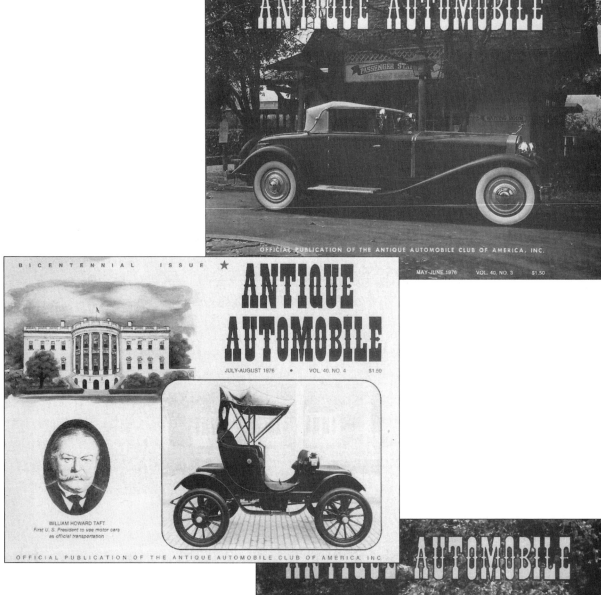

*May-June, July-August, and
November-December 1976.*

*January-February and
March-April 1977.*

July-August 1977: Allan C. Myers' 1929 Pierce-Arrow.

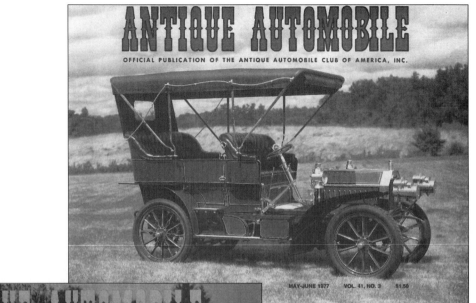

July-August, September-October, and November-December 1977.

March-April 1978: Harry B. Johnson's 1911 Pope-Hartford.

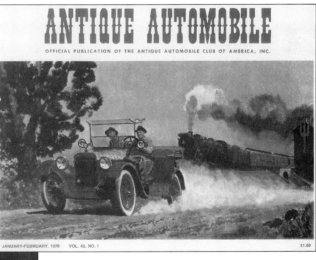

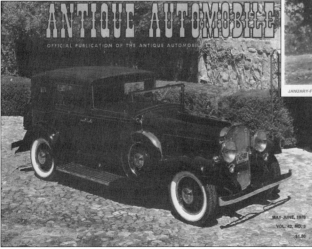

January-February and
May-June 1978.

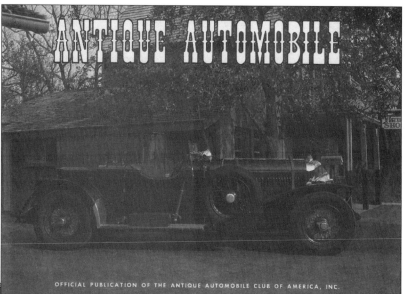

ANTIQUE AUTOMOBILE

OFFICIAL PUBLICATION OF THE ANTIQUE AUTOMOBILE CLUB OF AMERICA, INC.

JULY-AUGUST, 1978   VOL. 42, NO. 4 $1.50

SEPTEMBER-OCTOBER, 1978   VOL. 42, NO. 5 $1.50

*July-August, September-
October, and November-
December 1978.*

NOVEMBER-DECEMBER, 1978   VOL. 42, NO. 6 $1.50

January-February and
March-April 1979.

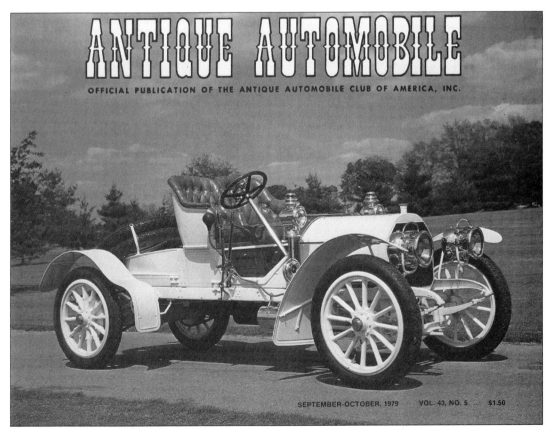

September-October 1979: Mahlon E. Patton's 1904 Mercedes.

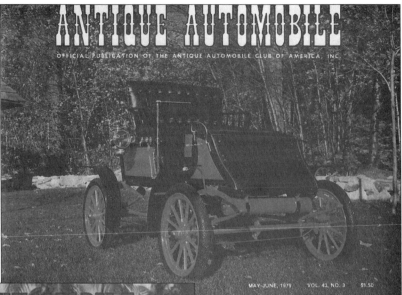

*May-June, July-August, and
November-December 1979.*

*January-February and
March-April 1980.*

September-October 1980: Lehman Mengel's 1933 LaSalle.

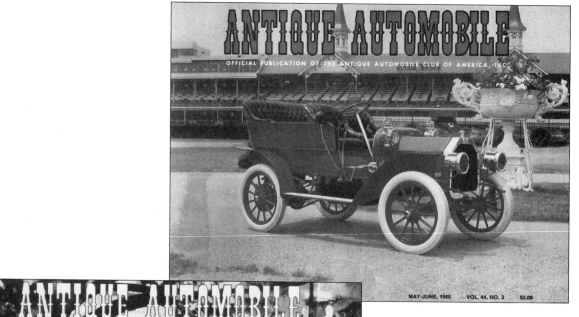

May-June, July-August, and
November-December 1980.

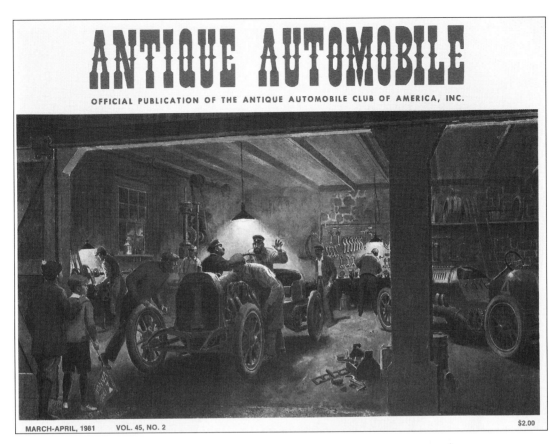

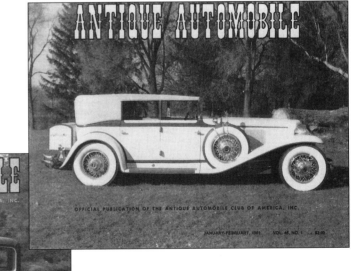

March-April 1981: Featured Peter Helck's "The Night Before The Big Race."

January-February and May-June 1981.

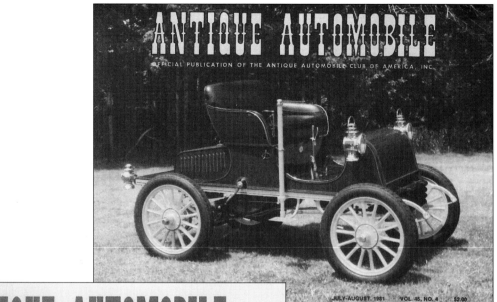

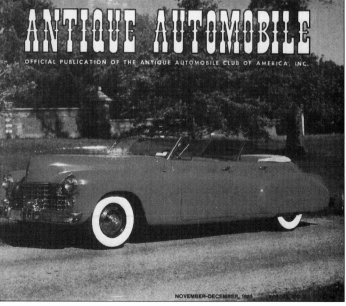

*July-August, September-
October, and November-
December 1981.*

476

*January-February and
March-April 1982.*

November-December 1982: Jean and Al Sergiacomi's 1932 Chevrolet.

May-June, July-August, and
September-October 1982.

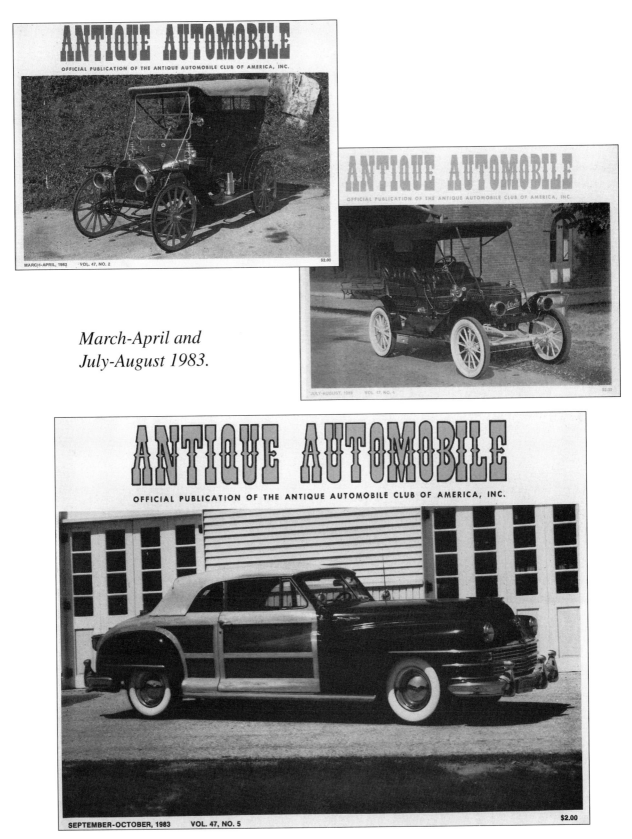

March-April and
July-August 1983.

September-October 1983: Richard L. Scott's 1947 Chrysler Town &
Country.

March-April 1984: The Henry Ford Museum's Bugatti Royale.

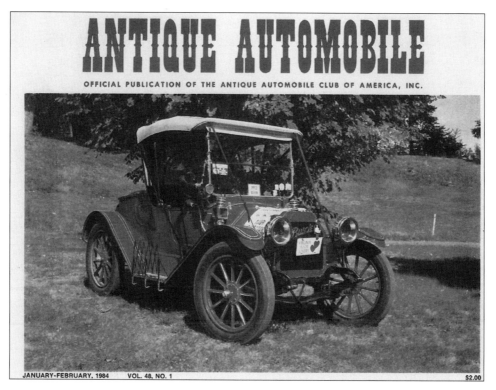

July-August 1984.

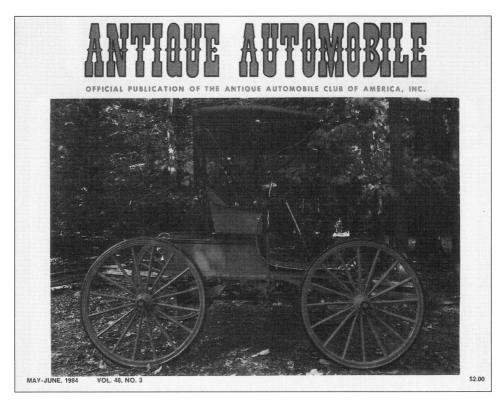

May-June 1984.

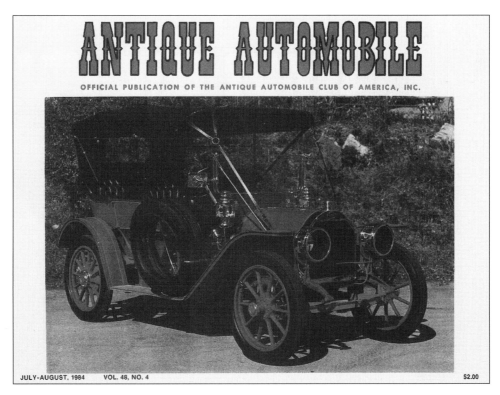

July-August 1984.

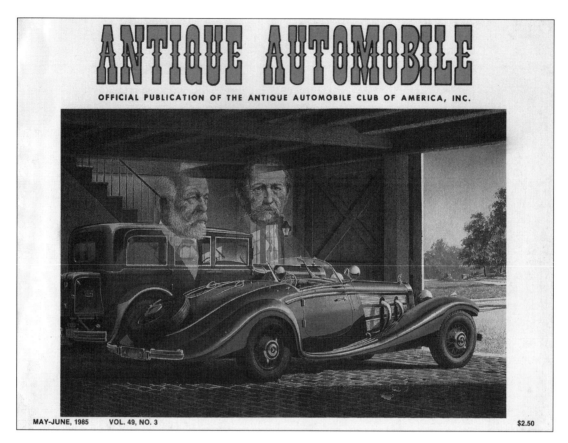

May-June 1985: Painting celebrating the 100th Anniversary of Mercedes-Benz by artist Charles L. Peterson for Richard Hoyersman.

July-August 1985.

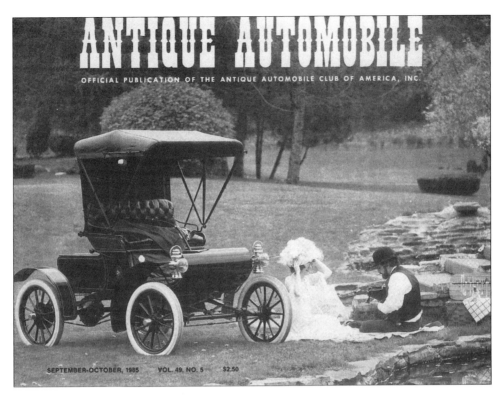

September-October 1985.

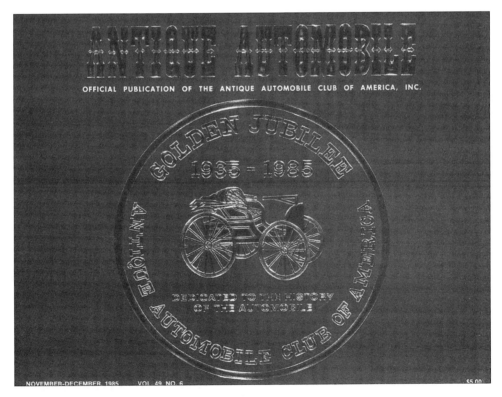

November-December 1985.

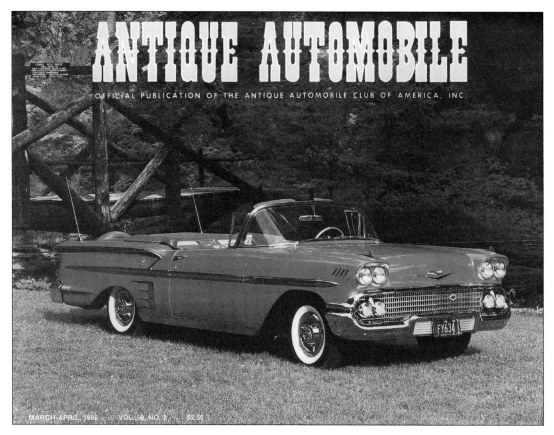

March-April 1986: John W. Larson's 1958 Chevrolet Impala.

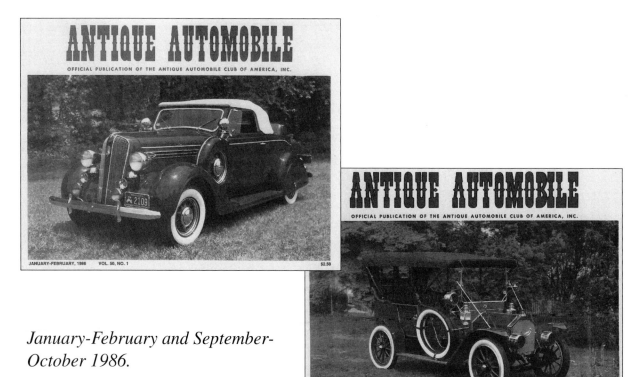

January-February and September-October 1986.

July-August 1987: Ethel and James A. Land's 1931 Ford Model A.

March-April and
September-October 1987.

485

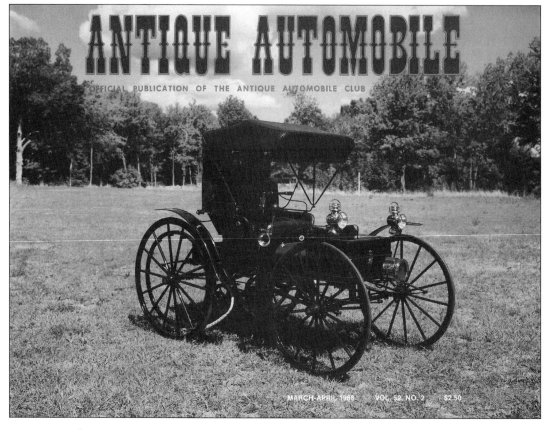

March-April 1988: Diane L. Burghardt's 1906 Holsman.

January-February and May-June 1988.

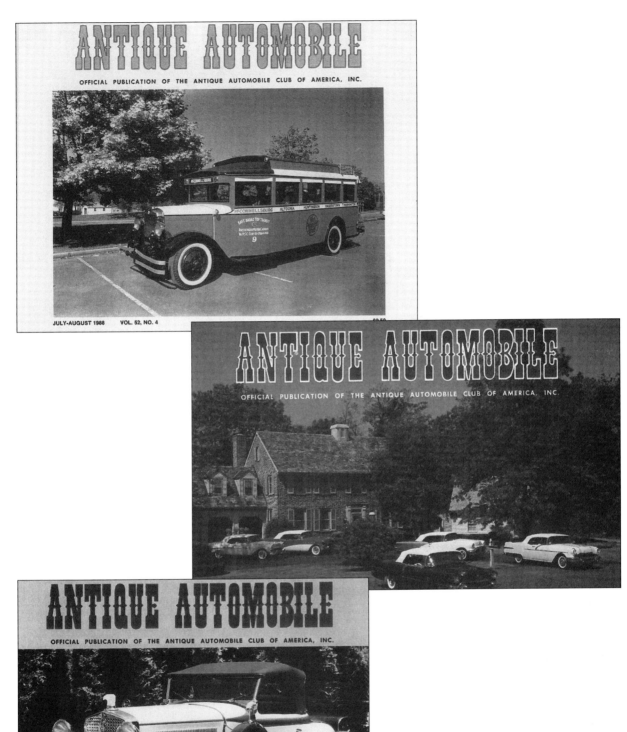

July-August, September-October, and November-December 1988.

March-April 1989: James Romonella's 1929 Ford Model A.

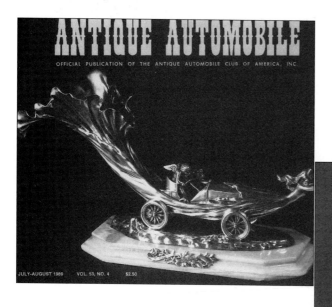

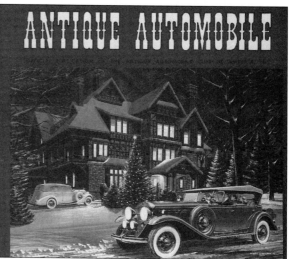

July-August and
November-December
1989.

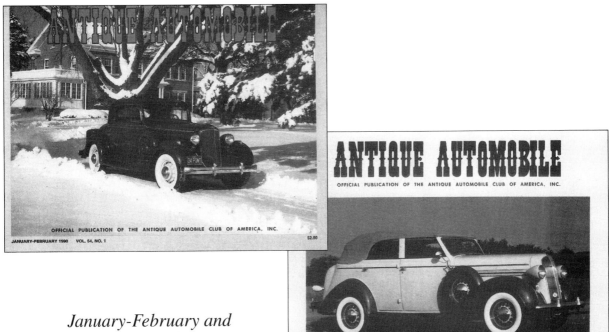

January-February and
March-April 1990.

May-June 1990: J. Stanley Stratton's 1910 Ford Model T.

DISASTER ALMOST STRIKES
ANTIQUE AUTOMOBILE

McFarland Publishing Co. was printing the *Antique Automobile* for many years prior to 1990. It had just completed printing the September-October 1990 issue, when a frantic call was made to Bill Smith. He was informed that the company had just declared bankruptcy. The entire shipment of magazines was on the loading dock and AACA had just 24 hours to pick them up before the courts locked up the site. When he arrived at the printers, Smith found the building had already been locked. There were some hasty negotiations with the bank lawyers and they agreed to release the magazines if AACA would immediately pay for the printing.

Smith managed to round up some volunteers to retrieve the magazines and get them to another company for mailing. But this was only one of the many problems to be resolved -- immediately! The November-December issue was almost ready to go to press and there was no printer. BSC Litho came to the rescue. It met the deadline for the next issue and has been the *Antique Automobile* printer ever since.

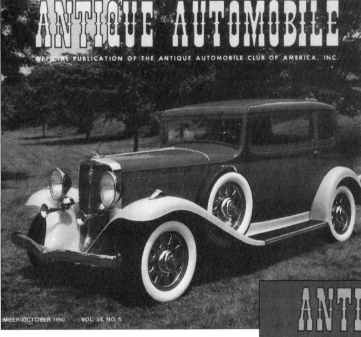

July-August, September-October, and November-December 1990.

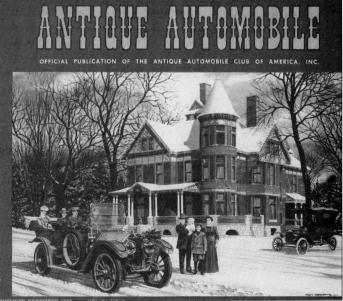

491

January-February 1991.

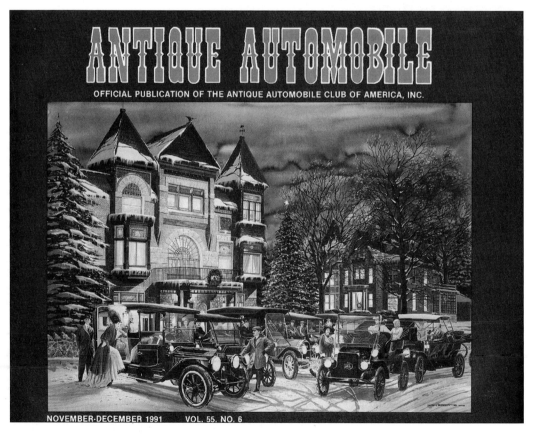

November-December 1991: Christmas painting by Ken Eberts.

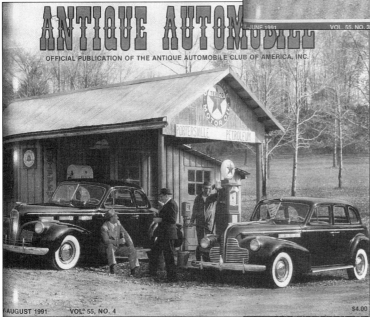

May-June, July-August, and September-October 1991.

January-February 1992.

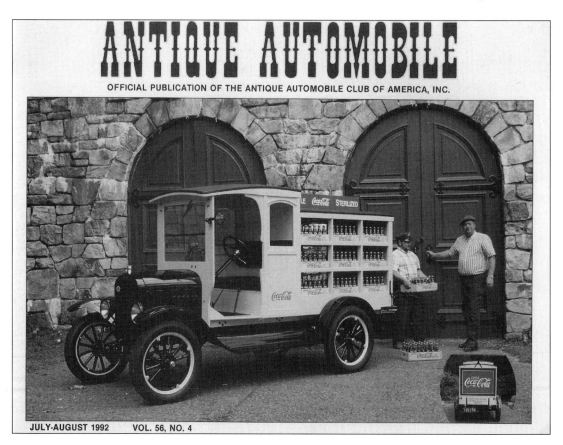

July-August 1992: Frankie Easterday's 1925 Ford Model T.

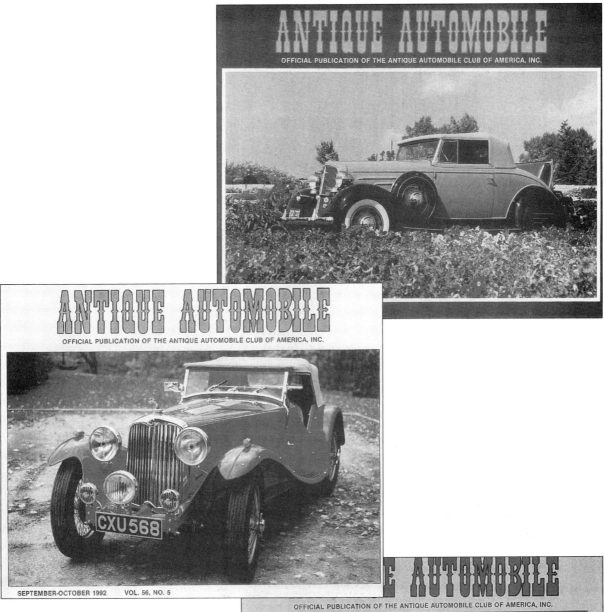

May-June, and September-October, and November-December 1992.

January-February 1993: MBNA Collection's 1929 Duesenberg SJ.

July-August and November-December 1993.

January-February 1994.

May-June 1994: Roy Graden's 1930 Ford Model A.

March-April 1994.

July-August 1994.

May-June 1995.

July-August 1995.

January-February 1996: Robert F. Kullman's 1930 Cadillac.

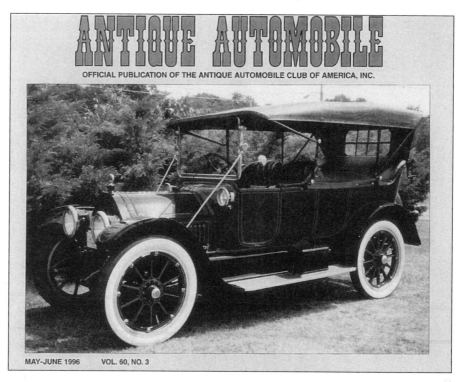

May-June 1996.

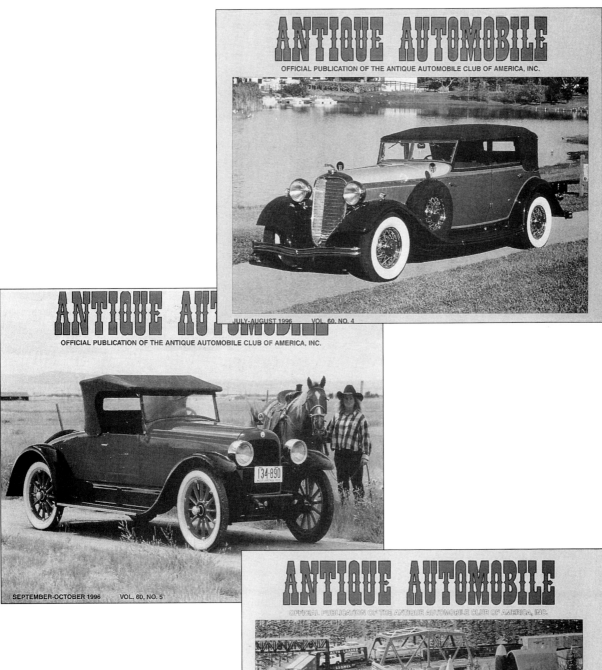

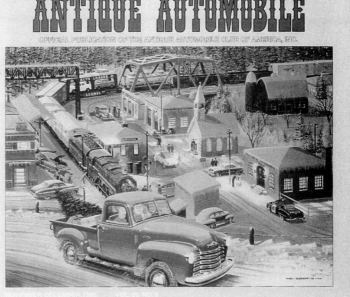

July-August, September-October, and November-December 1996.

January-February 1997: Louis R. Biondi's 1906 Pope-Hartford.

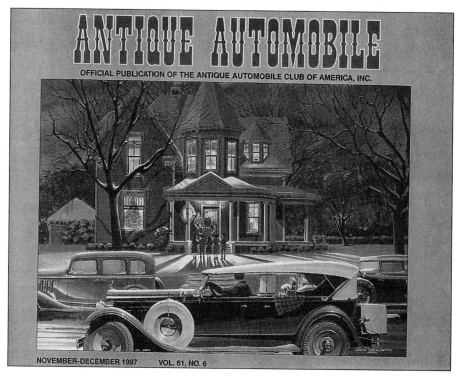

November-December 1997.

January-February 1998.

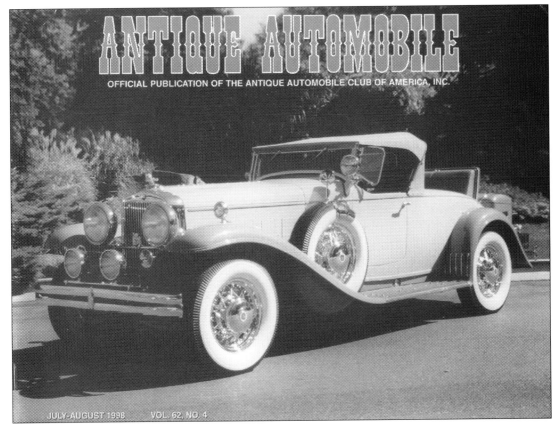

July-August 1998.

Policy and Procedures Manual

This manual was initially published to provide guidance for the operations of AACA and affiliated regions and chapters. It is a primary source for the organizational structure and policies of the national organizations; policies related to region and chapters, library and research center and other club business.

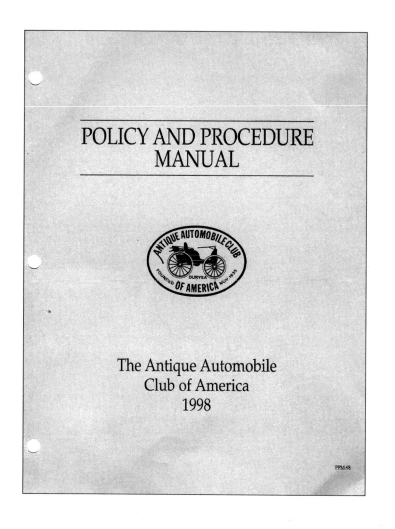

POLICY AND PROCEDURE MANUAL

The Antique Automobile Club of America 1998

PPM-98

The Chair of Policy and Procedures is an appointed position on the AACA Board of Directors and is responsible for compiling the information deemed appropriate to ensure adequate guidelines for all activities of the AACA. There was a total revision in the late 1980s to make the sections of the manual more consistent and current.

Over the years, separate guidelines were distributed to cover meets and different types of tours. Revisions to these guidelines were not well managed and frequently contained inconsistent levels of detail and contradictory information. To complicate matters, different editions of these guidelines were distributed without regard to which one was most current. In 1993, guidelines for meets and tours were updated in the *Policy and Procedures Manual* and all other separate guidelines were destroyed. From then on, there was one "official" set of guidelines.

This is one of the most important AACA publications since it basically controls the operations of the club. It is distributed to each region and chapter and copies can be obtained from National Headquarters.

AACA Roster

In the formative years of AACA, the roster of members was published as a part of *The Bulletin*. As new members were added, their names would be listed in the subsequent issues. As the membership grew, this became a difficult way to let the readers know who the members were. By the 1980s, it became necessary to publish a separate roster of membership.

The roster of AACA members is published annually. On even numbered years, it listed the members' names, addresses and membership alphabetically. On odd numbered years, it listed the members alphabetically by state.

National AACA First Junior, Senior, Preservation, Grand National and Annual Trophy Award Winners

The title of this publication, if a bit lengthy, says it all. It contains a list, by class of all the National First Prize Winners from 1952 to the current year of publication. Junior/Senior class judging as we know it started in 1952.

The book includes the year and make of each car winning the award, the owner's name and location where the First Junior was won, the year it was won and indicates if the vehicle subsequently won Senior, Preservation and Annual Grand National Meet (AGNM) awards. These awards are presented at each National Meet of AGNM.

There is also a section that lists the Annual Trophy Award Winners dating back to when the individual awards were started. These awards are presented at the Annual Meeting in Philadelphia, Pennsylvania, and the winners are selected by the National Awards Committee, Publications Committees or the AACA Board of Directors, as applies. The *Policy and Procedure Manual* contains a description of each award and identifies the procedures for determining the winners.

This softbound document is compiled by the National Awards Committee and is updated annually to keep it current. It is a valuable historical reference for AACA and is available from National Headquarters in Hershey, Pennsylvania.

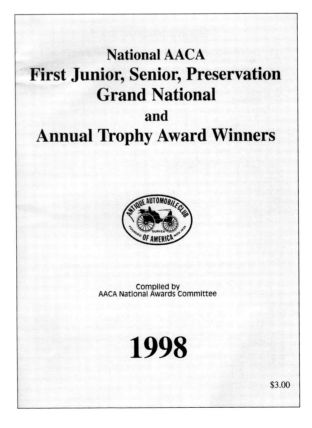

National AACA
First Junior, Senior, Preservation
Grand National
and
Annual Trophy Award Winners

Compiled by
AACA National Awards Committee

1998

$3.00

Newsletter Editor's Manual

This manual was prepared by the members of the AACA Regions Committee and Publications Committee in 1989 to assist region and chapter newsletter editors in their efforts to produce effective communications. It was primarily intended to address the needs of "soon-to-be" or new editors in the hope that the content would also be beneficial to experienced editors as well.

In a survey of AACA region and chapter presidents and editors, one thing stood out: The AACA regions and chapters that were strongly supported by their members also happened to be clubs with strong local newsletters. Did the strong region or chapter create the strong newsletter, or was it the other way around? Regardless of the "chicken-or-the-egg-first" question, the editors made it clear that they wanted more guidance to get started or to improve their publications.

The manual gave helpful suggestions for getting started if the club did not already have a newsletter as well as guidance related to identifying sources for newsletter content. It then provided hints on various layout formats, preparation for printing and subsequent distribution of the newsletters. The content was derived from a number of sources. Questions and responses were compiled from newsletter seminars at the Philadelphia Annual Meeting. There was an evaluation of the "best approaches" taken by the successful newsletters that were submitted for the newsletter contest. And, finally, there was the valuable input from Pat Locke, editor and project manager for the manual, and contributors Ed Rouze and Nancy Wright. Wright provided most of the excellent graphics that made the manual a truly educational document. Each of these newsletter editors had previously received Master Editor Awards and were recognized authorities in the field.

At the time of publication of the *Newsletter Editor's Manual*, most editors generated their text on a typewriter, used available clip art, and put the newsletter together with the outmoded "cut-and-paste" technique. Few of the editors had progressed to desktop publishing programs on personal computers. During the intervening years, more and more of the editors have shifted to computer generated newsletters, thus a revision is being planned to update this important manual.

Official Judging Manual

The manual is the responsibility of the AACA Class Judging Committee and serves as the guide for organizing the judging program for National Meets and provides standards, procedures and guidelines for AACA judges. The first *Official Judging Manual* was written in 1966 and consisted of eight pages. Since three of these pages were devoted to the Official Classification Guide, there was minimal room for judging procedures and procedures and instructions for organizing for a meet was limited. However, the manual was published in this format until 1984.

Official

JUDGING MANUAL

COPYRIGHT 1966

Antique Automobile Club of America
INCORPORATED
W. Derry Road, Hershey, Pennsylvania 17033
"America's Oldest and Largest Automotive Historical Society"

As the judging system evolved and became more structured, numerous mimeographed handouts were prepared to supplement the *Official Judging Manual* at the judging schools. The proliferation of these handouts led to confusion on the part of judges. If one handout contradicted another, which one was really official?

The AACA Judging Committee felt there was a need for a more comprehensive manual and in 1984, a new and improved manual was developed. Earl Beauchamp combined the best features of the existing manual with the appropriate portions of the various handouts and new information to generate a more effective publication. This helped organize the judging program at a meet and guide the actions of the judges. A more detailed description of the evaluations of this manual is contained in the judging chapter of this book.

Official Car Classifications

(Adopted Dec. 1951, Revised 1966.)

There are three main groups of cars: ANTIQUE cars are all pre-1930 models; CLASSIC and PRODUCTION cars are the later models. By definition "car" means *any* highway motor vehicle and "year" means *model* year.

Class	Type[a]	Group
1A	3-Wheel cars, Buckboards, Cyclecars	Through 1929
1B	Motorcycles	Through 1929
2	High-Wheel (solid tire), buggy-type cars	Through 1919
3	Electric cars	Through 1905
4	Electric cars	1906 Through 1929
5	Steam cars	Through 1905
6	None	
7	Steam cars	1906 Through 1914
8	Steam cars	1914 Through 1929
9A	Gas. cars, 1-cylinder	Through 1912
9B	Gas. cars, 2- and 3-cylinders	Through 1912
10A	Ford "T", brass radiator	1909 Through 1912
10B	Ford "T", brass radiator	1913 Through 1916
11	Ford "T", steel radiator shell	1917 Through 1927
12	Gas. cars, not previously classified	Through 1905
13A	Gas. cars, 4-cylinders	1906 Through 1909
13B	Gas. cars, 4-cylinders	1910 Through 1912
14	Gas. cars, more than 4-cylinders	1906 Through 1912
15	Gas. cars, 4-cylinders	1913 Through 1919
16	Gas. cars, more than 4-cylinders	1913 Through 1919
17A	Gas. cars, 2-wheel brakes, 4-cylinders	1920 Through 1929
17B	Gas. cars, 2-wheel brakes, more than 4-cylinders	1920 Through 1929
18A	Gas. cars, 4-wheel brakes, 4- and 6-cylinders [b]	1920 Through 1929
18B	Gas. cars, 4-wheel brakes, more than 6 cylinders [b]	1920 Through 1929
19A	Classic cars, specifically named	1930 Through 1933
19B	Classic cars, specifically named	1934 Through 1948
20	PRODUCTION cars	1930 Through 1935
21A	Ford "A"	1928 Through 1929
21B	Ford "A"	1930 Through 1931
22	Commercial cars, except hearses [c]	Through 1935

[a]Cars which may meet requirements for more than one class (for example, electric buckboards) shall be assigned to the *first* applicable class on the list, except commercial vehicles which must be entered in class 22.

[b]All cars originally produced with 2-wheel brakes, such as the Rolls-Royce Silver Ghosts, and to which factory front-wheel brakes were later added, are included in their original 2-wheel brake class.

[c]"Commercial" cars are basically trucks and busses of any kind but not taxicabs and station wagons which are classed as passenger cars.

Specified American Classic Cars

Auburn 8 and V-12	Lincoln Continental
Cadillac thru 1941	Locomobile—except Jr. 8 and
Chrysler—only LeBaron or	Lycoming engined models
Derham bodied	Marmon V-16
Cord	Packard—except 110 and 120
Cunningham	models—thru 1941
Duesenberg	Pierce-Arrow
duPont	Rolls-Royce—Springfield models
Franklin	Ruxton—only with original eng.
LaSalle	Stutz
Lincoln (not Zephyr)	

Specified Foreign Classic Cars

Alfa-Romeo	Delahaye	Mercedes (not diesel)
Bentley	Hispano-Suiza	Maybach
Bugatti	Horch	Minerva
Daimler	Isotta-Fraschini	Rolls Royce
Delage	Lagonda	Talbot Darracq
	Lancia	

Other makes of American or Foreign cars may be accepted by individual model upon written application to the Vice-President of Class Judging and approval by the Board of Directors.

PRIZES AWARDED AT AACA NATIONAL MEETS

In the SENIOR* category, there are no multiple prizes and a minimum of 360 points is required for first place. In the JUNIOR** category, multiple prizes are awarded for first, second and third place in each class. A minimum of 360 points is also required for first junior. The car scoring the highest over 360 is a first junior together with all other cars scoring within 5 points thereof. Of the remaining cars in the class, the next car will be a second junior together with all others scoring within 5 points thereof. Third junior is determined in the same way for those cars eligible after first and second places have been awarded. A minimum of 300 points is required for second and a minimum of 250 points is required for third.

*SENIOR cars are those which *have* won a First Prize at any previous National AACA Meet; these cars are *required* to display their "National First Prize" plaque. Sale or transfer of a Senior car does not change its Senior status.

**JUNIOR cars are all those which have *never* won a National First Prize.

Rummage Box

The *Rummage Box* was created by Jack Macy, vice-president regions in 1979 to improve the communications between the National organization and the Regions and Chapters. The first issues had a catchy subtitle, "A Collection of This and That Concerning AACA." This is a newsletter-style publication that is distributed to region and chapter president and newsletter editors.

From its inception, this publication had been the means by which the AACA Board of Directors and Region Committee provided important information to region and chapter presidents, newsletter editors and membership in general. All AACA officers are encouraged to submit articles related to their assigned areas of responsibility.

Several types of articles are included in the *Rummage Box*. Some are intended to convey specific information to the region and chapter presidents or newsletter editors. These include articles relating to affiliated club functions, newsletter contest information and important changes to AACA policy or procedures that apply to regions and chapters.

Some articles are of interest to the general membership, and newsletter editors are encouraged to reprint them. Also included have been puzzles, clip art and other items specifically for reprint. AACA does not copyright the *Rummage Box* just so editors can use its content in their publications.

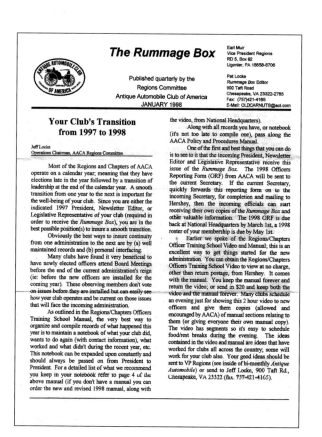

Another important source of articles has been the region and chapter newsletters. Newsletters that are submitted for the newsletter contest are reviewed and if articles are found that appear to have application for other clubs, they are frequently included in *Rummage Box*.

The *Rummage Box* was recently added to the AACA website. This makes the publication more readily available to the growing number of members with access to computers. It also allows newsletter editors to download articles of interest and insert them directly into their newsletters without having to retype the articles.

Wheels

One of the most frequently stated problems for the AACA and the hobby in general is the need to get young people interested in antique vehicles. The young members program was established in 1996, opening a special membership in the AACA to enthusiasts from eight to fifteen years old.

Wheels is a newsletter-formatted publication specifically for the AACA's young members. It is published quarterly and in its short history has become one of the most important methods of generating interest among the club's new generation of members.

What is it? You mean you haven't heard? "Cars and Their Parts" is the **HOTTEST** new program for Junior AACA Members.

At selected AACA National Meets across the country, junior members are invited to a short class about antique cars and how their parts work. After judging on show day, groups of interested junior members are formed. The groups, under the direction of National AACA Directors and members go out to the show field for a close look at selected cars and trucks.

The group is shown how specific parts of the car are connected and work together. Different models and different size vehicles are sometimes compared for a better understanding of the functions.

Did you ever want to get a close look under the beautiful cars that line the show field? Well, this is your chance. Doug Drake, AACA National Director, is the lead instructor, and Wheels will be there to catch your happy smiles.

"Cars and their Parts " class at AACA Eastern Fall National Meet at Hershey. More pictures inside.

Regions and Chapters Newsletters

Publication of a newsletter is one of the most important means to keep the members of a region and chapter up-to-date on what is happening with their club and aware of activities that have been scheduled by the club and neighboring organizations. It provides a way to dispense technical or social information, news items and other articles about members and items of general interest to the membership. This can run from technical articles to a favorite recipe. Most people like to see their name in print, even locally.

AACA recognized the important contribution that newsletters make by establishing the newsletter contest to reward editors. This contest was started in 1959 for the best newsletters in three categories based on the printing process used: printed, mimeographed or ditto and other processes. There was only one winner in each category; however, runner-ups and honorable mention editors were sometimes named.

In 1965, there was a major change in the newsletter awards. Under the new rules for the newsletter contest, the publications were recognized with three award levels: Merit, Distinguished and Excellence. Newsletters would be evaluated by a committee chaired by the Vice-President of Publications and designated as having achieved at these three levels.

There was one additional award given to the editor for the "Best Regional Publication." From 1966 to 1969, this top newsletter award was accompanied by a gift of a life membership for the editor.

Recognizing that single "Best Regional Publication" award was insufficient to honor certain outstanding efforts, the Publications Committee replaced that award with the Master Editor Award in 1970. A limited number of multiple awards could then be made to recognize the top editors whose newsletters had already achieved the Award of Excellence. Unfortunately for the new winners, the life membership gift was no longer provided.

The Ann S. Eady Memorial Award was created in 1983, and presented to the editor of a region or chapter newsletter for his/her contribution to the general welfare and sprit of the AACA. This award was sponsored by the Southeastern Region and the trophy itself is Ann S. Eady's typewriter, which she also used as editor of *Peachtree Parade* from 1965 to 1974. It should be noted that this is not an award necessarily for the "best" newsletter, but includes the overall contribution of the winner to the region or chapter as well as editing an outstanding newsletter. Traditionally one of the winners of a Master Editor award has been the recipient.

The newsletter contest has proven to be an excellent means in which to honor the individuals who contribute so much to the effective communications among AACA regions and chapters.

AACA
Library and Research Center

In 1948, Thomas McKean, the AACA's first Life Member, donated his entire literature collection to the Free Library of Philadelphia. He recognized its historic value and saw to it that the material was available to hobbyists for historic purposes. McKean was curator of the collection until his untimely death at the age of forty.

The AACA Library had been located in the second story of the National Headquarters at 501 W. Governor Road in Hershey. In 1977, the Alfred S. Lewerenz Collection was purchased by the library, which created the need for a new building. Members across the country came to the rescue with contributions of money and materials. The club broke ground for a new facility in 1985. The Library and Research Center building has been a wonderful resource for the club and automotive hobbyists and historians throughout the world. The library is also open to the public.

The AACA Library and Research Center is beautifully constructed of brick, totally compatible with the National Headquarters building it is attached to. (AACA photo)

The spacious and clean AACA Library and Research Center provides hobbyists and historians a wonderful atmosphere in which to look up critical information. (AACA photo)

The AACA Library and Research Center logo. (AACA)

William H. Smith was president of the AACA Library for the first five years. Since 1987, he has served as business manager overseeing the day-to-day operation of the library.

Librarian Kim Miller, recipient of the "High Achiever Award" from the Philadelphia Chapter of the Special Association, and her able staff help hobbyists research many aspects of their cars on a daily basis. The AACA Library and Research Center has become one of the most active automotive archives in the world. Copy machines are on the premises and copies for research purposes can usually be made on the spot. Quite a few hours researching this very book was done in the confines of the AACA Library and Research Center.

Thanks to Edward Peterson, the AACA Library and Research Center also houses the archives of SPAAMFAA (the Society for the Preservation and Appreciation of Antique Motor Fire Apparatus in America), which makes up a significant collection of material.

For a number of years, the AACA Library and Research Center and AACA Museum, Inc., have used a raffle car for fund raising. Ford Mustangs have proven to be the best for drawing the most club member interest in terms of raising dollars for the worthy cause.

In 1997, the AACA Library and Research Center saw as much of an increase in donations of materials as it did in usage. The Library and Research Center Endowment Fund continued to grow as well.

During 1997, the estate of revered member Benny Bootle donated funds, some of which was used for the purchase of a new color copier. The annual literature auction held in October raised more than $17,600 for the purchase of needed literature while the auction of parts, toys, and more added an additional $2,300.

William E. Bomgardner Hall

The Antique Automobile Club of America dedicates this building, housing the AACA Library and Research Center, as a tribute to the outstanding and dedicated service of its first Executive Director 1959-1986.

David Strong, president
December 5, 1986

A plaque inscribed with these words hangs in the AACA Library & Research Center in Hershey, Pennsylvania. David Strong was president of the organization at that time.

AACA
Museum, Inc.

For many years, the directors of the AACA held a dream of establishing a museum. Long under consideration by the club, the decision was made in the spring of 1993 to begin the process of creating a museum. The directors voted to form an independent Museum Board of Directors for the express purpose of moving forward with this project.

In the fall of 1993, the museum established its mission statement:

"Dedicated to the preservation and display of all forms of historic motor vehicles and related memorabilia, the AACA Museum exists to educate and provide enjoyment for the hobbyist and the public."

With this mission statement in mind, the Museum Board moved forward to develop and implement a plan for funding and sustaining a museum. As a large part of this plan, the solicitation of funds from individuals and interested parties became of utmost importance.

The museum became a registered, tax-exempt 501(c)(3) entity. From 1994 to 1996, the museum was successful in raising funds from many sources. The funds permitted the club to be able to purchase a parcel of land on Route 39, just over a mile from the site of the famous Hershey Fall Meet. This South Hanover Township site provides approximately 19 acres of rolling land that will afford the museum the necessary room needed for museum buildings as funds develop. A full-fledged museum, storage units, and more are planned for the facility. There are also plans to subdivide and develop sites for an AACA Hershey Region headquarters building and a commercial hotel.

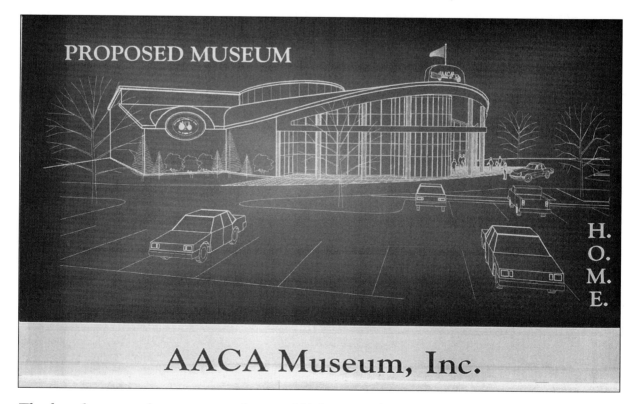

The brochure used to promote the establishment of the AACA Museum in Hershey, Pa., using the acronym HOME (Help Our Museum Evolve).

In the meantime, the AACA Museum has been receiving donations from members and friends. These donations have included everything from a fully-restored 1914 Woods Mobilette, to a late model 1965 Ford Falcon. Other gifts range from memorabilia to generous cash donations. Some of the donated vehicles are on temporary display in the lower level of the AACA Library and Research Center. By the end of 1997, the organization had thirty-one vehicles donated and promises of many more to come.

In an effort to help provide storage and support the AACA Museum project, the Canton Classic Car Museum in Canton, Ohio, accepted the 1914 Woods Mobilette on temporary loan from the museum. The museum displays the car on loan with literature about the future museum in Hershey.

While funds are being accumulated for these buildings and permanent quarters, a program is in place to endow the museum. A Museum Endowment Fund has been established and a program is in place to raise an initial $250,000. This endowment will ensure the museum's continuation and well-being into the future.

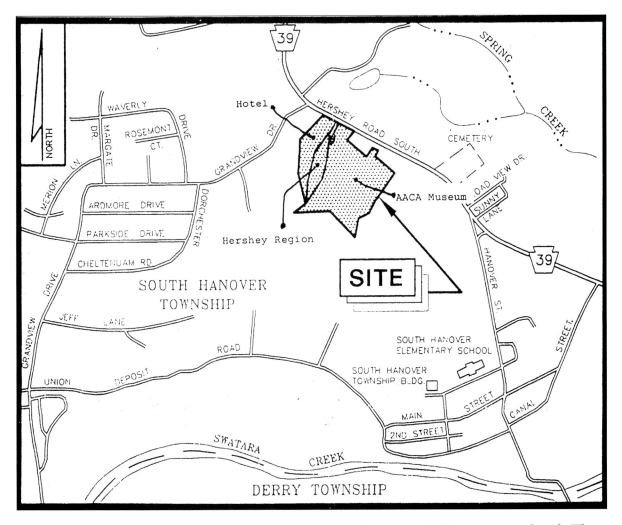

This is the map outlining the proposed use for the new AACA Museum land. The bulk would remain intact for the museum, with small portions devoted to the Hershey Region Headquarters and a new hotel complex. (The Sun)

In September 1997, an Endowment Fund Challenge was announced. A prominent AACA family agreed to donate $100,000 to the Endowment Fund, provided the club would raise a matching amount (or more) in increments of $500 or more by February 1999.

The museum hosted its third Auto Exposition during the first weekend in May 1998 at the site of the famous National Fall Meet in Hershey, Pennsylvania. The event was considered a success and a repeat performance is to be held in 1999.

The AACA Museum, Inc. is a member in good standing of the National Association of Automobile Museums, a professional association of dedicated museums across the United States. The organization includes many other top-level museums including the Blackhawk Automotive Museum, Canton Classic Car Museum, Henry Ford Museum & Greenfield Village, Imperial Palace Auto Collection, National Automotive Museum, The Peterson Museum, S. Ray Miller Collection, National Studebaker Museum, and the Sloan Museum, among others.

The AACA Museum, Inc. is directed by the club's Executive Director, William H. Smith, and the AACA Museum Board of Directors.

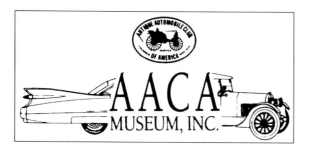

Museum logo.

Museum ribbon cutting.

Museum dedication.

Tuckers donated to AACA Museum

The AACA Museum, Inc. received from the William J. Cammack Supporting Organization three rare Tucker automobiles, memorabilia and an endowment for their preservation and maintenance. The gift included Tucker automobiles numbers 1001, 1022 and 1026 as well as a vast collection of Tucker memorabilia, including seven Tucker engines and the Tucker test chassis from the collection of David Cammack of Alexandria, Virginia. The collection also includes a 1939 Bantam roadster, 1939 Bantam two-door coupe, 1941 Crosley convertible, 1941 Crosley station wagon, 1952 Crosley Farm-O-Road, 1920 Ford Model T truck, 1941 Mercury station wagon, and a 1936 Packard convertible sedan as well as an LGB train collection, Indian artifact collection, and assorted model trucks, cars, and memorabilia.

The William J. Cammack Support Organization also made a substantial contribution to help facilitate the development of the museum. A portion of this money is designated for the museum construction with the remainder earmarked to house the vehicles, memorabilia and collection.

William H. Smith, AACA executive director, was ecstatic about the generous contribution and expressed that he, too, hoped it would set an example for others to follow in building this dream museum. He thanks the family of Mr. Cammack and those involved in the donation's implementation. Those listed in the AACA press release are, in addition to the Cammacks and Mr. Smith, the AACA Museum Board of Directors, 1996 Museum President Richard H. Taylor, 1997 Museum President Al D. Edmond, John P. Dedon, legal counsel for the William J. Cammack Supporting Organization, and Neil Hendershot, legal counsel for the AACA Museum Inc.

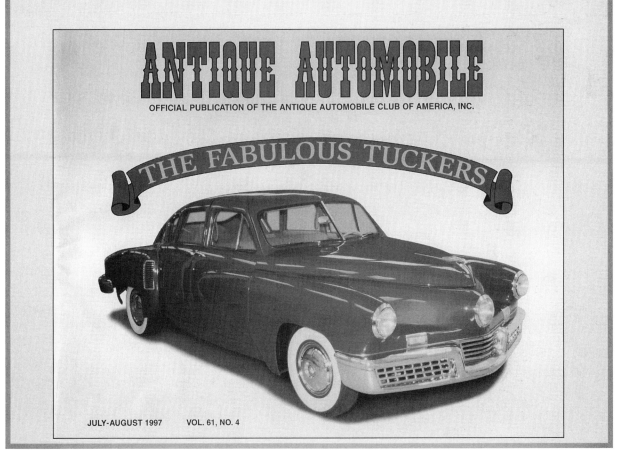

ANTIQUE AUTOMOBILE

OFFICIAL PUBLICATION OF THE ANTIQUE AUTOMOBILE CLUB OF AMERICA, INC.

THE FABULOUS TUCKERS

JULY-AUGUST 1997   VOL. 61, NO. 4

The Future

The future looks bright for the AACA. A legislative committee has established a network of legislative leads in all areas of the country. They are currently having success with communications and are responding to state and local issues.

The AACA continues programs to include our youth, tours being held include cars of our younger members, and the continuation of the "25 year rule." All point to growth and an organization that will be geared toward the needs of future car enthusiasts for years to come.

That does not mean that as hobbyists we are not responsible for spreading the word about antique car collecting, restoring, touring, and camaraderie, though. We must show our cars and share our interests with as many people as possible, especially our youth. Belonging to a dynamic organization like the AACA is just a start. Get those old cars out on the road and in front of the public so they can experience the sight, sound, and smell of the vehicles that have excited enthusiasts for more than 100 years!

AACA on
the Internet

The Internet...the AACA moves into the electronic age

The AACA was one of the first antique automobile clubs to have a presence on the World Wide Web (Internet). The club's establishment of a website came in January 1996. AACA member Peter Gariepy, of Tucson, Arizona, initiated the site and has been Webmaster ever since.

The AACA Board of Directors appointed an Internet Committee to oversee the content and help Gariepy obtain the appropriate information and documentation needed to make the site valuable for AACA members and potential members.

The site provides up-to-date information on the organization's leadership, judging, legislation, publications, and many other topics of interest. A list of all national events for the upcoming year is posted. Detailed information about the museum project can be found, complete with news of the latest acquisitions and color photos. The AACA Annual Report is also listed on the site. There is even a full list of films and videos the AACA offers on loan to regions and chapters for entertainment. An entire section is devoted to *Wheels*, the official publication of the Junior Members of the AACA. *Wheels* offers kids up to 15 years old an in-depth look at car collecting and the AACA. Also, links are provided to numerous single marque clubs for members who want information about specific brands of vehicles.

The website also lists all AACA regions and chapters and offers a free homepage connection for any region or chapter which wants to develop its own site. The St. Lawrence-Adirondack Regions and the North Alabama Region were the first two AACA regions to take advantage of the opportunity.

In 1997, the AACA website had approximately 45,000 visitors, up 125 percent from the previous year.

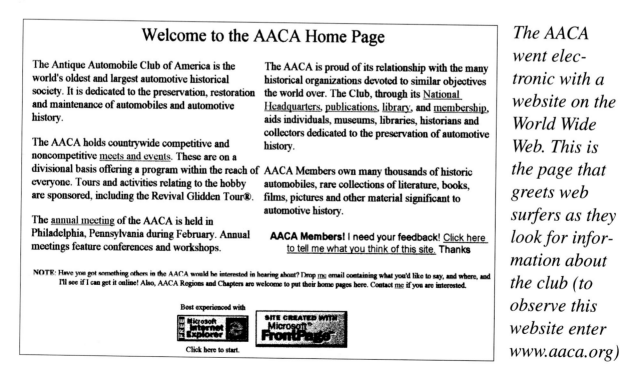

The AACA went electronic with a website on the World Wide Web. This is the page that greets web surfers as they look for information about the club (to observe this website enter www.aaca.org)

AACA
Films and
Video Program

Officers

Bibliography

Index

Please complete and print this Film/Video Request and return it to the
following :

Antique Automobile Club of America
501 W. Governor Rd.
P.O. Box 417
Hershey, PA 17033
PHONE: (717)534-1910 FAX: (717)534-9101

Film List

Video List

Film/Video Request Form

NOTE: You must be an AACA Region or Chapter President to place a film or video order.

Order Date:

Exact Show Date:

President's Name:

Region/Chapter Name:

President's Address:

Ship To: (If different)

Film/Video Requested

	Film or Video?	Film/Video #	Film/Video Title
1st Choice:	○ Film ○ Video		
2nd Choice:	○ Film ○ Video		
3rd Choice:	○ Film ○ Video		

All requests must be made 4 weeks prior to show date: Requests will be acknowledged. File/Video will be sent 10 days prior to shoe date and must be returned next mailing day after the show date. Failure to do so could result in suspension of ording privileges. When returning file/video to AACA National Headquarters, insure each iten for a minimum of $100. If using United Parcel Service, $100 insurance is automatically included. Substitutions will be made when necessary at the discretion of the film librarian.

NOTE: This form is to be printed and returned. You can not submit your request electronically.

INSTRUCTIONS FOR USING AACA FILMS

All films in the AACA Film Library are 16mm. Films will be mailed postpaid by AACA National Headquarters to the president of any recognized AACA region or chapter or to the program chairman at the direction of the president. All requests must be made by the president four (4) weeks prior and include show date. Film request forms are available from AACA National Headquarters. Films must be returned next mailing day after show date. Failure to do so may result in suspension of ordering privileges.

If the film is damaged during use, report such damages on the card enclosed with the film. Secure end of films with masking tape before mailing. Keep a minimum of three (3) feet of header on films at all times. CAUTION: Due to copyrights and regulations on AACA films, no admission charge or fund raising projects may be made when showing AACA films. Film showing time is not to exceed 60 minutes for each showing. When returning films to AACA National Headquarters, insure each film for a minimum of $100.00. If using United Parcel Service to return films, $100.00 insurance is automatically included.

To order a film complete and return the Film/Video Request Form.

1. 1948 GLIDDEN TOUR™ - Filmed by Tydol. Color, Silent, 25 minutes.
2. 1951 GLIDDEN TOUR™ - Filmed by Gulf Oil. B&W, Sound, 10 minutes.
3. MAKE WAY FOR YESTERDAY - VMCCA Silver Jubilee Rally 1955, filmed by Regent Oil Company. Color, Sound, 40 minutes.
4. GOGGLES AND GAUNTLETS - 1953 Glidden Tour™, filmed by Firestone Tire & Rubber Company. Color, Sound, 15 minutes.
5. LEST WE FORGET - filmed by General Motors Corporation. Opens with first auto show. Lively comedy in antique autos. B&W, Sound, 15 minutes.
6. VINTAGE CAR FILM - 1954 Anglo-American Car Rally. B&W. Sound, 15 minutes.
7. HEY! GET A HORSE! - 6th Annual Hamilton-Fairfield Parade Exhibition, 1960. Gift of Antique & Classic Car Club of Butler County. Color, Silent, 20 minutes.
8. 1956 VMCCA GLIDDEN TOUR™ AT FRENCH LICK, NC. - Filmed by Leonard Rhinehart. Color, Silent, 20 minutes.
9. 1957 GLIDDEN TOUR™ FROM ROANOKE, VA. TO HERSHEY - Filmed by Leonard Rhinehart. Color, Silent, 20 minutes.
10. THRU A REAR-VIEW MIRROR - 1957 Glidden Tour™, filmed by Firestone Tire & Rubber Company, Color, Sound, 20 minutes.
11. ORMOND BEACH ANTIQUE CAR SHOW - Gift to "The Birth Place of Speed," 1960 Antique Car Show. Color, Sound, 12 minutes.
12. TOURING 'ROUND TAHOE - HCCA 1960 Tour. Gift to AACA by Horseless Carriage Club of America. Color, Sound, 35 minutes.
13. 1958 VMCCA GLIDDEN TOUR™ IN NEW ENGLAND - Including Lake Forest AACA Meet and Virginia Meet of Classic Car Club, filmed by Leonard Rhinehart. Color. Silent, 45 minutes.
14. 1959 GLIDDEN TOUR™ FROM CINCINNATI TO DETROIT - Consists of three films, each of which shows the entire tour. Color, Silent, one hour.
15. 1959 AACA LONDON TO BRIGHTON ENTRY - Central Park competition and Brighton Run in England by official U.S. entry. Color. Silent, 15 minutes.
16. 1960 BRIGHTON ELIMINATION TRIALS AT HERSHEY - Filmed by Mrs. William Klein, Jr. Color, Silent, 15 minutes.
17. 1905 THE FIRST GLIDDEN TOUR™ - B&W, Silent, 12 minutes.
18. THE FIRST INDIANAPOLIS 500 - B&W, Silent, 12 minutes.
19. 1960 SCOTTISH VETERAN CAR RALLY - Gift of National Benzole Company, Ltd. Color, Sound, 20 minutes.

20. AACA EUROPEAN TRIP & RUN - Filmed by Leonard Rhinehart. Color, Silent, 30 minutes.
21. THE THREE POINTED STAR - History of Mercedes Daimler, Benz Company from 1885 to date, Grand Prix Races, factory production of present Mercedes cars. Gift of Mercedes Benz. Color, Sound, 35 minutes.
22. 1964 GLIDDEN TOUR™ - Filmed by Conoco Gas at Pikes Peak, Colorado. B&W, Sound, 30 minutes.
23. BEAUTY IN TRUST - Gift of National Benzole Company, Ltd. Views of English homes and castles. Color, Sound, 20 minutes
24. SAFETY FIRST - A gift of Mercedes Benz. How to drive safely shows results of accidents in Mercedes testing. B&W, Sound, 12 minutes.
25. 1964 GETTYSBURG SPRING MEET - Filmed by John A. Brown. Color, Sound, 16 minutes.
26. RACELAND - Framingham; Massachusetts & New York World's Fair 1940 VMCCA day. B&W, Silent, 20 minutes.
27. MONTAGUE MUSEUM - Official opening of the museum in England. Color, Sound, 20 minutes.
28. LET'S GO GLIDDEN IN 1965 - Filmed by Robert Buckley in Virginia and West Virginia. Color, 45 minutes.
29. BLOW YOUR HORN - 1966 Reno Tour. Gift of Horseless Carriage Club through Bill Harrah, a Mike Roberts production. Color, Sound, 45 minutes.
31. THE AMERICAN ROAD - History of Ford Motor Company from first car through the "Ts" till today. Donation of a permanent loan from Ford Company. B&W, Sound, 40 minutes.
32. 1909 AUTO RACE - Along with re-run 50 years later. Donation of a permanent loan from Ford Company. Color, Sound, 20 minutes.
33. HORSES TO HORSEPOWER - History of Flint, Michigan from carriages to cars of today. History of G.M. B&W, Sound, 60 minutes.
34. 1966 AACA EUROPEAN TOUR - By Richard Minnick. AACA tour in Europe back of Iron Curtain. Color, Silent, 50 minutes.
35. 1967 GLIDDEN TOUR™ - In Michigan by Richard Minnick. 1967 Glidden as traveled through Michigan. Color, Silent, 40 minutes. AACA film.
36. 1967 GLIDDEN TOUR™ - In Michigan as filmed by WKYC-TV station. Color. Sound, 20 minutes.
37. 1947 FALL OUTING AACA - Devon, Pennsylvania. Color, Silent, 15 minutes.
38. FIRST MOVIES OF AACA MEETS - 1939 Meet in Marion - First Annual Banquet at Bookbinders, Philadelphia. Color, Silent, 20 minutes.
39. 1949 GLIDDEN TOUR™ - An Indianapolis review. Color, Silent, 20 minutes.
40. GADGETS GALORE - Early auto history. B&W, Sound, 12 minutes.
41. 1900 AUTO PARADE - 1901 CONEY ISLAND PARADE - 1904 ORMOND BEACH FLORIDA RACE - 1904 VANDERBILT CUP RACE - 1904 MT. WASHINGTON HILL CLIMB. B&W. Silent, 25 minutes.
42. HISTORY ON WHEELS - From carriages through to today. B&W, Sound, 15 minutes.
43. AUTO BIOGRAPHY - A 20th Century Production of CBS narrated by Walter Cronkite (Auto History from the start). B&W, Sound, 30 minutes.
44. MERRILY WE ROLL ALONG - With Groucho Marx, an NBC-TV production, early auto history through changing America till today along with comedy. B&W, Sound, 55 minutes.
45. OUR OLD CAR - Family cars from 1905 to 1936, MGM Production. B&W, Sound, 12 minutes.
46. 1950-51 DEVON MEET - 1951 YORKLYN DELAWARE MEET - By Stanley Wilkinson. Color, Silent, 20 minutes.
47. 1951 POTTSTOWN MEET - OLD DOMINION MEET - WAYNESBORO 1954 - By Stanley Wilkinson. Color, Silent, 20 minutes.
48. HOW TO PHOTOGRAPH ANTIQUE CARS - 35mm slides of antique cars, showing how to photograph them.
49. STYLING AND THE EXPERIMENTAL CAR - By Ford Motor Company. Color, Sound, 20 minutes.
50. 1969 GLIDDEN TOUR™ IN TENNESSEE - By Roland Dunkelberger and Ray Campbell. Color, Silent, 60 minutes.
51. TWO TARS - Laurel & Hardy. Two sailors rent a Model T and wreck about every car in sight. B&W, Silent, 30 minutes.

52. BARNEY OLDFIELD'S RACE FOR A LIFE - Ford Sterling, Mack Sennett & Oldfield. B&W, Silent, 12 minutes.
53. ALL WET - Charlie Chase comedy. B&W, Silent, 15 minutes.
54. NON-SKID KID - Eddie Boland. B&W. Silent. 15 minutes.
55. CALIFORNIA OR BUST - Snub Pollard. B&W, Silent, 30 minutes.
56. STEPPING ON THE GAS - Milburn Morante. B&W, Silent, 30 minutes.
57. A WEEK END DRIVER - A hair raising chase with airplanes and flivvers. B&W, Silent, 15 minutes.
58. THE RECKLESS DRIVER - Woody Woodpecker Cartoon. B&W, Sound. 8 minutes.
59. WANDERING WILLIES - Andy Clyde. B&W, Silent, 30 minutes.
60. THE FIREMAN - Charlie Chaplin. B&W, Silent, 30 minutes.
61. A TWO CYLINDER ROMANCE - Billie Rhodes. B&W, Silent, 15 minutes.
62. LOVE, SPEED AND THRILLS - Chester Conklin. B&W. Silent, 15 minutes.
63. HAVE BADGE, WILL CHASE - Abbott and Costello. B&W, Sound, 10 minutes.
64. BIG BUSINESS - Laurel & Hardy selling Christmas trees from a Model T. B&W. Silent, 30 minutes.
65. CHAMPS OF THE CHASE - Abbott and Costello. B&W, Sound, 8 minutes.
66. DOUBLE WHOOPEE - Laurel & Hardy as Hotel Footman and Doorman. B&W. Silent, 30 minutes.
67. WIFE AND AUTO TROUBLE - Willie Coller who takes the secretary out in a new T. B&W, Silent, 15 minutes.
68. HURRY/HURRY - W. C. Fields in the maddest motorcar merrymaking ever filmed. B&W, Sound, 8 minutes.
69. ROARING WHEELS - Shows building and operating miniature race cars, Soap Box Derby and early racing cars. B&W, Sound, 8 minutes.
70. T'WAS HENRY'S FAULT - How mass production of the T changed things. B&W, Silent, 20 minutes.
71. YESTERDAY LIVES AGAIN - Shows Wright Brothers, San Francisco earthquake, Lillian Russell and Buffalo Bill. B&W, Sound, 8 minutes.
72. THE GREAT CHASE - W.C. Fields drives a get-away car for a pair of bank robbers in a madcap escape. B&W, Sound, 8 minutes.
73. THE DESPERATE SCOUNDREL - Ford Sterling and Keystone Cops, comedy. B&W, Silent, 30 minutes.
74. THRILLS ON WHEELS - An amazing hair raising picture. B&W, Sound, 8 minutes.
75. AUTO INTOXICATION - Ford Sterling. What happens when you buy an auto. B&W, Sound, 15 minutes.
76. TEDDY AT THE THROTTLE - Gloria Swanson and Wallace Berry. Hero rescues heroine from railroad tracks, auto chases, close calls with trains. B&W, Silent, 35 minutes.
77. THE 13TH ALARM - Chester Conklin, as a member of fire company who even starts a fire. B&W, Sound, 16 minutes.
78. THE MUSIC BOX - Laurel & Hardy. Their funniest comedy, all about delivering a new piano on top of a hill. B&W, Sound, 35 minutes.
79. GAY NINETIES LIVE AGAIN - 90's highlights. B&W, Sound, 20 minutes.
80. BUSY BODIES - Laurel & Hardy comedy in which their T finally ends up by being sawed in two. B&W, Sound, 20 minutes.
81. MEET THE SENATOR - Heinie Conklin. A Mack Sennett comedy ends with a car chase. B&W, Sound, 20 minutes.
82. THE MESSENGER BOY - A Benny Rubin comedy, real action. B&W, Sound, 20 minutes.
83. HOG WILD - Laurel & Hardy comedy. Trying to put up an aerial when the ladder gets stuck on a T and the fun starts. B&W, Sound, 20 minutes.
84. HOT ROD HUCKSTER - A Woody Woodpecker cartoon. B&W, Sound, 10 minutes.
85. THE LION TAMER - Amos and Andy in the circus. B&W, Sound, 10 minutes.
86. OUR DAREDEVIL CHIEF - Ford Sterling as chief of Keystone Kops. B&W, Silent, 20 minutes.
87. A JITNEY ELOPEMENT - Just that in a Model T. B&W, Silent, 25 minutes.
89. ONE GOOD TURN - Laurel & Hardy off to see America in a Model T. B&W, Sound, 20 minutes.
90. MIDNIGHT PATROL - Laurel & Hardy as policemen on night squad car duty. B&W, Sound, 20 minutes.
91. THE SPEED KINGS - Early auto racing. B&W, Sound, 10 minutes.

92. HOLLYWOOD OR BUST - Abbott & Costello. B&W, Sound, 10 minutes.
93. YOSEMITE NATIONAL PARK - By Ford Motor Company Tour through the park. Color, Sound, 20 minutes.
94. AIKAI IKES AUTO - Horse. car comedy. B&W, Silent, 20 minutes.
95. ON THE WRONG TREK - What happens when you take your mother-in-law on your vacation in the old car. B&W, Sound, 20 minutes.
96. SUPER-HOOPER-DYNE-LIZZIES - A Mack Senett comedy when radio controlled Model T's take over. B&W, Silent, 25 minutes.
97. TOUR KENTUCKY TOUR - Filmed and donated by Widen DuRand III, 1969 Model T tour through Kentucky. Color, Sound, 25 minutes.
98. THE CHANGING ARCHITECTURE OF THE AUTOMOBILE BODY - A GM production showing the changing of early body style of cars, sport cars and special bodies. Color, Sound, 30 minutes.
99. PERFECT DAY - Laurel & Hardy comedy when the family goes on a Sunday outing in the T. B&W, Sound, 20 minutes.
100. SCENES OF THE 68 GLIDDEN IN VERMONT AND 69 STEAM MEET IN CAPE COD - Color, Silent, 20 minutes. Donated to AACA.
101. FLIGHT OF THE ARROW - Story of the 1933 V-12 Pierce Arrow Roadster, 24 hour run in salt flats at Bonneville. 45 minutes, B&W, Sound.
102. 1970 AACA SPRING MEET AT CHAPEL HILL, N.C. - 20 minutes, B&W, and Color, Silent. Can be used on single drive sprocket (sound) projectors only.
103. LIZZIES OF THE FIELD - An early auto race that is really wild. B&W, Silent, 20 minutes.
104. LOVE, LOOT AND CRASH - When the cook is tired and the crooks take over the Model T race is on. B&W, Silent, 25 minutes.
105. THE HOOSEGOW - Laurel & Hardy get started when arrested during prohibition. B&W, Sound, 20 minutes.
106. COUNTY HOSPITAL - Laurel & Hardy comedy. An accident starts it all. B&W, Sound. 20 minutes.
107. THE 3 SPRING MEETS OF 1971 - (75th Anniversary Year) By Roland Dunkelberger. Color, Silent, 20 minutes.
108. DAYTONA BEACH ANTIQUE CAR MEET - Color, Sound, 20 minutes.
109. BLOTTO - Laurel & Hardy comedy. How to step out on your wife and what she does to your T. B&W, Sound, 30 minutes.
110. AN AUTO NUT - Sid and Paul comedy. How to get your wife a new car. B&W, silent, 15 minutes.
111. THE BLACKSMITH - Buster Keaton comedy. Ruins the good old cars. B&W, Silent, 30 minutes.
112. CHICKENS COME HOME - Laurel & Hardy comedy. The past will catch up with you and trouble begins. B&W, Sound, 30 minutes.
113. WILBER SHOWS AUTO RACING HISTORY - B&W, Sound, 20 minutes.
114. DON'T PARK HERE - Charlie Dorety shows how to start the old cars, comedy. B&W, Silent, 30 minutes.
115. IF I HAD A MILLION - Comedy W. C. Fields takes that million, buys old cars and demolishes them. B&W, Sound, 10 minutes.
116. YOUNG OLDFIELD - And his racing career. B&W, Silent. 10 minutes.
117. BOB'S BUSY DAY - Bob Hope with his problems with old cars and girls, comedy. B&W. Sound, 10 minutes.
118. HOBOKEN TO HOLLYWOOD - Billy Beven and Vernon Dent comedy. Cross country trip in a 1922 Essex and mobile home, plus a short on Hollywood today (1920 that is). B&W, Silent. 20 minutes.
119. TAXI TRIANGLE - With Jack Benny, comedy. How to get married and divorced while waiting for the light to change. B&W, Sound, 10 minutes.
120. BREEZING ALONG - Lloyd Hamilton as the chauffeur who does it all wrong comedy. B&W, Silent, 25 minutes.
121. CALIFORNIA BOUND - W. C. Fields comedy when he heads west to his orange grove oasis!! B&W, Sound, 10 minutes.
122. ANY OLD PART - Laurel and Hardy comedy. Just into trouble with a maiden in distress. B&W, Sound, 20 minutes.
123. FATAL GLASS OF BEER - W. C. Fields comedy. B&W, Sound, 20 minutes.

124. HIS MARRIAGE VOW - Harry Longdon comedy. B&W, Silent, 20 minutes.
125. THE PHARMOCIST - W.C. Fields comedy, gunfight and bootlegging. B&W, Sound, 20 minutes.
126. PERILS OF PAULINE - Pat Boone. 1917 Hudson Super 6 Touring in car chase. B&W, Silent. 12 minutes.
128. SATURDAY AFTERNOON - Vernon Dent comedy. What happens when you step out on your wife with the car. B&W, Sound, 10 minutes.
129. RACK FOR LIFE - Barney Oldfield. 1913 races to the girl tied to the tracks. B&W. Silent, 12 minutes.
130. NO INDIANS PLEASE - Abbott & Costello comedy. The Indians chase that Model A. B&W, Sound, 10 minutes.
131. HIS FIRST FLAT TIRE - Sid Smith. Comedy. What happens when you stop at the bank while it is being robbed. B&W, Silent, 15 minutes.
132. DEVIL DRIVERS - Early Auto Racing. Monte Carlo, Grand Prix, dirt track, Indianapolis. B&W, Sound, 10 minutes.
133. ON THEIR WAY - Eddie Boland comedy. 1920 Sports Van (Model T) equipped for camping! B&W, Silent. 12 minutes.
134. DONT PARK THERE - Will Rogers comedy. A country boy going to town with horse and wagon, buys T and trouble starts. B&W, Sound. 30 minutes.
135. A HASH HORSE FRAUD - Comedy. They try to sell the beanery, the purchaser calls the Keystone Kops. B&W, Silent. 12 minutes.
136. FAST AND FARIOUS - Lidge Conley. Slapstick old car action (twin 6 Packard, T's). B&W, Silent, 30 minutes.
137. 1971 AACA GLIDDEN TOUR™ - Ottawa, Canada. Color, Sound, one hour. By Roland Dunkelberger.
138. SKYLARKING - Mack Sennett comedy with flying 1923 Model T. Sound, 12 minutes.
139. TAKE NEXT CAR - Hal Roach comedy. Race between horse drawn trolley and 1923 Reo Jitney. Sound. 12 minutes.
140. GASALOONS' - 1934 RKO Radio Production. Ed Kennedy drops a windshield nut, comedy. Sound, 20 minutes.
141. WHAT PRICE TAXI - Gilbert Cook comedy. Problems of the taxi drivers in early 30's. B&W, Sound, 20 minutes.
142. GENTS OF LEISURE - Chester Conkin. Leisure life interrupted by the old steam train and cars. B&W, Sound, 20 minutes.
143. THE MECHANIC - Donald Duck shows how to fix your car. B&W, Sound, 10 minutes.
144. 1972 AACA RELIABLITY TOUR - Lake Geneva, Wisconsin. Color, 25 minutes, Sound.
145. MIDGET CAR MANIACS - Comedy. Abbott & Costello. B&W, Sound, 12 minutes.
146. CHICAGO TO EVANSTON RACE - As rerun in 1945. Color, Silent, 20 minutes.
147. FASHION BY FUNCTION - Chrysler Airflow story. B&W, Sound, 20 minutes.
148. HERITAGE PLANTATION - Story of the Heritage Plantation in Sandwich, Massachusetts, includes Antique Auto Museum. Color, Sound, 20 minutes.
149. THE FAST LADY - A full length feature. Story of a Bentley Racer filmed in England. Rated "G." Color, Sound, One hour and 45 minutes.
150. 1973 GEORGIA GLIDDEN TOUR™ - Color 60 minutes.
151. BEYOND A PROMISE - Story of Studebaker. B&W, Sound, 20 minutes.
152. 1956 AACA EAGLE ROCK HILL CLIMB - Color, Silent, 15 minutes.
153. 1949 FORD NEW CAR SALESMAN - Color, Sound, 15 minutes.
154. DOLLARS & SENSE - Mack Sennett Comedy. Romance triangle with Keystone Kops to the rescue. B&W, Sound, 20 minutes.
155. SATURDAY AFTERNOON - Harry Landon comedy with the girls on a car ride. B&W, Sound, 20 minutes.
156. TOWED INTO A HOLE - Laurel and Hardy comedy with their boat and Model T. B&W, Sound, 20 minutes.
157. TAKE BUS, PAY LATER - Abbott & Costello comedy. B&W, Sound, 8 minutes.
158. 1975 GLIDDEN TOUR™ - Canandaigua, New York. Color. Sound, 25 minutes.
159. 140 - 35mm slides of the 1975 Glidden Tour™ mounted in one round Kodak Carousel. 140 Slide tray.
160. GETTING A TICKET - Eddie Cantor gets picked up in his 1925 Rolls. B&W, Sound, 20 minutes.

161. CAR TROUBLE - When a Model A is hemmed in by two cars. And HORN HEROES - Laurel & Hardy in a brass horn factory. The two shorts are B&W, Sound, 15 minutes.
162. KEYSTONE KOPS - Original Keystone Kops on foot. B&W, Sound, 15 minutes.
163. KID SPEED - Larry Semon & Oliver Hardy. Early race cars and garage comedy. B&W, 20 minutes.
164. LOVES INTRIQUE - Garage mechanic boxes champion over girl, with old car and train chase. B&W. Sound, 30 minutes.
165. PARDON MY BACKFIRE - Three Stooges run a garage!!! B&W, Sound, 20 minutes.
166. UNCOVERED WAGON - A Model T caravan with prairie schooner tops. B&W, Sound, 15 minutes.
167. POPEYE'S USED CAR AND POPEYE'S MOTOR KNOCKS - Comedy cartoons. B&W, Sound, 10 minutes.
168. SPEEDWAY MAGOO & MOTHER'S LITTLE HELPER - B&W, Sound. 10 minutes.
169. TOONERVILLE TROLLEY - Famous Old Trolley Car with Kitraka Animated, Color. Sound. 10 minutes
170. BIMBO'S AUTO - Bimbo Trades old for new then goes back to the old. Cartoon. Animated Color. Sound, 10 minutes.
171. THE STOLEN JOOLS - A guessing game for over 70 old time movie stars of the 30's appear in this film. Car Chase. B&W, Sound, 20 minutes.
172. COPS - Buster Keaton and Virginia Fox comedy. Cops and Action. B&W, Sound, Music Track, 20 minutes.
174. MATCHING THE HARD ONES - Newest techniques in repairing lacquers. Color, Sound, 20 minutes.
175. BEFORE YOU SPRAY - Products to use and procedures to follow in preparing surfaces before you spray color coats. Color. Sound. 15 minutes.
176. THE GOLDEN AGE OF THE AUTOMOBILE - Traces the colorful story of the automobile to today. Color, Sound, 30 minutes.
177. STORY OF THE 1918 MAXWELL - B&W, Silent. 15 minutes.
178. 1976 VMCCA GLIDDEN TOUR™ - Colorado Springs, Color, Sound, 30 minutes.
179. THE STORY OF THE 1915 BUICK - ACROSS PIKE'S PEAK TO CALIFORNIA, B&W, Silent, 15 minutes.
180. EARLY AMERICAN AUTO RACING - 1930 to 1956 FOXTONE NEWS REELS, B&W, Sound, 20 minutes.
181. 1976 RELIABILITY TOUR - Orillia, Ontario, Canada, 25 minutes, Silent.
182. AACA 1977 GLIDDEN TOUR™, Part I (10 minutes) Part II (45 minutes). Silent, 55 minutes total.
183. STUDEBAKER FILM - Testing of 1935 models - new and durable body and ride, B&W, Sound, 10 minutes - Second part, story and demonstrations of Studebaker's Weasel Cargo & Personnel carrier built for the Army, 1842-1844, Color, Sound. 20 minutes.
184. AN AMERICAN LOVE AFFAIR - American Motors, 15 minutes, Color, Sound.
185. SMART WORK - What happens when your wife buys a new car for your birthday and you do not know it. B&W, Sound, 12 minutes.
186. 1981 LONG ISLAND GLIDDEN TOUR™ - Silent, 45 minutes.
187. 1964 INDY 500 RACE - Color, Sound, 28 minutes.
188. 1973 INDIANAPOLIS 500 RACE - Color, Sound, 30 minutes.
189. 1982 RELIABILITY TOUR - B&W, Silent, 20 minutes. Filmed and donated by Roland Dunkelberger.
190. 1983 BLUE RIDGE GLIDDEN TOUR™ - Silent, Color, 45 minutes.
191. Magic of a Shadow (Rolls Royce) - Sound, Color, 20 minutes.

INSTRUCTIONS FOR USE OF AACA VIDEO

All videos in the AACA Video Center are VHS. A video will be mailed postpaid by AACA National Headquarters to the president of any recognized AACA Region or Chapter or to the program chairman at the direction of the president. All requests must be made by the president four (4) weeks prior and include show date. Film/Video request forms are available from AACA National Headquarters. A video must be returned next mailing day after show date. Failure to do so may result in suspension of ordering privileges.

If the video is damaged during use, report such damages on the card enclosed with the video. Rewind video before returning. CAUTION: Due to copyrights and regulations on the AACA Video Center, no admission charge or fund raising projects may be made when showing any of the AACA videos. When returning video to AACA National Headquarters, insure each video for a minimum of $100.00. If using United Parcel Service to return video, $100.00 insurance is automatically included.

To order a film complete and return the Film/Video Request Form.

1. AACA Film 17: THE FIRST GLIDDEN TOUR™ OF 1905, Silent: AACA Film 91: THE SPEED KINGS, a 1913 comedy, Sound, and AACA Film 68: HURRY, HURRY, a 1940 W. C. Fields film, Sound, 30 Min.
2. AACA Film 180: EARLY AMERICAN RACING 1930-1956. Sound - and AACA Film 132: DEVIL DRIVERS, early auto racing, Sound, 30 Min.
3. AACA Film 5: LEST WE FORGET, Sound, and AACA Film 6: 1954 ENGLISH/AMERICAN ANTIQUE CAR RALLY, Sound, 30 Min.
4. AACA Film 163: KID SPEED, Silent; and AACA Film 143: AUTO MECHANIC, Walt Disney Cartoon, Sound, 30 Min.
5. AACA Film 41: ANTIQUE AUTOS ON PARADE 1900-1904 - B&W, Silent, 25 Min. AACA Film 51: TWO TARS - B&W, Silent, 30 Min.
7. BACK IN TIME IN 89 - AACA National Fall Meet 1989 (Hershey) 35 Min.
8. 1988 GLIDDEN TOUR™ - Grand Rapids, MI - VMCCA, 1 Hr. 35 Min.
9. 1990 AACA RELIABILITY TOUR - Burnsville, MN.
10. AACA NATIONAL FALL MEET 1990 (Hershey), 30 Min.
11. THE ROMANCE OF RESTORATION - CLASSIC CARS REBORN - 18 Min. Donated by White Post Restorations.
12. 1990 GLIDDEN TOUR™ - Colorado Springs, CO - VMCCA, 32 Min.
13. 1963 GLIDDEN TOUR™ - Finger Lakes of New York State - Filmed in Newark, NY.
14. AUTO BODY REPAIR BASIC METAL STRAIGHTENING TECHNIQUES - By Vern Phillips, 30 Min. Donated by Hershey Region - AACA.
15. AUTO BODY REPAIR THE STECK PULLROD PROCESS - By Vern Phillips, 30 Min. Donated by Hershey Region - AACA.
16. THE SIGNS & RHYMES OF BURMA-SHAVE - 60 Min.
17. 1991 AACA ANNUAL GRAND NATIONAL MEET - 45 Min.
18. FORD AND THE AMERICAN DREAM - 50 Min.
19. HEARTBEAT OF THE WORLD - AACA National Fall Meet 1991 (Hershey) 30 Min.
20. HISTORIC MOTORCAR JOURNAL Auburn-Cord-Duesenberg Museum - 28 Min.
21. LONDON-BRIGHTON TOUR - November 1990.
22. THE STORY OF MUSTANG - 30 Min.
23. THE STORY OF CORVETTE - 30 Min.
24. WHEELS THE JOY OF CARS - 54 Min.
25. 1991 GLIDDEN TOUR™ Seven Springs, PA. AACA, 1 Hr. 30 Min.
26. RICHARD PETTY THE LEGEND - 1958-1992 (Volume I & II) 2 Hr. 12 Min.

27. 1964 AACA - GETTYSBURG SPRING MEET - Silent, 12 Min.
28. AACA Film 176: THE GOLDEN AGE OF THE AUTOMOBILE - Color, Sound, 30 Min.
29. AACA Film 174: MATCHING THE HARD ONES - Color, Sound, 20 Min.
30. MINNESOTA REGION JUDGING MEET, Rochester, MN, June 1991 - 30 Min. Donated by John Rivers - Minnesota Region.
31. MINNESOTA REGION PIONEER CHAPTER TOUR - June 1991 25 Min. Donated by John Rivers - Minnesota Region.
32. AACA Film 134: DON'T PARK THERE - B&W. Sound, 30 Min.
33. CAR COMMERCIALS OF THE 1950's - 2 Hrs.
34. AACA Film 29: BLOW YOUR HORN - Color, Sound, 45 Min.
35-1. AACA Film 43: AUTOBIOGRAPHY - B&W, Sound, 30 Min.
35-2. AACA Film 4: GOGGLES AND GAUNTLETS - Color, Sound, 15 Min.
36. AACA Film 171: THE STOLEN JOOLS - B&W, Sound, 20 Min.
37. AACA Film 156: TOWED INTO A HOLE - B&W, Sound, 20 Min.
38. AACA Film 10: THRU A REAR-VIEW MIRROR - Color, Sound, 20 Min.
39. AACA Film 188: 1973 INDIANAPOLIS 500 RACE (GENERATIONS IN SPEED) - Color, Sound, 30 Min.
40. AACA Film 18: THE FIRST INDIANAPOLIS 500 - B&W, Silent, 12 Min.
41-1. 1992 VMCCA BLUEGRASS Bicentennial GLIDDEN TOUR™ Lexington, KY - Sept. 27-Oct. 2, 1992.
41-2. AACA Film 151: BEYOND A PROMISE - B&W, Sound, 20 Min.
42-1. GENEVIEVE - A comedy about two friendly rivals who engage in a race of their own on the way back from the Brighton Veteran Car Rally. - Color, Sound, 86 Min.
42-2. AACA Film 42: HISTORY ON WHEELS - B&W, Sound, 15 Min.
43-1. MEMORIES AND YOU IN '92 - AACA National Fall Meet 1992 (Hershey) - 38 Min.
43-2. AACA Film 83: HOG WILD - B&W, Sound, 20 Min.
44-1. 1992 RELIABILITY TOUR - Houghton Lake, MI August 16-21.
44-2. AACA Film 44: MERRILY WE ROLL ALONG - B&W, Sound, 55 Min.
45. AACA Film 32: 1909 AUTO RACE - Color, Sound, 20 Min.
46. AACA Film 98: THE CHANGING ARCHITECTURE OF THE AUTOMOBILE BODY - Color, Sound, 30 Min.
47. AACA Film 101: FLIGHT OF THE ARROW - B&W, Sound, 45 Min.
48. AACA Film 175: BEFORE YOU SPRAY - Color, Sound, 15 Min.
49. AACA Film 49: STYLING AND THE EXPERIMENTAL CAR - Color, Sound, 20 Min.
50. AACA Film 75: AUTO INTOXICATION - B&W, Sound. 15 Min.
51. AACA Film 31: THE AMERICAN ROAD - B&W, Sound, 40 Min.
52. AACA Film 38: FIRST MOVIES OF AACA MEETS - Color, Silent, 20 Min.
53. THE '49 FORD IN YOUR FUTURE - Video includes fascinating manufacture and assembly operations, plus all passenger models and the car's debut at the Detroit Auto Show. Color (some B&W), 43 Min.
54. FORD CLASSICS OF THE FIFTIES - 1956 MARK 11, 1957 Retractable, and 1958 Edsel star in this edit of the original files that introduced them. - 60 Min.
55. THE 1950-51 FORDS - A compilation of all 1950-51 Ford Films that appeared in the Ford Show Quarterly - 60 Min.
56. THE 1953-54 FORDS - An edit of company films about how cars are produced and 50th Anniversary plans. Includes a lively series of TV commercials and a great 1954 tour of Rotunda and Rouge assembly lines. - 60 Min.
57. THE 1955-56 FORDS - Highlights production in 1955, followed by a collection of 1955-56 Ford Car TV commercials. Includes race track scenes, classy showroom cars. - 60 Min.
58. THE 1955-66 THUNDERBIRDS - Collection of TV commercials. Includes 1956-57 Daytona speed trials. - 60 Min.
59. THE 1957-59 FORDS - Series of company film clips and TV ads. 60 Min.
60. GETTING STARTED/BACK ON TRACK - Restoration video, Vol. 1.
61. CHASSIS & RUNNING GEAR - Restoration video, Vol. 2.

62. PATCHWORK & METAL FINISHING - Restoration video, Vol. 3.
63. LEADWORK & PLASTIC FILLERS - Restoration video, Vol. 4.
64. PAINTING & WOOD GRAINING - Restoration video, Vol. 5.
65. METAL TRIM & CHROME PREPARATION - Restoration video, Vol. 6.
66. THE LONG, LONG TRAILER - Lucille Ball and Desi Arnaz hit every hilarious pothole on the road to marital bliss when they take their honeymoon in "The Long, Long Trailer" - 97 Min. Donation from Roland Dunkelberger
67. HISTORY OF THE MOTOR CAR
Part I - THE DAWN OF MOTORING - Covers the evolution of the motor car from the invention of the wheel until 1895. Wind machines, steam carriages, gas engines and bicycles all form part of a story which includes the experimental vehicles of Benz.
Part II - THE VETERANS - This tells the story of the development of the motor car between 1895 and 1914. - 60 Min.
68. HISTORY OF THE MOTOR CAR
Part III - THE VINTAGE YEARS - This continues the story after World War I and through the Twenties. This was the age of the Bugatti, of flamboyant Fiats and supercharged Mercedes, of Alpha Romeos and three litre Bentleys.
Part IV - THE THIRTIES - "The   Thirties" covers the age when cars were at their most exotic. This was the time of the Cord, the Duesenberg, the Daimler Straight Eight, the V12 Pierce Silver Arrow and V16 Cadillac. It was also the time when Ford introduced the V8 for people of lesser means. - 60 Min.
69. HISTORY OF THE MOTOR CAR
Part V - CARS, CARS AND MORE CARS - This episode covers the Forties and Fifties. Some of the cars shown include the Healey, the Mark Seven Jaguar, the Studebaker and the Ford Thunderbird.
Part VI - THE YEARS OF PLENTY - This final episode tells the story of the automobile during the Sixties and Seventies. Included are many of the popular cars of the period, some of the expensive and less well-known and a number of designer's dream cars. - 60 Min.
70. 1993 GLIDDEN TOUR™ - A hub tour in southern Delaware, the lower eastern shore of Maryland and the eastern shore of Virginia. Includes vehicles through 1935. Sept. 19-24, 1993. Approx. 60 Min.
71. SEVENTH ANNUAL NEW LONDON-NEW BRIGHTON Antique car run. August 25-28, 1993 - 59 Min.
72. PIONEER CHAPTER/MN REGION 2-DAY TOUR - Duluth, MN June 26 & 27, 1993 - 27 Min.
73. MINNESOTA REGION JUDGING MEET - St. James, MN June 5, 1993 - 34 Min.
74. AACA Film 146: CHICAGO TO EVANSTON RACE - Color, Silent, 20 Min.
75. CONCOURS D'ELEGANCE OF THE EASTERN UNITED STATES - Fabulous Cars of Famous People - The 3rd annual Concours d'Elegance features a display of 85 rare automobiles owned by such celebrities as Rudolf Valentino, Woodrow Wilson and Tony Curtis. The event takes place in 1992 on the grounds of the Penn State, Berks campus in Reading, PA - 50 Min.
76. OXY-FUEL SAFETY IT'S UP TO YOU - Sound, Color, 30 Min.
77. SAFETY IN OXY - FUEL WELDING - 30 Min.
78. AACA Film 1: 1948 GLIDDEN TOUR™ - Color, Silent, 25 Min.
79. AACA Film 2: 1951 GLIDDEN TOUR™ - B&W, Sound, 10 Min.
80. AACA Film 3: MAKE WAY FOR YESTERDAY - Color, Sound, 40 Min.
81. AACA Film 7: HEY! GET A HORSE! - Color, Silent, 20 Min.
82. AACA Film 8: 1956 VMCCA GLIDDEN TOUR™ AT FRENCH LICK, NC. - Color, Silent, 20 Min.
83. AACA Film 9: 1957 GLIDDEN TOUR™ FROM ROANOKE VA TO HERSHEY - Color, Silent, 20 Min.
84. AACA Film 11: ORMOND BEACH ANTIQUE CAR SHOW Color, Sound, 12 Min.
85. AACA Film 12: TOURING ROUND TAHOE - Color, Sound, 35 Min.
86. AACA Film 13: 1958 VMCCA GLIDDEN TOUR™ IN NEW ENGLAND - Color, Silent, 45 Min.
87. AACA Film 14: 1959 GLIDDEN TOUR™ FROM CINCINNATI TO DETROIT - Color, Silent, 60 Min.
88. AACA Film 15: 1959 LONDON TO BRIGHTON ENTRY - Color, Silent, 15 Min.
89. AACA Film 16: 1960 LONDON-BRIGHTON RUN - Color, Silent, 15 Min.
90. AACA Film 19: 1959 SCOTTISH VETERAN CAR RALLY - Color, Sound, 20 Min.
91. AACA Film 20: AACA EUROPEAN TRIP & BRIGHTON RUN - Color, Silent, 30 Min.

92. 1994 VMCCA GLIDDEN TOUR™, KERRVILLE, TX - Color, Sound, 55 Min.
93. 1994 LONDON TO BRIGHTON RUN - Color, Sound, 35 Min.
94. AACA Film 36: 1967 GLIDDEN TOUR™ - Color, Sound, 20 Min.
95. AACA Film 191: THE MAGIC OF A SHADOW - Color, Sound, 20 Min.
96. FORD DIESEL POWER DRIVE - In the winter of 1992, Ford Heavy Truck invited a group of people to put its new midrange diesel engines to the test. - 15:31 Min.
97. MANUFACTURING THE NEW FORD DIESELS - AN INTERVIEW WITH THE PLANT MANAGER - Ford's new FD-1460 and FD-1060 engines are built at Consolidated Diesel Co. in North Carolina. This video takes viewers inside the plant to visit with its manager - 10:37 Min.
98. THE NEW FORD DIESELS SALES AND MARKETING STRATEGY - 40 Min.
99. FORD HEAVY TRUCK MEDIUM/HEAVY MARKET OPPORTUNITIES - 30 Min.
100. FORD HEAVY TRUCK CLASS 8 MARKET OPPORTUNITIES - 22 Min.
101. HERSHEY AND MORE IN '94 - 1994 Eastern Division AACA National Fall Meet in Hershey, PA - 56 Min.
102. AACA REGIONS' OFFICER'S TRAINING
103. 1994 NATIONAL RELIABILITY TOUR - July 24-29, 1994 in Charlotte, North Carolina.
104. THE 30TH INTERNATIONAL STUDEBAKER DRIVERS CLUB MEET - To commemorate its 30th year of International Meets, The Studebaker Drivers Club gathered in Bloomington, MN. This tape chronicles the 30th S.D.C. Meet in a wonderfully entertaining style, ... not just for Studebaker enthusiasts, but for the delight of anyone with a passion for the automobile and truck. - 52 Min.
105. AUBURN, CORD, DUESENBERG - The Cars 'The History' The Owners * The Festival 'The Museum' - 56 Min.
106. HENRY FORD - Biography - This video looks at the driving forces of this dynamic industrialist, philanthropist and automotive autocrat. - 50 Min.
107. THE 1995 GREAT NORTH AMERICAN RACE - An ESPN Special - Approx. 45 Min.
108. 1995 GLIDDEN TOUR™ - The 50th Glidden Tour™ hosted by the Pottstown Region - AACA. Headquartered in Reading, PA, the tour traveled to different locations in Berks and Lancaster County as well as Valley Forge National Park. Sept. 17-22, 1995.
109. KEEPING THE HOBBY ALIVE IN '95 - 1995 Eastern Division AACA National Fall Meet in Hershey, PA - 43 Min.

AACA PAST PRESIDENTS

1936-37-38	Frank Abramson	1971	Frederick L. VanWinkle
1939-40-41	George M. Hughes*	1972	Harold L. Coker
1942	Hyde W. Ballard*	1973	Jerry L. Hodges
1943-44	George M. Hughes*	1975-76	Franklin B. Tucker
1945	George Gerenbeck, Jr.	1977	Herman L. Smith*
1946-47	Thomas McKean, Jr.*	1978	Henry E. Krusen
1948	M.J. Duryea*	1979-80	William H. Smith
1949-50	D. Clarence Marshall*	1981	Richard H. Taylor
1951	James Melton*	1982	Arthur L. Bragg
1952	T. Clarence Marshall*	1983	Jack Macy
1953	S. Howard Brown*	1984	Robert N. Garrison
1954-55	Lesley R. Henry	1985	M.G. Randall
1956-57	William E. Swigart, Jr.	1986	David K. Strong
1958-59	William Pollock	1987	Al D. Edmond
1960	George R. Norton, Jr.	1988-89	Howard V. Scotland, Jr.
1961	Mahlon E. Patton*	1990	J. Stanley Stratton
1962	J. Leonard Rhinehart*	1991	Ronald V. Barnett
1963-64	Edgar E. Rohr*	1992	C. Robert Belier
1965	Ralph O. Majors*	1993	Lloyd Riggs
1966	Hyde W. Ballard*	1994	Roy Graden
1967	Ray E. Henry*	1995	Benny Bootle*
1968	John J. Lambert, Jr.*	1996	Edward B. Baines
1969	Albert Whiting*	1997	Samuel H. High, III
1970	Morris E. Kunkle	1998	Thomas F. Howard

* Deceased

AACA NATIONAL DIRECTORS

Frank Abramson PA 1935-1939
Charles H. Adams GA 1978-1980
A.R. Allison CA 1979-1984
Donald M. Anderson TN 1965-1967
V.O. Anderson IA 1966-1971
Bayard Badenhausen PA 1947-1948
L. Scott Bailey NY 1957-1959
Samuel E. Baily PA 1943; 1947; 1950-1966
Edward B. Baines OH 1984-1986; 1992-1997
Hyde W. Ballard PA 1938-1942; 1946; 1956-1976
Ronald V. Barnett AL 1986-1998*
Earl D. Beauchamp, Jr. VA 1995-1998*
C. Robert Belier CAN 1984-1992; 1994-1995
David A. Berg PA 1997-1998*
James Beun VA 1958-1960
Milton R. Binger WY 1981-1984
Curtis L. Blake MA 1958-1960
William J. Boden, Jr. PA 1954-1962
Terry Bond VA 1997-1998*
Benny T. Bootle SC 1988-1996
Carl Boyd KY 1993-1998*
Arthur L. Bragg VA 1976-1990
Theodore B. Brooks PA 1935-1948; 1951-1954; 1956-1958

Edwin A. Brossman PA 1945
John A. Brown VA 1958-1975
S. Howard Brown PA 1950-1955
Frank Buck PA 1977-1983
Ralph T. Buckley NJ 1951-1957
Kenneth B. Butler IL 1961-1963
Paul H. Cadwell PA 1947-1948; 1951-1953; 1955-1957
Chuck G. Carisch DE 1986-1988
C. Albert Clemens PA 1953-1954
Harold L. Coker TN 1969-1974
George C. Corson PA 1954-1956
Lloyd J. Davis MD 1996-1998*
Charles E. Dearnley, Jr. PA 1948-1953
John F. Dietz, Jr. WI 1966-1968; 1971-1981
George W. Dohn PA 1967; 1979-1981
Douglas D. Drake NY 1989-1998*
E. Paul du Pont DE 1949-1950
Paul L. Dudek MN 1989-1994
Nancy Dunn SC 1995-1997
M.J. Duryea MA 1946-1957
Earle S. Eckel NJ 1935-1938; 1948-1955
Al D. Edmond IA 1983-1997
Henry L. Feinsinger PA 1961-1972
Theodore Fiala PA 1935-1940; 1947-1948

AACA NATIONAL DIRECTORS (cont.)

Russell J. Fisher WI 1998*
Jerry S. Foley, III FL 1961-1963
Donald A. Gallager PA 1947-1952
Robert N. Garrison GA 1974-1988
George Gerenbeck, Jr. PA 1940-1945
Roy Graden PA 1987-1998*
James H. Gray WV 1963-1965
Marshall I. Groff PA 1947-1950
W. Harrison Hall, Jr. PA 1954-1956
Ralph Harms CA 1995-1996
Henry B. Harper IL 1970-1974
Walter W. Heckman TN 1980-1985; 1988-1990
J. Russell Heitman IL 1943-1944
Harold E. Henry MD 1995-1998*
Leslie R. Henry MI 1951-1983
Ray M. Henry OH 1963-1977
Samuel H. High, III PA 1987-1998*
Bill Hinkle WY 1986-1991
Jerry L. Hodge TN 1970-1978
Thomas F. Howard TN 1991-1998*
George M. Hughes PA 1938-1948; 1950-1953
Henry Krusen PA 1973-1981
Morris E. Kunkle, Jr. PA 1966-1976
James W. Ladd PA 1958-1959
Thomas Ladson, Jr. MD 1962-1967
John J. Lambert, Jr. NY 1964-1969
Robert C. Laurens PA 1950-1953
Carl C. Law, Jr. OH 1964-1969
Leonard Le Crone PA 1968-1973
Robert C. Lea, Jr. PA 1946-1949
C. Raymond Levis PA 1955
Jack Macy IN 1978-1980; 1982-1993
Ralph O. Majors CA 1960-1965
T. Clarence Marshall DE 1949-1957
Thomas McKean, Jr. PA 1938-1941; 1946-1949
Joseph R. McNutt OH 1974-1975
James Melton CT 1949-1954
W. Jay Milligan NY 1959-1964
G. Richard Minnick MD 1972-1974
Theodore D. Moore NJ 1951-1952; 1953-1955
Earl L. Muir PA 1993-1998*
Joseph J. Murchio NY 1954-1956
John P. Myer AL 1993-1998*
George R. Norton, Jr. PA 1957-1968
L. Edward Pamphilon MD 1947-1964
Seth E. Pancoast PA 1970-1973
Fred Parsons PA 1935-1937
Mahlon E. Patton PA 1958-1975
Parry Paul PA 1943
D. Cameron Peck IL 1949-1954
Clifford D. Phipps MN 1986
William Pollock PA 1956-1964
James A. Raines NC 1998*

M.G. Randall MI 1980-1994
Tom Reese MN 1973-1987
J. Leonard Rhinehart MD 1959-1970
F. Earl Richardson OH 1955-1957
Janet M. Ricketts FL 1991-1998*
Lloyd Riggs CA 1987-1995
Henry W. Roever PA 1941
Ray W. Rogers OH 1957-1962
Edgar E. Rohr VA 1960-1983
William E. Rowland PA 1949-1954
Howard V. Scotland, Jr. MD 1983-1996
Herbert Singe, Jr. NJ 1955-1966
George R. Smith TN 1987-1992
Herman L. Smith CAN 1973-1987
Stanley B. Smith PA 1955-1966
William H. Smith PA 1975-1986
Murrell E. Smith, Sr. MD 1978-1992
William P. Snyder, III PA 1953-1953
Ruth Franklin Sommerlad OH 1953-1961
William C. Spear NH 1948-1950
William Sprague MA 1982-1983
Robert C. Sprague, Jr. MA 1977-1979
John Paul Stack NY 1951-1952
Anna W. Stanley VA 1975-1983
Kenneth H. Stauffer PA 1969-1977
J. Stanley Stratton PA 1985-1998*
Roland P. Stratton NJ 1967-1972; 1975-1976
Ronald A. Stringer IL 1981-1986
David K. Strong MN 1975-1977; 1979-1990
Sidney M. Strong MN 1955-1957
Bob Swanson CT 1992-1994
William E. Swigart, Jr. PA 1951-1985
Carter Taylor TX 1990-1992
Richard H. Taylor OH 1977-1991
Franklin B. Tucker NJ 1965-1985
Frederick Van Winkle PA 1967-1978
Joseph B. VanSciver PA 1947
Joseph S. Vicini NJ 1998*
Sterling E. Walsh, Sr. MD 1993-1998*
Ralph R. Weeks PA 1943-1945; 1951-1955
Warren S. Weiant, Jr. OH 1951-1953
Thomas J. Wells PA 1976-1978
A. Frederic Wetherill PA 1947-1949
Duane C. White MA 1956-1958
Albert W. Whiting PA 1964-1970
Hanna Whitworth CA 1985-1986
John Widdel, Jr. SD 1984-1989; 1991-1998*
Dan C. Williams TX 1958-1960
Joseph C. Williams PA 1935-1937
Dudley C. Wilson PA 1946-1947
Gerald S. Wright CA 1968-1979
David L. Zimmerman NJ 1997-1998*

* Incumbent at time of publication.

AACA MUSEUM, INC., DIRECTORS

Edward B. Baines OH 1996
Donald R. Barlup PA 1997-1998*
Ronald V. Barnett AL 1997-1998*
Benny T. Bootle SC 1995-1996
David Cammack VA 1997-1998*
Robert H. Dare PA 1997-1998*
Al D. Edmond IA 1993-1997
Louis E. Fritz, Sr. MD 1997-1998*
Robert N. Garrison GA 1993-1994
Roy Graden PA 1993-1998*
Samuel H. High, III PA 1997

Thomas F. Howard TN 1998
Paul A. Ianuario SC 1997-1998*
John P. Myer AL 1993-1998*
Nelson E. Neff PA 1998
Jim Nowak PA 1993-1995
Lloyd Riggs CA 1993-1995
William H. Smith PA 1993-1998*
Dr. J. Stanley Stratton PA 1996-1997
Richard H. Taylor OH 1993-1998*
Joseph S. Vicini NJ 1997-1998*
Sterling E. Walsh, Sr. MD 1993-1998*

* Incumbent at time of publication.

AACA LIBRARY & RESEARCH CENTER DIRECTORS

Edward B. Baines OH 1993-1995
Donald R. Barlup PA 1997-1998*
Ronald V. Barnett AL 1988-1990; 1993-1994
Earl D. Beauchamp, Jr. VA 1995-1997
C. Robert Belier CAN 1995
Paul P. Bell PA 1989-1995
David A. Berg PA 1998*
Terry Bond VA 1998*
Benny T. Bootle SC 1989-1994
James P. Butler PA 1990-1992
John Caperton KY 1990-1992
Henry Austin Clark NY 1982-1987
James Conant OH 1982-1986
John S. Conde MI 1982-1985
David Cummings PA 1982-1983
George W. Dohn PA 1984-1988
Paul L. Dudek MN 1991-1994
Helen J. Earley MI 1988-1990
Al D. Edmond IA 1996-1997
Russell J. Fisher WI 1998*
Robert N. Garrison GA 1982-1988; 1991-1996
James E. Gillenwaters, Jr. TN 1998*
Roy Graden PA 1992-1993
Ralph Harms CA 1995-1996
Bert Harrington GA 1982-1987
Thomas S. Heckman PA 1987-1989
Harold E. Henry MD 1995-1997
Leslie Henry MI 1982-1983

Samuel H. High, III PA 1994
John J. Lambert NY 1985-1994
Lorraine M. Logan NY 1982-1991
Earl L. Muir PA 1995
Nelson E. Neff PA 1994-1998*
James R. Nowak PA 1989-1998*
John N. Packard MD 1997-1998*
Ralph B. Price MD 1992-1994
M. G. "Pinky" Randall MI 1988-1992
Robert Robinson PA 1987-1988
Arthur C. Rutledge MD 1982-1993; 1995-1998*
Bernard Schukraft IL 1995-1997
Richard E. Slichter PA 1995-1997
Herman L. Smith CAN 1982-1987
William H. Smith PA 1982-1986
Robert Sovis MI 1982-1984; 1988-1989; 1995-1996
Kenneth Stauffer PA 1982-1986
J. Stanley Stratton PA 1986-1989; 1991-1998*
Ronald A. Stringer IL 1982-1984
David K. Strong MN 1987-1990
William E. Swigart, Jr. PA 1982-1985
Carter Taylor TX 1982; 1990-1992
Richard H. Taylor OH 1984-1991; 1993-1998*
Franklin B. Tucker NJ 1982-1994
Margaret M. Vitale NY 1998*
Sterling E. Walsh MD 1996-1998*
Shirley M. Wise MD 1993-1998*
David L. Zimmerman NJ 1997-1998*

* Incumbent at time of publication.

1998 Officers

AACA National Directors

1996-1998	**1997-1999**	**1998-2000**
Carl R. Boyd	Terry Bond	Ronald V. Barnett
Lloyd Davis	David A. Berg	Earl D. Beauchamp, Jr.
Roy Graden	Thomas F. Howard	Douglas D. Drake
Samuel H. High III	Janet M. Ricketts	Harold E. Henry
Earl L. Muir	Dr. J. Stanley Stratton	Joseph S. Vicini
John P. Myer	John "Jack" Widdel, Jr.	Russell J. Fisher
Sterling E. Walsh, Sr.	David L. Zimmerman	James A. Raines

President
Thomas F. Howard

Secretary/Treasurer
Douglas D. Drake

Ass't Treasurer
William H. Smith

Executive Vice-President
Janet M. Ricketts

Ass't. Secretary
Sterling E. Walsh

Executive Director
William H. Smith

Vice-Presidents
Presidential Appointments

Assistant Vice-Presidents

Class Judging	Carl R. Boyd	David A. Berg
Finance & Budget	John P. Myer	Samuel H. High, III
Membership	David L. Zimmerman	Earl D. Beauchamp, Jr.
National Activities	Earl D. Beauchamp, Jr.	Terry L. Bond
National Awards	Harold E. Henry	Joseph F. Vicini
National Headquarters	Samuel H. High, III	Earl L. Muir
Publications	Terry L. Bond	Sterling E. Walsh
Regions	Earl L. Muir	Harold E. Henry
Legislation	Sterling E. Walsh	Jack Widdel
Library & Research	J. Stanley Stratton	Russell J. Fisher
Senior Car Awards	Roy Graden	Carl R. Boyd
Technical Matters	John "Jack" Widdell, Jr.	James A. Raines
Public Relations & Communications	Lloyd J. Davis	David L. Zimmerman
AACA Museum, Inc.	Ronald V. Barnett	Roy M. Graden

Chairpeople

Director 1999 Annual Meeting	Samuel H. High, II	
1999 Annual Meeting	Seth E. Pancoast, Jr.	
Chief Teller	William H. Smith	
Chaplain	J. Stanley Stratton	
Editor, Antique Automobile	William H. Smith	
Film Library & Trophies	William H. Smith	
Director 1998 Founders Tour	Douglas D. Drake	
Director 1998 Reliability Tour	Earl L. Muir	
Director 1998 AGNM	Earl D. Beauchamp, Jr.	
Director 1999 Founders Tour	Roy M. Graden	
Director 1999 Glidden Tour™	Earl D. Beauchamp, Jr.	
Director 1999 AGNM	James A. Raines	
Director 2000 Founders Tour	Terry L. Bond	
Director 2000 Reliability Tour	Thomas F. Howard	
Director 2000 AGNM	Harold E. Henry	

National Activities-Eastern	Ernest N. Screen, Jr.
National Activities-SE	Ernie Stoffel
National Activities-Central	Joseph Gagliano
National Activities-Western	Raymond Fairfield
Chairman-Speakers Bureau, Eastern	John L. Walker
Chairman-Speakers Bureau, SE	George R. Smith
Chairman-Speakers Bureau, Central	Nate Gunderson
Chairman-Speakers Bureau, Western	Frank T. Snyder, III
Chairman-Grievance	Roy M. Graden
Chairman-Policy and Procedure	Joseph S. Vicini
Chairman-National Judges Training	Ronald S. Rubinstein
Chairman-Judges Records	Sandra F. Neidigh
Chairman-Judges Administration	David A. Berg
Chairman-Class Certification	Douglas Van Duser

Bibliography

Magazines and Periodicals:

The Antique Automobile. Every issue of the *Bulletin* and *Antique Automobile* and many articles were consulted (too numerous to individually list). If you can find a copy, we recommend the following issues for club history:

        10th Anniversary issue, 1945

        25th Anniversary issue, 1960

        50th Anniversary issue, 1995

Antique Automobile Club of America, Eastern Fall Meet Program, October 1995.

Many AACA regional and chapter newsletters contain excellent sources for historic data on the club. Once again, the resource is too large to list individually.

History of the Deep South Region, 1997, Ernie Youens.

Old Cars Weekly, Oct. 1993, Hershey Coverage.

Quatrefoil, by The Automobile Quarterly, L. Scott Bailey, Fall-Winter 1976.

Wheels, by the AACA, Volume 1, Number 1, Ronald N. Moskalczak. Published as the official publication of the Junior Members of the Antique Automobile Club of America.

Index